Reading *Capital* Today

Reading *Capital* Today

Marx after 150 Years

Edited by
Ingo Schmidt and Carlo Fanelli

PlutoPress
www.plutobooks.com

First published 2017 by Pluto Press
345 Archway Road, London N6 5AA

www.plutobooks.com

Copyright © Ingo Schmidt and Carlo Fanelli 2017

The right of the individual contributors to be identified as the authors of this work
has been asserted by them in accordance with the Copyright, Designs and Patents
Act 1988.

British Library Cataloguing in Publication Data
A catalogue record for this book is available from the British Library

ISBN   978 0 7453 9973 7   Hardback
ISBN   978 0 7453 9971 3   Paperback
ISBN   978 1 7868 0084 8   PDF eBook
ISBN   978 1 7868 0086 2   Kindle eBook
ISBN   978 1 7868 0085 5   EPUB eBook

This book is printed on paper suitable for recycling and made from fully managed and
sustained forest sources. Logging, pulping and manufacturing processes are expected
to conform to the environmental standards of the country of origin.

Typeset by Stanford DTP Services, Northampton, England

Simultaneously printed in the United Kingdom and United States of America

Contents

Introduction: *Capital* After 150 Years

Ingo Schmidt and Carlo Fanelli

Why read *Capital*? After its publication in 1867, increasing numbers of socialists turned to *Capital*, or introductions to its ideas written by Engels and Kautsky, to understand what they were up against. Yet the revolution that mostly Western European socialists had been preparing for during the days of the First and Second Internationals happened in Russia, a country where the logic of capital that Marx had revealed had barely started to develop. Its supposed gravediggers, the industrial working class, even less so. The 1917 revolution truly was, to borrow Gramsci's term, a revolution against *Capital*.

Another 50 years later, a new generation of leftists, inspired by anti-colonial revolutions in the South and discontented with the administered worlds of Soviet communism and Western capitalism, turned to *Capital* and other Marxist texts outside the Soviet orthodoxy in search of ideas for how to restart the revolutionary process in the East and West. Not long after a New Left had started discovering new sides of Marx's works, it seemed as if capitalists, concerned with the conjunction of social unrest and economic crises in the 1970s, had also taken a look at *Capital* to find ways of getting more surplus value for less money out of workers in old and new industrial districts.

Indeed, the neoliberal counter-reforms the capitalist classes unleashed against New and Old Lefts from the 1980s onwards created a world after *Capital's* image. This was particularly true after the Soviet Union collapsed under the weight of its own bureaucracy, and the Chinese communists' decided to follow into the service of capital accumulation. One hundred years after the revolution against *Capital*, the world looks much more like the one portrayed by Marx 150 years ago. But it wasn't just the need for a constantly expanding market that spread capital over the entire surface of the globe, it was also the effort to bypass workers' organizations of any kind that prompted capitalists to move operations to locations previously untouched by capitalist relations of production or socialist agitators.

Reading *Capital* in Changing Historical Contexts

The Russian revolution against *Capital*, along with other revolutions that followed in its wake, failed to develop an egalitarian alternative model of development. Welfare states, built as part of post-Second World War efforts to contain the further spread of communism, have since seen their social safety nets much reduced. Both labour and other social movements organizing around issues historically neglected by Marxists have also reached an impasse having been unable to stop, let alone reverse, decades of concerted capitalist class war from above. Nevertheless, there is little doubt that twentieth-century struggles to overcome or at least tame capitalism did as much in shaping today's global capitalism as the unfolding logic of capital did. Reading *Capital* today – against the background of class struggles that moved history forward since its publication and, more significantly, the revolution against it – may help us to understand why twentieth-century socialisms failed and why capitalism was triumphant, but also how new socialisms, drawing on the experiences of past socialisms and the discontent produced by capitalism's current crises, might be built. These experiences include reorientations and adaptations of socialist strategy at different social conjunctures. Debates around *Capital* played their part in these searches for strategic renewal. The late nineteenth-century debate between Bernstein, Kautsky and Luxemburg about the need to abandon socialist politics based on Marx's analysis of capitalism pretty much set the tone for debates about the need for strategic reorientation in the twentieth century.

There were always some, following Bernstein, who argued that Marx's analysis of capitalism, and the socialist politics based on this analysis, might have been appropriate in Marx's time but that actually existing capitalism was entirely different and thus required a non-Marxist socialism. The irony of these repeated efforts to abandon Marxist socialism by relegating *Capital* to the dusty shelves of outdated history books is that latter-day revisionists glossed over the changes in capitalism that led Bernstein to turn against Marxist analysis and socialism. In their view, the entire nineteenth century was the classical age of capitalism and Marx was its analyst. Changes that could not be explained within the framework established by *Capital*, notably the interventionist state and waves of automation in the production process, emerged, according to these latter-day revisionists, only in the twentieth century.

Marxists often responded defensively to the revisionist challenge by declaring that Marx was right and did not need any updating. Yet, as *Capital* was elevated to Holy Scripture status it also became detached from socialist politics as practice. Henceforth voluntaristic practices, whose twists and turns were driven by whatever reasoning but certainly not by theoretically guided understandings of respective junctures of capitalist development, could be wrapped into endless Marx quotes. The irony of this response is that Kautsky, who invented this method in an effort to reconcile the Marxist left with the revisionist right inside the German Social Democratic Party, was often seen as just another revisionist by latter-day defenders of true Marxism. Endlessly repeating Lenin's charge against his former role model, Soviet Marxists saw nothing but a renegade in Kautsky. Western Marxists, who had little political practice they could hide behind Marxian orthodoxies, accused Kautsky, often in tandem with Engels, of falsifying Marx's critical theory into a positivist cookbook for political strategies. Both charges, however, rest on a separation of theory and practice.

A different response to the revisionist challenge came from Luxemburg and was later adopted by Lenin and Trotsky. Recognizing that revisionists had a point when they proclaimed the inability of received Marxist wisdom to explain recent capitalist developments or aspects of capitalism that Marx simply had not dealt with, they drew on *Capital* and other of Marx's writings to come up with new theories that were closer to empirical realities than Kautsky's orthodoxy, but also allowed for more systematic strategizing than did Bernstein's abandonment of Marxism. However, to gain credibility for their revisionist Marxism they thought it better to label their original ideas as orthodox Marxism, therein competing with Kautsky's and other Marxists' claims of being the true heirs of Karl. Whatever the value of their theoretical and strategic inventions, engaging in a competition for the title of true heir did a lot to make Marxism look like a scholastic exercise to anyone but the already initiated. Moreover, by hiding the light of their inventions under claims to orthodoxy they might have discouraged many likeminded critical spirits and determined socialists from also developing new ideas. With hindsight, it is hard to understand why original thinkers like Luxemburg, Lenin and Trotsky were so anxious not to be seen as revisionists. If they did not understand that a general theory of capitalism like the one Marx had advanced in *Capital* needed to be articulated with changing historical appearances, they would not have been able to further develop Marxist theory like they did.

All said, there is a possibility of learning from past debates about *Capital* in order to better understand today's capitalism but also a danger of getting stuck with quarrels as to who the truest follower of Marx is. To get past this danger, the old debates need to be put into their respective historical contexts. New interpretations of *Capital* always came up when socialist strategies ran into problems that could not be explained by earlier theories. Understanding the concrete historical conditions under which each new reading of *Capital* occurred also helps us to understand what might be learnt from those readings under today's different conditions. In other words, considering the historical contexts of the recurrent waves of debate around *Capital* helps us to distinguish between those aspects of *Capital* and its various interpretations that apply to the capitalist mode of production in general and others that are specific to certain times and places. It also enables us to identify issues that were largely ignored, or only dealt with *en passant*, but that could possibly be better understood in accordance with a new reading of *Capital*.

Capital in the Age of Capital

What were the historical contexts in which *Capital* was written and read? Marx worked on *Capital* after the defeat of the 1848 revolutions, a defeat that marked the passing, in Hobsbawm's terms, from the 'age of revolution' to the 'age of capital'. Though Marx's stated goal in the foreword to *Capital* was to 'reveal the law of motion of modern society', its underlying purpose, as is quite clear from many of his letters and his involvement with the First International, was to understand the emergence of industrial working classes that Marx and Engels had already identified as agents of revolutionary change in the run-up to the 1848 revolutions. They saw the defeat of these revolutions as confirmation of their argument that it was time to move from cross-class alliances struggling against feudal rulers to independent working-class movements. *Capital* was all about understanding the conditions under which workers could form such movements.

Drawing on *Capital*, Engels, Kautsky and others in the First and Second Internationals wrote popular texts that could be used for educational purposes in burgeoning workers' organizations. Texts such as Engel's *Anti-Dühring* or Kautsky's *Economic Doctrines of Karl Marx* do not have the critical depth of *Capital* but without them Marxist socialism would never have become a mass movement. The difference between the critique of political economy Marx advanced in *Capital* and popular expositions of this critique points to the dual character of all political projects which, following in the tracks of the Enlightenment one way or another, see an understanding of the world as a prerequisite for changing it. All these projects, Marxism no less than liberalism, rely on critical analysis as much as on mass support rallied around a set of ideas and collective identities.

Paraphrasing Marx's analysis of commodities and labour in the first chapter of *Capital*, we might say that theory has a dual character. We might also say that theory producing labour has a dual character: it produces knowledge value, expressed in abstract terms, and legitimation value, used for concrete political mobilization. These two sides of theory exist in an uneasy relationship. If the production of knowledge retreats in ever more abstract formulations, it generates nothing but dogmas cut off from reality checks, but it will be also too bloodless to rally support for the cause the theory allegedly advances. If, on the other hand, political mobilization severs ties with a movement's theoretical foundations or reduces theory to the role of a slogan-delivering machine, the movement's inner cohesion and appeal to outsiders will deteriorate. Ideally, questions that are relevant to the movement are picked up by theoreticians to further develop their analysis and discuss refined versions with movement militants. In this way, a continuing dialogue between theory and practice would be established.

Sadly, the history of Marxism is full of examples showing that it does not always work this way. Efforts to organize emerging industrial working classes, theoretically supported by *Capital*'s focus on the role these classes play in enriching capitalists and driving capitalist development forward through their struggles for shorter hours and better pay, made it difficult for socialist parties and unions in Western Europe to recognize the significance of the colonial expansion and imperialist rivalries that eventually exploded in the First World War. Left-wingers in the Second International tried to rally workers against colonial conquest as well as against the arms race and war-mongering amongst the imperial powers. However, their appeals to international-ism had an idealist ring that could not compete with the seemingly realistic prospect, advocated by right-wing social democrats, of reaping material gains for Western working classes from colonial exploitation. The divide between anti- and pro-imperialist currents in the Second International made effective opposition against imperialist war efforts impossible. Eventually, the pro-imperialist currents supported their respective ruling classes during the First World War, while theoretical inventions made by the left in support of opposition to colonialism and war would later become signposts for communist and left-socialist strategies. This is particularly true for Lenin's *Imperialism: The Highest Stage of Imperialism*, published in 1916. It portrayed capitalism as a decaying system in which the breaking of the weakest link of the imperialist chain, Russia, could lead to the unravelling of capitalist rule in the imperialist centres. Later, when the hopes for revolution in the West had already been disappointed, the same portrait of capitalism, coupled with Lenin's plea for the Right of Nations to Self-Determination, served as the larger context within which postcolonial regimes embarked on developmentalist projects.

Capital in the Age of Imperialism

Without having a similar impact on socialist, developmentalist or any other progressive projects as did Lenin's intervention, Hilferding's *Finance Capital* and Luxemburg's *Accumulation of Capital*, published in 1911 and 1913 respectively, were much closer to Marx's *Capital*. Hilferding drew mostly on Marx's analysis of money and finance in Volumes 1 and 3 of *Capital* to analyse what he saw as a merger between industries and banks into finance capital and the imperialist policies the newly created finance capitalists pursued. He understood the categories that Marx had developed in *Capital* as being specific to the concrete forms in which capitalism appeared in Marx's day. As these forms developed, Hilferding thought, Marx's categories also had to be further developed. Where Hilferding saw the need to adjust Marx's categories to keep up with historical changes, Luxemburg considered Marx's work as unfinished because its analytical apparatus rested on the simplifying assumption of a pure capitalism in which only capitalists and workers existed, with no traces of non-capitalist modes of production. Recognizing that Marx left *Capital* unfinished, Volumes 2 and 3 were published on the basis of incomplete manuscripts by Engels in 1885 and 1894, respectively. Luxemburg thought the next step necessary to complete Marx's work was to demonstrate how capitalism developed historically within a non-capitalist world. Starting with a critique of Marx's schemes of reproduction, which suggest that capitalist accumulation is not constrained by a lack of effective demand, Luxemburg developed the argument that capitalist expansion into non-capitalist milieus, advanced by means of credit and military force, creates the markets necessary to realize surplus value produced under capitalist relations of production. Her key argument, which she developed against Marx, was that accumulation in a purely capitalist economy would be constrained by insufficient effective demand and that, therefore, capitalism is bound to economic stagnation unless capitalists find markets in non-capitalist social milieus.

Finance and the capitalist expansion into non-capitalist milieus were aspects of capitalist development before and after Hilferding and Luxemburg wrote their respective works on these issues. The attention they attracted in socialist circles after the publication of *Finance Capital* and *Accumulation of Capital* was short-lived, as the First World War and the Russian Revolution confronted socialists with new and urgent challenges. However, after the collapse of Soviet communism, when finance was at the helm of restructuring capitalism globally and territories that the Russian and other revolutions had turned into no-go areas for capitalists were reintegrated into the world market, the issues raised by Hilferding and Luxemburg once again reappeared on leftist radar screens. By then, finance had taken on much larger and opaque forms compared to the marriage between bankers and industrialists that Hilferding had tried to understand, and capitalist expansion no longer took the specific form of colonial conquest, which had attracted most of Luxemburg's attention. But the questions both had asked took on a new urgency after communist regimes coming out of the revolution against *Capital* had collapsed or, as in China and Vietnam, turned onto the road to capitalism. At the time the revolution happened, though, it helped to establish a new brand of Marxist socialism after the Second International's support for national war efforts from 1914 onwards had discredited that original brand of organized Marxist socialism.

Capital and Soviet Communism

The Russian Revolution induced new readings of *Capital* in order to solve practical problems. The establishment of workers' councils, or Soviets, posed the question of whether these new forms of exerting political power could be developed into devices through which workers could self-manage collectively owned means of production and thereby overcome the rule of the law of value exerted by a small number of private owners of the means of production over the dispossessed working-class majority under capitalism. Dealing with that question required a sharp distinction between the productive forces and relations of production that characterize the capitalist mode of production and the respective forces and relations in non-capitalist modes of production. Works like Rubin's *Essays on Marx's Theory of Value* and Pashukanis' *General Theory of Law and Marxism*, both published in 1924, used *Capital* to stress the specific capitalist forms in which economic activity unfolds and political power is executed. Despite being highly abstract, these works supported left currents in the Bolshevik Party that sought to develop genuinely socialist relations of production. These aspirations were at odds with other currents in the party that made the development of the productive forces the number one priority. To achieve this goal, individuals belonging to these productivist currents sought to turn theoretical concepts that Marx had used to analyse the capitalist mode of production into tools for economic planning.

Marx's analysis of the primitive accumulation of capital, which transformed feudalist into capitalist relations of production, was translated into the need for socialist accumulation of capital in order to establish the basis for the future growth of industrial production, an idea originally advanced by Preobrazhensky in his *New Economics* in 1926. The reproduction schemes Marx used to analyse accumulation in an economy divided into sectors producing means of production and means of consumption, respectively, and that had been the analytical backbone of much of the Marxist debate on imperialism since Hilferding's *Finance Capital* and Luxemburg's *Accumulation of Capital*, became the core of the Five-Year Plans that were used to allocate economic resources in the Soviet Union from 1928 onwards. Rather than overcoming the rule of the law of value this approach aimed at allowing economic planners to consciously apply this law in order to avoid the waste of human and non-human resources associated with the anarchy of market production, an expression of the unconscious rule of the law of value, under capitalist relations of production. The consolidation of bureaucratic rule in the Soviet Union firmly established this latter reading of *Capital* as the basis of Soviet economic policies, whereas ideas such as those advanced by Rubin and Pashukanis, who were both executed in 1937, were brutally suppressed. Preobrazhensky, who belonged to the Left Opposition around Trotsky, was murdered a year after Stalin had appropriated his ideas and started to apply them ruthlessly way beyond Preobrazhensky's original proposals concerning the conversion of the peasantry into an industrial working class and the speed of building industrial capacity.

Capital and the New Lefts

Of course, the counterrevolution that culminated in Stalin's reign of terror as much as the failure of revolution in the industrialized West, which the Bolsheviks had sought to unleash by their own taking of power in 1917, posed new questions for socialists of all strands. However, debates over these questions were subdued when the Great Depression seemed to confirm the bleakest conclusions one could possibly draw from Marx's theories of crises. Moreover, the role of the Red Army in defeating the Nazi Wehrmacht gave the Soviets a second lease on legitimacy, despite the Stalinist terror. It wasn't until the 1960s that, under radically different economic and political conditions, a new generation of socialist activists and intellectuals picked up the question about the relations between capitalist development and revolution. During a period of unprecedented economic prosperity, claims referring to a close connection between crises, the intensification of class struggles and eventually revolution, were dropped. Such claims had been a staple of the original Marxism of the Second International, and seemed more than appropriate in the days of the Comintern and the Great Depression, but they now appeared outdated in the new age of welfare capitalism.

Many new leftists considered anti-imperialist struggles in the peripheries instead of crises in the capitalist heartlands as triggers for revolution. But to the degree these struggles diminished the size of the capitalist world market, the basis for prosperity in the West would be undermined. In turn, the taming of class conflict based on prosperity might also be unsettled. Thus, there was a line from fighting against the imperialist exploitation of Southern peripheries to unlocking class struggles in the West. Lenin, who also saw the plunder of the colonial world as an economic basis for labour aristocracies favouring class collaboration over class struggle, had already made this argument in embryonic form. But now, at a time when the imperialist centres were striving to maintain control over peripheries despite decolonization and the struggles of some of the postcolonial regimes to move from political to economic independence, works such as Gunder Frank's *Development of Underdevelopment* and Emmanuel's *Unequal Exchange*, published in 1967 and 1969 respectively, offered much more elaborate and empirically updated versions of Lenin's original argument.

Theories of unequal exchange especially underpinned Lenin's argument by adapting Marx's labour theory of value to a real world in which Western and Southern labour were anything but equal. Another significant difference between the classical and new theories of imperialism was that the former were mostly interested in the effects that colonial expansion would have on capital accumulation in the imperial centres. The new theories of imperialism, on the other hand, also recognized the class alliances pushing liberation movements and subsequent developmentalist projects forward as agents of change in their own right. In view of anti-imperialist struggles from Vietnam to Algeria and Cuba, to name only those receiving most attention in the West, it was the obvious thing to consider the suppressed peoples of the South rather than Western working classes, the latter apparently subdued by social reform and consumerism, as vanguards of revolutionary change.

However, there were also New Left currents that detected revolutionary potential under the political conditions of Western welfare states and the surface appearances of commodity exchange. Drawing on Marx's early writings on alienation, the critique of a totally administered world advanced by critical theorists like Adorno and Marcuse, and Marx's analysis of the factory regime in *Capital* and *Grundrisse*, these new leftists argued that the contradiction between courting workers as valued customers and exploiting them behind factory gates would reignite revolutionary fervour. This line of reasoning did not rely on wage pressures and the threat of unemployment, which had been a key focus of the Old Left, but on the basis that liberal claims to equality flew in the face of dictatorial rule in the workplace. This shift of focus from economic conditions to hierarchies of power made these arguments also applicable to communist countries, where politburo members celebrated the superiority of Eastern working-class rule over worker's exploitation in the capitalist West while bossing around actually existing workers in ways not much different from the management regimes under which Western workers were toiling away. A wave of workers' rebellions, going as far back as the early 1950s in Eastern Europe and taking off in Western Europe in the late 1960s, gave credence to this kind of analysis.

Although one could have assumed that the turn from prosperity to crisis in the mid-1970s would provide workers with additional reasons to struggle, the opposite was true. Labour militancy remained high across most of Western Europe until the late 1970s and in some cases into the early 1980s, but after the world recession in the mid-1970s, the character of workers' struggles changed. The playfulness of the prosperity days, when fear of job loss did not haunt workers as much, was replaced by a sense that this might be the last chance to make any gains. This turn from optimistic exuberance to a more pessimistic outlook seemed to confirm readings of *Capital* that, going back to the 1960s and most notably Althusser's *Reading Capital*, thought that workers, like anybody else, were hopelessly caught in the roles they were playing in the reproduction of the capitalist mode of production. Agency had been overwhelmed by structure – the logic of capital had triumphed over class struggle. Or so it seemed.

Capital and the New Social Movements

At the same time that Marxists saw their political hopes fading along with a receding wave of labour militancy, new social movements with little interest in Marx's *Capital* or actually existing capitalism burst onto the scene. Although there was some overlap with Marxist socialism, most of the activists and intellectuals struggling for women's rights or against racism or ecological destruction did not struggle against the capitalist owners of the means of production. Their adversaries were the sexists, racists and megalomaniac industrialists that could be found in actually existing capitalism and socialism alike. These movements rallied thousands of people in support of the legalization of abortions, against the legal discrimination of ethnic or sexual minorities, or to stop nuclear power and the arms race. However, bereft of any vision of turning sometime protestors into long-term activists, these mobilizing successes were short-lived. The new social movements quickly disintegrated into single-issue campaigns sustained by the new world of non-governmental organizations that was at least as arcane as that of the Marxist circles hanging on to their ideas.

Together, from the mid-1960s to the early 1980s, the various New Lefts and new social movements were strong enough to unsettle the welfare capitalism that had developed after the end of the Second World War. Already in the 1960s, when the long postwar boom was still in full swing, capitalists had viewed most of the claims made by these movements as a threat to their profits. Once the boom turned bust in the mid-1970s, they were convinced that it was time to end the welfare state compromise in order to restore profits threatened by social movements and capitalist crisis alike. Subsequently, they launched, in Gramsci's terms, a passive revolution that appropriated some of the ideas around which the New Lefts and new social movements had rallied. Most significantly, the call for liberation, originally launched against the rule of corporate elites and state bureaucrats but also branded as a call for national and women's liberation, was reinvented as a call by corporate elites to liberate everyone from union bosses and welfare bureaucracies. The new call for market liberation resonated even amongst many working-class people who actually benefited from the social protections that were rolled back in the name of individual freedom and choice from the early 1980s onwards. However, the issues raised by the left movements that were defeated, marginalized or co-opted by an emergent neoliberal bloc are as urgent as they were when leftists originally raised them, from the times of the First and Second Internationals to the new social movements of the 1970s.

Readings of *Capital* in this Volume

In Chapter 1, Ingo Schmidt shows how Marx's *Capital* influenced a range of thinkers and political movements from communists to social democrats and anti-colonialists. Their interpretations sought to create a common language, shape collective identities and legitimate socialist strategies. Yet, despite a range of victories now and then, these movements ultimately reached an impasse by the 1980s, as global capitalism transcended domestic barriers to accumulation. An increasingly disorganized working class, having exhausted both the limitations of 'capitalism with a human face' and the strategies linked to these interpretations, struggled to respond to the challenges in a coherent way. The analyses that guided these failures are key to understanding the present conditions of workers around the world in all their diversity. If new roads to socialism are to be found, dissident voices of the past informed by present realities may be useful starting points for the remaking of a working-class politics in a way that Marx and others had envisioned during the First International.

In Chapter 2, William Pelz emphasizes the importance of the International Working Men's Association (IWMA), later known as the First International, to the formation of *Capital*. He argues that the two projects were intertwined – one intellectual and literary, the other political and practical – with the aim of winning workers over to the ideas of internationalism and labour activism. In this regard, just as Marx's ideas were transmitted to the International, the activities of the International shaped and influenced Marx's writings.

In Chapter 3, Anej Korsika examines the lasting legacy of the Bolshevik revolution against *Capital*. Although *Capital* was, as Marx put it, initially met with a 'conspiracy of silence', one of the few places where it received serious attention was in Tsarist Russia. The October Revolution was one of the first attempts to integrate Marx's theoretical insights with the practical problems posed by capitalism.

As Korsika argues, despite a variety of strategies none of them actually succeeded in abolishing capitalism. Instead, Soviet communism was swallowed by capitalism. Despite the ultimate failure of the Soviet socialist experiment, a close historical reading nevertheless provides important insights that could contribute to contemporary struggles against capitalist exploitation.

In Chapter 4, Prabhat Patnaik shows how the Labour Theory of Value (LTV) is often assumed to explain the relative prices between numerous non-monetary commodities in terms of the money commodity. However, for Patnaik, this interpretation is largely erroneous. In his view, the LTV was never meant as an explanation of the relative prices of commodities but rather, in the words of Marx, as a 'first approximation'. He makes the argument that the LTV is largely concerned with the relative exchange ratio between the money commodity, on the one hand, and the world of non-money commodities taken together, on the other. Understood this way, since money is necessarily a form in which wealth is held under capitalism, a rise in money wages, or in the money prices of scarce raw materials, must lower the given-output-rate-of-profit of the system to keep alive this form-of-wealth role of money.

Although *Capital* did not deal with gender and the family directly, in Chapter 5 Silvia Federici shows how Marx's historical materialist method made a significant contribution to the development of feminist theory, most notably around the construction of gender hierarchies and identities. Here, Federici notes two different Marxes, with two different viewpoints on gender and class struggles. One left the question of gender largely untheorized, naturalizing women's domestic work and idealizing industrial labour as the normative form of social production and a potential leveller of social inequalities. The other Marx was discovered by feminists in the 1970s, who revolted against housework, domesticity and economic dependence on men as they sought a theory capable of explaining the root causes of women's oppression from a class perspective. As Federici shows, the result of this synthesis was a theoretical revolution that changed both Marxism and feminism.

In Chapter 6, Peter Gose and Justin Paulson examine the various economic laws identified in *Capital* from an anti-determinist philosophy of praxis perspective. They distinguish between six meanings of 'law' in *Capital* and explore how they interrelate in the book's defining arguments. Gose and Paulson demonstrate that Marx's laws derive from historical conditions that are themselves outcomes of class struggle. Laws exist midway up an explanatory hierarchy and are bound up with exactly the same objective conditions as praxis, such that they are two sides of the same coin. They conclude by showing how this reconciliation of specific historical determination with general ontological open-endedness remains one of Marx's greatest and most distinctive achievements.

In Chapter 7, Paul Thompson and Chris Smith examine theories of so-called cognitive capitalism contending that the accumulation of knowledge and information (i.e. immaterial labour) has displaced struggles over production and the labour process. Rooted in the traditions of Italian *operaismo* and the French regulation school, proponents of cognitive capitalism argue that capitalism is in the midst of a third major transition centred on the accumulation of immaterial assets, the previous two phases having transitioned away from mercantilism and industrial capitalism. In critiquing these views, Thompson and Smith demonstrate the continuing relevance of Marx's writings on the labour process in *Capital*. While Marx's *magnum opus* doesn't have all the answers, it remains an indispensable tool for analysing capital-labour relations in the production process, as well as examining the contested terrain around control over the working day, particularly in relation to new technologies and science.

In Chapter 8, Carlo Fanelli and Jeff Noonan argue that at the heart of *Capital* is an exploration of an emergent world capitalism, rather than questions of workers' struggles or trade unions as agents of political transformation. While organizing workers at the point of production is not only important but necessary, Marx (and Engels) argued that in failing to come to terms with the root sectionalism of trade unionism organized labour risked impeding the formation of an alternative political and class project. Challenging the entrenched power of capital and the state required the development of a class-oriented trade unionism that responded to the undemocratic and alienating structures upon which capitalism depends in ways that built upon the radical potential of the working class as a whole. Fanelli and Noonan argue that a key task of the left must be to draw out this implicitly radical contestation, and connect success in the struggle to control ever more of the social surplus to a long-term struggle for socialism.

In Chapter 9, Hannah Holleman illustrates the importance of Marx's writings for the global environmental movement. She shows how, in the absence of an historical analysis such as that presented in *Capital*, issues of mass displacement, species extinction, climate change and inequality seem a natural and inevitable feature of modern society. This obscures the ways in which capitalism is inherently environmentally destructive. Holleman shows how *Capital* provides a strong foundation for developing a deeper understanding of the core of capitalism's ecological rift, as well as insights for developing a movement that challenges continued socio-ecological degradation.

Finally, in Chapter 10, Peter Hudis imagines society beyond *Capital* – that is to say, the conditions under which a transformative socialist project may emerge. In this regard, Marx's writings provide fertile ground from which to begin. Hudis shows how Marx's body of thought contains crucial elements for discussions of a socialist society that both proponents and opponents alike have overlooked. Drawing on both published and unpublished works now made available with the publication of the *Gesaumtausgabe* (MEGA-2), Hudis contends that it is now possible to reconstruct an outline of Marx's concept of a postcapitalist society with an eye to how it addresses today's search for pathways beyond the dead-end of capitalist production.

Reading *Capital* Today

Reading *Capital* today allows us to learn from the experiences of socialists and other left activists of the past, understand how present-day capitalism came into being, and develop socialist strategies for the future. In other words, reading *Capital* today is a political project. In this regard, while this collection of essays is meant for students and researchers alike, it also aims to inform a range of labour and other social movements in all their diversity. The different theoretical and political traditions that the contributors to this volume come from shape the way they read *Capital* and the way they interpret the respective issues addressed. This book neither claims to address every issue relevant to the making of a new socialist left nor does it suggest a particular interpretation of *Capital*. Quite the contrary, it is an invitation to use *Capital* as a common point of reference that allows us to put different issues into context, discuss alternate points of view, and build unity in diversity.

1

Capital and the History of Class Struggle

Ingo Schmidt

'[I]t is the ultimate aim of this work to reveal the law of motion of modern society', Marx explained to his German readers in the preface to the first edition of *Capital*. The first chapter of the actual text makes clear that he understands 'modern society' as one 'in which the capitalist mode of production prevails' (Marx 1976: 92, 125). Over the next 24 chapters he analyses commodity exchange, money and capital, the production of surplus value and capital accumulation, in a model in which only two classes exist: capitalists and workers. He illustrates this highly abstract model with experiences from England where, at the time, the capitalist mode of production had made deeper inroads into non-capitalist modes of production than anywhere else. England is also the example Marx uses to explain the historical origins of the division between workers and capitalists. The final eight chapters of *Capital* are devoted to this process of, in Marx's terms, 'so-called primitive accumulation'.

Yet, he derives the 'general law of capitalist accumulation' in Chapter 25 from an abstract model before looking into the historical origins of the capitalist mode of production. Moreover, in *Capital* we find workers struggling against capitalists' quest for lower wages, longer hours and harder work but, even when they had some success in these struggles, we see them failing in some other respect. From skilled workers they are downgraded to appendices of machines owned and controlled by capitalists, many are pushed into an industrial reserve army of labour that keeps a lid on the wage demands of the active army of workers. Although Marx sees workers as a 'class constantly increasing in numbers, ... trained, united and organized by the ... capitalist process of production' (1976: 899, 929), their 'dependence on capital' appears so overpowering that it is difficult to see how the same workers will ever be able to overthrow capitalist rule.

In the *Communist Manifesto*, Marx and Engels declared that 'the history of all hitherto existing society is the history of class struggles' (1998: 2); in *Capital* we find abstract laws but little class struggle and history. Yet, despite being so strangely removed from history and class struggle, *Capital*, along with other of Marx's and Engels' writings, did inspire revolutionary movements – just not, as Marx had expected, in countries like England where industrial capitalism developed but in largely agrarian and non-capitalist countries from Russia to China, Cuba and Vietnam. The perceived threat from the 'Revolution Against *Capital*' (Gramsci 2000) in these countries, along with domestic pressure from unions and social democratic parties, led to the emergence of a welfare capitalism looking very different from the brutal exploitation of workers Marx described in *Capital*. Marx's speculations about workers' revolutions were turned upside down when capitalists felt that social reform had gone too far and turned to class struggle from above to restore their power. The collapse of Soviet communism looked like a late confirmation of Marx's original proposition that socialist revolutions can only succeed on the basis of an industrial economy. This collapse greatly facilitated capitalist efforts to roll back social reforms in the West and thereby recreate capitalism after the image of *Capital*, but with industrial working classes largely relocated from the North to the postcolonial South.

Even though actually existing capitalism today looks more like the capitalism Marx depicted in *Capital*, the latter is still, and probably will be as long as capitalism exists, an abstraction reminiscent of, but not identical with, capitalist realities. Maybe it is precisely this dissonance between empirical capitalism and the abstract laws revealed by Marx that made *Capital* attractive to generations of socialists who sought to understand capitalism in order to overcome it. This dissonance opened the space for them to adjust their interpretations to the changes coming with capitalist development and to adjust socialist strategies accordingly. This chapter outlines the key interpretations of *Capital* from 1867 until today, along with the strategies derived from them. It will show that ideas devised in *Capital* and other Marxist writings gripped the masses, to paraphrase Marx, and therefore became a material force. This is true for social democracy, even after shaking off its Marxist roots; for communism, even though Soviet realities replaced Marx's ideas about workers' self-liberation with the dictatorship of the politburo; and it is also true for some anti-colonial movements, even though Marx said hardly anything, and certainly not in *Capital*, about the colonial world. This outline will also show that dissident Marxists, whose ideas were never widely circulated enough to grip the masses, played important roles in unsettling dominant interpretations of *Capital* when the strategies linked to those interpretations became stuck in dead-ends. After all hitherto dominant interpretations of *Capital* and Marxist politics have been defeated, and while capitalism produces increasing levels of discontent, dissident voices of the past may provide starting points for the remaking of working-class politics in a way that Marx and his comrades envisioned during the First International, only now on a much more global scale.

Capital for the Socialist Workers' Movement

Marx begins his analysis of the inner workings of the capitalist mode of production with the most common and seemingly simple thing one finds in societies associated with the capitalist mode of production: the commodity. Searching for the laws governing commodity exchanges, Marx deciphers abstract labour as the source of value and surplus value that is produced by workers who have to sell their labour power to acquire their means of subsistence. The surplus value is appropriated by the buyers of labour power: as owners of the means of production and managers of the labour power they have bought, they pocket the revenue from the sale of commodities made by the workers. This revenue recovers the costs of labour power and means of production used in the production process and the creation of surplus value. This is so because the use value of labour power for the capitalist lies in the fact that it can produce a value greater than its exchange value or wage. Marx then shows why the accumulation of capital, i.e. the reinvestment of surplus value, leads to the concentration and centralization of capital, why it produces recurrent crises and deepening inequalities between workers and capitalists.

In Volume 2 of *Capital*, Marx looks at the conditions under which the exchange between producers of means of production and means of consumption, respectively, allow the continued accumulation of capital, but he also ponders the possibilities why these conditions may not be fulfilled, i.e. why crises may interrupt the process of accumulation. In Volume 3, Marx demonstrates how competition leads to a uniform rate of profit across industries operating under different economic conditions and discusses the question whether this profit rate has a tendency to fall. He then shows how commercial capital, money capital and landowners get their share of the surplus value produced under the command of productive capital. The final chapter on classes ends after a page and a half with a comment by Engels, who assembled Volumes 2 and 3 from Marx's unfinished manuscripts, saying: 'At this point the manuscript breaks off' (Marx 1981: 1025). As more of Marx's original manuscripts became accessible, beginning with the *Grundrisse* published in Moscow in 1939, Marxists spent much time pondering the degree to which Engels' editing of Volumes 2 and 3 changed their content compared to Marx's intentions, and whether Marx was still planning to write a book on wage labour as originally planned or whether his arguments about wage labour were actually moved into the three volumes of *Capital* (see, for example: Rosdolsky 1977; Lebowitz 1992).

Be that as it may, what we find in *Capital*, notably Volume 1, is a detailed analysis of the ways capital exploits workers in the production process and how a reserve army of labour is created that ensures that the supply of labour power is large and cheap enough to allow the continued production of surplus value. We also find hints at workers' struggles for shorter hours and higher wages. Yet, every victory in these struggles becomes a reason for capitalists to replace skilled workers and their workplace bargaining power with machines and unskilled workers who can easily be hired and fired. In short, we see the constant transformation of labour power into variable capital and the latter's key role in producing surplus value, but we don't see the possessors of this labour power, the workers, acting as individuals having ideas and aspirations cutting through the laws governing capitalist production. We also don't see workers acting outside the production process or hear anything about the lives of unemployed workers or family members performing unpaid household labour. Reading *Capital* tells us nothing about the making of working classes as collective agents of change. But it did help activists who read it in building workers movements that could, more or less legitimately, claim to articulate working-class interests. In fact, Marx himself was a part of this process. He started work on actual economic development and political economic theories, which formed the basis for *Capital*, after the defeat of the 1848 revolutions.

The dominance that an expanding capitalist mode of production had gained over its opponents is reflected in the subordinate role workers play in *Capital*. However, the world described in it rang true to many workers and thus provided fertile ground for socialist strategies that can be derived from it, even though such strategies are not presented in *Capital*. The First and Second Internationals created the organizational framework in which workers' experiences on the one hand and Marx's scientific analysis of the capitalist mode of production on the other could be mediated. This mediation process contributed to the formation of collective identities and a strategic vision for the industrial working classes of Western Europe (Steenson 1991). The long boom following the defeat of the 1848 revolutions confirmed Marx's argument that capital accumulation would turn increasing numbers of people into workers; his prediction of increasing working-class misery was confirmed by the subsequent depression of the early 1870s to the early 1890s.

That depression was followed by another long boom during which the factory regime that Marx had identified in *Capital* as the core of capitalist rule extended its hold over increasing sections of Western European populations. But at the same time, the real wages of skilled and organized workers were rising. The idea that union organizing would allow only temporary material gains but prepare workers for the final battle in the face of escalating working-class misery, with which Marx had concluded Volume 1 of *Capital*, lost its persuasiveness. Increasingly it was replaced by the idea that capitalism could gradually be transformed into socialism, one reform at a time. The new boom coincided with the last wave of colonial expansion that raised the question whether, and if so, to what degree, the exploitation of popular classes in the colonial world was the basis for rising real wages in the industrial world. *Capital*, narrowly focusing on industrial capitalism, had no answers to the questions of colonial exploitation and even less to the related question of imperialist rivalry that culminated in the First World War and another shift from long boom to long downturn. The Marxism around which the Second International was built faced two moments of crises: one when the long boom and rising real wages refuted the expectation of capitalist decline and increasing pauperization of the working class, and another when the boom was ended not by the unfolding of the general law of capitalist accumulation but by great power conflict and war.

Revolution Against *Capital*

Rosa Luxemburg (2003, 2011) offers the clearest example how reading *Capital* can help in finding new strategies when old ones are at an impasse. She reminded her comrades that Marx left non-capitalist modes of production out of his analysis. She argued that this was necessary to reveal the law of modern, i.e. capitalist, society but also that the image of capitalism arising from *Capital* should not be mistaken for capitalist reality. In order to bring insights derived from *Capital* closer to reality it would be necessary to analyse the relationships between the capitalist mode of production and non-capitalist modes of production, within which capitalism has developed historically. More specifically, she maintained that Marx, in order to show the conditions under which capital could continuously accumulate, had constructed numerical examples that illustrated such a possibility. Yet, according to Luxemburg, he had not shown why there would always have been enough effective demand to realize all of the surplus value that has been produced. In her view, such realization, and thus the accumulation of capital, depends on purchases from non-capitalist social strata. This argument allowed her to understand capital accumulation as a process progressively replacing non-capitalist modes of production. Considered from this angle, colonial expansion at the end of the nineteenth century was the means that overcame the depression from the 1870s to the early 1890s. Rising real wages, then, were reliant on working-class complicity with colonialism but came at the price of also fighting the wars of their respective national bourgeoisies, once the outward expansion turned into imperialist infighting. Based on this analysis, political strategy shifted from social reform to anti-imperialism and, once the First World War began, opposition to war and the revolutionary overthrow of political regimes.

In a more eclectic analysis, drawing on the Marxist Hilferding as much as the proto-Keynesian Hobson, Lenin (2010) arrived at similar conclusions. Luxemburg, writing in industrialized Germany, sought to reinvent working-class politics as an alternative to the class collaboration advocated and practised by revisionist social democrats and union leaders, a collaboration in which she saw the origins of social democracy's support for imperial war. Lenin, writing in agrarian Russia with only few pockets of industrial production, sought to establish a revolutionary form of class collaboration between workers and peasants. He went to great pains to demonstrate that capitalism had established roots in Russia's vast agricultural sector but that this agrarian capitalism was very different from the industrial capitalism Marx had analysed in *Capital* (Lenin 2004). The uneven development between industrial capitalism, applying the latest technology in firms much larger than most in industrialized England, and agrarian capitalism, still laden with remnants of feudal rule, made Russian capitalism more vulnerable to economic and political crisis. Lenin therefore identified Russia as the weakest link in the imperialist chain. He expected that the breaking of this chain would lead to the unravelling of capitalism in its most industrialized centres with their working-class majorities.

By seeing the development of industrial capitalism as part of a larger process of the penetration of non-capitalist social strata and regions Luxemburg and Lenin were able to understand the unevenness of capitalism on a world scale as much as within individual countries. By 'deprovincializing Marx' (Harootunian 2015), they departed from the mechanistic interpretations of *Capital* that had played such a big role in the making of First and, on a much larger scale, Second International socialism. However, they shared with Marx the conviction that the decisive battle for socialism would be fought in the centres, not the peripheries. The Marxism they had advanced was in crisis once it became clear that the Russian Revolution was not going to be followed by a successful revolution in the West. If Gramsci called the Russian Revolution a revolution against *Capital*, the failure of revolution in the West and the crisis of Marxism this failure triggered led to reinterpretations of *Capital* that were even further removed from Marx's abstract model of Western European capitalism than Luxemburg's and Lenin's.

In the West, Marxists had to understand why the revolutionary uprisings from 1918 to 1923 failed before they could possibly think about new strategies for socialist transformation. To do so, they shifted their focus from capital accumulation and crises as breeding grounds for revolutionary fervour to the question of how capitalism could maintain a certain level of legitimacy despite the hardships every crisis inflicts on the working classes. To this effect, Gramsci (2000) developed the concepts of civil society and hegemony, Adorno and Horkheimer (2007: 94–136) conceived of mass deception, and Althusser (2008: 1–60) pondered on the effects of ideological state apparatuses. A new reading of *Capital* since the 1960s, for which Althusser's 1965 work *Reading Capital* served as a catalyst, used the concept of fetishism (for which neither Kautsky, Luxemburg nor Lenin had had much use) to understand the ideological reproduction of capitalism. Meanwhile, Marxists in the East turned Marx's analysis of the capitalist mode of production, derived in large part from a critique of classical political economy, into a guidebook for industrialization in agrarian countries.

When Marx explained to his German readers why they should be interested in capitalist development in England, he famously declared that the 'country that is more developed industrially only shows, to the less developed, the image of its own future' (1976: 92). Once his notebooks became available it became clear that Marx did not think this dictum should be generalized beyond Western Europe (Anderson 2010). It was no surprise, though, that Soviet leaders, urgently needing an economic strategy to overcome the devastation brought about by war, civil war and foreign intervention, were looking at capitalist industrialization in the West. There was a readily available model they thought they could follow, replacing private property and capitalist rule with state property and Communist Party rule, in order to build an economy in which, after a phase of original socialist accumulation, everyone's material needs could be satisfied. Controversy over the speed with which industrialization could be pushed and by how much consumption had to be restrained during the transition period aside, the goal of modernizing the Soviet economy in the tracks of capitalist industrialization was shared across the factions struggling for power in the Soviet Union (Erlich 1967). In turn, Soviet-style industrialization became a model for many postcolonial regimes in the South. Far from being the opening shot for revolution in the industrialized West, Russia's revolution against *Capital* was the precursor for revolutions in other agrarian societies, most notably in China, Cuba and Vietnam.

Social Reform Against *Capital*

That the revolution started in the East and then moved to the South, rather than the West, was one side of refuting Marx's argument about capital accumulation, crises and revolution in industrialized countries. The other was that, after two world wars, revolutions, counterrevolutions and the Great Depression, capitalism in the West grew faster than ever before and was transformed by social reforms that turned the failed liberal capitalism of old into an organized capitalism seemingly capable of reconciling efficiency with equity. Welfare capitalism in the post-Second World War era had more in common with the political vision that the revisionist Hilferding had developed in the 1920s (Smaldone 1988) than with the revolutionary conclusions Marx had drawn from *Capital*. Ironically, though, *Capital* was also Hilferding's starting point, but his conclusions were different from Marx's. Contrary to Luxemburg, who argued that an equilibrium between total production and total demand was an assumption Marx had made in order to develop a theoretical model to analyse the reality of insufficient demand, Hilferding argued that such an equilibrium could exist in reality. In the early days of capitalism, large numbers of firms competed with each other; they increased production when prices went up, and scaled production down once it outpaced sales. However, the concentration and centralization of capital had reduced the number of firms to such a level that competition could be replaced by cooperation.

Furthermore, the increasing volume of credit and stock markets allowed a smooth transition of production capacities from shrinking to expanding sectors of the economy. Continued full employment thus became a possibility. If, at the time Hilferding wrote *Finance Capital*, this wasn't a reality it was because the leaders of the cartels and trusts that dominated the economy chose to make money by boosting prices beyond the costs and profit margins firms in a competitive market could make. They further chose to invest in colonial conquest rather than domestic economies. Yet, in a democratic republic, social democratic parties and unions, Hilferding thought, could serve as countervailing powers and force capitalists to manage the economy in way that would replace capital exports and imperialist conquest by production for domestic use. Starting from *Capital*, Hilferding arrived at a political concept that anticipated much of Keynesianism, which delivered guidance for postwar social democrats. However, the Keynesian compact in the West only became possible because Soviet communism had developed into a formidable challenge to capitalist rule and because new markets, ranging from the beginnings of industrialization in the postcolonial South to the capitalist penetration of private households, created sufficient demand to keep accumulation going (Schmidt 2014).

While the Cold War and its proxy wars in the South were raging, the contending regimes in the East and West had some things in common that led to new interpretations of *Capital* on both sides of the iron curtain and also to an unexpected convergence of workers' struggles. By the mid twentieth century, the factory regime whose embryonic forms Marx had analysed in Volume 1 of *Capital* (1976: Chapter 15) had developed into a much more detailed division of labour; more rigid control of the labour process was supplemented by large-scale bureaucracies extending beyond the factory into state apparatuses. Soviet communists, always eager to mimic the allegedly more advanced forces of production of the West, had designed production complexes in which the experiences of shop-floor workers were similar to those of their Western counterparts. A new generation of activists, disgusted with bureaucratic rule, sought a strategy for shop-floor rebellion against this rule. To do so, they drew on Marx's concept of alienation (Marx 1980) but also began to read *Capital* politically (Cleaver 1979), understanding the day-to-day struggles over wages, hours and working conditions as an attack on the heart of the capitalist system or, in the East, the dictatorship of the politburo.

Labour rebellions in the East were met with a mix of state repression and efforts to expand the supply of consumer goods even at the price of financing them with credits from Western capitalists. Labour rebellions in the West, which had benefited from the exceptional conditions of full employment, ended when the end of the long boom led to the restoration of a reserve army of labour. At this point, Marxists rediscovered theories of crises that had been developed in the 1920s and 1930s (Grossman 1992; Varga 1935), a time when the general crisis of capitalism seemed imminent. However, unlike in the days when capitalist crises could be considered a springboard for socialist transformation, this was no longer the case in the 1970s. Stalinist terror and post-Stalinist bureaucratic rule had exhausted Soviet communism as a role model for socialists in the West. Efforts to build a New Left beyond social democracy and Soviet communism had failed too. Their fixation on alienation, which was quite understandable and convincing during the days of prosperity, had nothing to say about socialist politics in times of economic crisis. None of the strategies advanced by the left could cope with harsh economic realities. Therefore, the 1970s crisis of capitalism turned into a crisis of Marxism, which, unlike previous ones, didn't lead to renewal of Marxist ideas and socialist strategy but to 'post-Marxism' and a farewell to the working class.

Capital's Counter-Offensive

The defeat of Old and New Left movements commonly associated with 1968 (Horn 2008) bore some resemblance to the defeat of the 1848 revolutions. Both defeats removed political barriers to further capital accumulation. The former had removed pretty much any opposition to the expansion of capital, conditions reflected in *Capital*'s treatment of labour more as variable capital than as autonomous agent, whereas the latter turned the tide from gradual advance of social reform and anti-colonial revolution to neoliberal counter-reform across the capitalist world and, after the collapse of the Soviet Union, the entire globe. Among the movements defeated over the course of the 1970s were, as noted above, the rank-and-file rebellions against the factory regime represented by capitalists but also unions and the state. These workers' movements had some overlap with movements of women and ethnic minorities who, to the degree they were part of the workforce, held the lowest paying jobs under the most hazardous conditions. However, women's and ethnic minority movements extended way beyond struggles at the point of production, including struggles for legal and social rights and against capitalist penetration of every aspect of life. This latter aspect was most obvious in women's struggles over the recognition of household labour. Ecological movements, in a similar vein, fought against further capitalist penetration of nature.

These new social movements posed a challenge for various forms of Marxist politics. The 'new workerism' focused on workers' experiences at the point of production represented an alternative to the fixation on parties, unions and state shared by social democrats and Soviet communists. But it had nothing to say about the concerns of the new social movements that lay beyond the labour process. Ironically, the new workers shared this silence with social democratic and Soviet Marxists and even dissident currents such as the Trotskyists. The institutionalization of the old social movement, i.e. the transformation of liberal into organized capitalism, posed another challenge for Marxism. Greatly extended state intervention clearly changed the ways in which the logic of capital could unfold. More specifically, welfare state expansion created new layers of workers in the public sector whose pay was dependent on the state's ability to raise taxes. The struggle between private sector wages and profits that *Capital* was concerned about was thus supplemented by the struggle over the sharing of the tax burden and access to public services financed by these taxes. In organized capitalism workers had won some institutionalized power so that the three-way struggles over wages, profits and taxes could trigger inflation and fiscal crises.

Marxists did theorize the changes that distinguished organized from liberal capitalism (Boddy and Crotty 1976; O'Connor 1973), and also tried to understand the concerns of the new social movements within Marxist frameworks (Menon 1982; O'Connor 1988). But it never became clear whether, and if so how, these innovations would fit into the context of Marx's general theory of accumulation and crises. Some argued that the laws identified by Marx would govern capitalist development in new institutional forms, whereas others thought organized capitalism was governed by different laws, in which case they found it hard to explain why they didn't abandon Marx like most social democrats had already done when organized capitalism began establishing its reign in the 1950s. Marxists attempted to break new theoretical and political ground during the 1960s and 1970s, but their failure to come up with a strategy as coherent as those of social democrats and Soviet communists in the 1920s and 1930s indicated that the historical bloc that held organized capitalism together, itself an outcome of the crises and class struggles of the 'Age of Catastrophe' from 1914 to 1945, had begun to fracture (Schmidt 2011). However, at the time it was anything but clear that this fracture would deepen and eventually lead to the replacement of the welfare state bloc by a neoliberal bloc.

With strikes and protests flaring up in many places across the Western world, capitalists in the 1970s had every reason to be concerned that Old and New Left movements would find common ground, in which case the profit squeeze they complained about loudly would have become reality. However, before that happened the capitalist elites reoriented themselves, moving from an accommodation of social movement demands to a counteroffensive. This included repression of the most radical elements of left movements, the co-optation of moderate elements of new social movements, and the rollback of the welfare state and organized labour. The turn to austerity turned cyclical unemployment into a permanent reserve army of labour whose ranks were further filled by a new wave of automation of production processes and office work and the relocation of manufacturing to low-wage areas. The result was that the working classes made in the days of the First and Second Internationals and later integrated into organized capitalism were unmade one counter-reform at a time. Investment in new technologies, production facilities and the logistics networks connecting them created demand effective enough to keep accumulation going despite the assault on wages and social spending.

The privatization of public enterprises and services created further investment opportunities, notably in logistics and information industries, i.e. the areas crucial for the establishment of global production networks capable of bypassing the still existing bastions of organized labour. These networks, controlled by multinational corporations almost exclusively headquartered in the West, also played a central role in the reestablishment of capitalist and imperialist control in the South where they had been challenged by the radicalization of anti-colonial movements in the wake of the Cuban Revolution. Capitalist efforts to regain and consolidate their class power over workers globally eventually culminated in the reintegration of formerly communist countries into the capitalist world-system. This global capitalism developed out of the defeat of social democracy, with its roots in the Second International and Soviet communism and revolutions in the South that were inspired by the Soviet experience. It further developed out of the failures to forge a New Left beyond the shortcomings of social democracy and Soviet communism that became so apparent with the diversity of social movements during the 1970s. Ironically, this global capitalism resembles the capitalism presented in *Capital* more than the organized capitalism that arose out of the crisis of liberal capitalism and under the influence of socialist movements inspired, one way or the other, by *Capital*.

Capital Against Global Capitalism

In global capital, it seems, the logic of capital has triumphed over workers' struggles against capital. The labour processes in today's sweatshops are strikingly similar to those Marx analysed in Volume 1 of *Capital* and Engels had already portrayed in great empirical detail in his 1845 *Condition of the Working Class in England*. However, during the time of Marx and Engels England was the workshop of the world while other Western European countries and North America were industrial laggards and the rest of the world fell victim to Western colonization. Today, most manufacturing is located in the postcolonial South, with China playing a key role not only as the new workshop of the world but also as a rising political power potentially challenging Western dominance. This new role of China is somewhat ironic considering that its industrialization was spurred by a revolution that was even more against *Capital* than the Russian Revolution. The Chinese Revolution wasn't won by mass strikes, protests and eventually a carefully planned insurrection, as in Russia, but by a prolonged war of peasant guerrillas against foreign occupation and troops loyal to the domestic capitalist regime.

Thus, despite the apparent similarities between nineteenth-century and present-day factory regimes, it would be misleading to go back to *Capital* and abandon later innovations in Marxist theory. To fully understand the labour processes of today, their analysis needs to be put in the context of changes in the capitalist world-system. More specifically, the relocation of production from the imperialist centres to Southern peripheries and China's escape from peripheral status require an analysis of imperialism and the development of anti-systemic revolution. Such an analysis might start from the classical works of Luxemburg, Lenin and their contemporaries. However, these works shared Marx's assumption that industrial production lies at the heart of capitalist wealth and power and that the main sites of production were also the centres of capitalism. This poses the question of whether the old centres can retain their dominant position within global capitalism after so much production has been moved to the postcolonial world. Answering these questions requires updating the classical theories of imperialism, just as Marx's analysis of the labour process needs an update.

The factories of *The Condition of the Working Class in England* and of *Capital* were independent economic units. Hilferding had already pointed at cartels and trusts superseding such independent units, and Marxists in the 1970s (Braverman 1974) examined the changes in the labour process in monopoly capitalism. Yet, the vertically integrated corporations that had replaced large numbers of independent factories gave way to globally networked production, which raises questions about the location of power and competition within these networks. Closely related to these questions are the roles of the state and finance in today's global system. Notwithstanding the anti-state rhetoric that accompanied the neoliberal globalization of capitalism, shares of taxes and public spending in GDP barely shrank compared to the 1970s heyday of welfare state expansion. States also play a key role in finance, as bond-selling market participants, as rule-makers, and through their central banks. The analysis of finance in Volume 3 of *Capital* is one place from which an analysis of finance today might start; Hilferding's *Finance Capital*, with its analysis of the merger of industrial and money capital, is another. But, as in the case of imperialism, competition and monopoly, changes in actually existing capitalism require adjustments of older analytical tools and possibly the invention of new ones too. The transformations and crises of capitalism from 1867 to the present went hand in hand with as many transformations and crises of Marxism. If the latter is to serve as a guide for socialist politics in the future, as it did in the past, further innovation is required to move beyond the most recent crisis of Marxism triggered by the defeat of the movements of 1968. Such innovation further requires incorporating issues into Marxist analysis that lay beyond the scope of *Capital*, notably the non-capitalist worlds of nature, household labour and subsistence production.

As far as interpreting capitalism goes, reading *Capital* and works developed in the tracks of it at various later turns of capitalist development is a good basis for constructing an up-to-date critique of political economy. The defeats and failures of socialist strategies derived from Marxist analyses after *Capital* do not mean that there is nothing to be learned from the analyses that inspired socialisms from Lenin's Bolshevism to social democratic welfare states and anti-colonial revolutions or New Left efforts to move beyond the three aforementioned roads to socialism. Though all of these socialisms ultimately failed, they left their marks on today's global capitalism. Therefore, the analyses that guided these socialisms are a key to understanding the present condition of the workers of the world in all their diversity. Theoretically, there is no going back to *Capital* untainted by the failures and defeats of socialist strategies derived from it at various points in time. Practically, though, there might be a going back to the politics of *Capital* precisely because of those failures and defeats.

Capital, and all socialist pamphlets, leaflets and speeches drawing on it one way or another, did play a role in the making of the working classes and socialist movements from 1867 onwards. They created a common language in which to discuss strategy, helped to shape collective identities, and produced, at least for certain periods of time, legitimate socialist strategies. Yet, the defeat of these movements and strategies led to the unmaking of working classes as we knew them from the nineteenth century until the 1980s. The development of global capitalism since then has produced a variety of protest and strike movements throughout the world, but the discontent underlying these protests and strikes has not yet consolidated into new working classes capable of challenging the rule of global capital. If *Capital* contributed to the making of working classes in the past because it gave the everyday experiences of workers a somewhat coherent framework from which political strategies and visions of alternatives to capitalism could be derived, the same may be true in the future. For this, reading *Capital* isn't enough; it requires us to take ideas that draw on it and other Marxist works into the realm of organizing and mobilizing for socialist change, just as Marx took his own ideas about *Capital* into the First International.

References

Adorno, T. and Horkheimer, M. (2007 [1944]). *Dialectic of Enlightenment*. Stanford: Stanford University Press.
Althusser, L. (2008 [1970]). Ideology and Ideological State Apparatuses. In *On Ideology*. London and New York: Verso, 1–60.

Althusser, L. (2009 [1965]). *Reading Capital*. London and New York: Verso.

Anderson, K. (2010). *Marx on the Margins*. Chicago: University of Chicago Press.

Boddy, R. and Crotty, J. (1976). Wages, Prices, and the Profit Squeeze. *Review of Radical Political Economics*, 8: 63–7.

Braverman, H. (1974). *Labor and Monopoly Capitalism*. New York: Monthly Review Press.

Cleaver, H. (1979). *Reading Capital Politically*. Austin: University of Texas Press.

Engels, F. (1975 [1845]). The Condition of the Working Class in England. In *Marx and Engels Collected Works*, Vol. 4, New York: International Publishers, 295–596.

Erlich, A. (1967). *The Soviet Industrialization Debate, 1924–1928*. Cambridge, MA: Harvard University Press.

Gramsci, A. (2000 [1917]). The Revolution Against *Capital*. In *The Antonio Gramsci Reader, Selected Writings 1916–1935*, New York: New York University Press, 32–6.

Gramsci, A. (2000 [1929–35]). Hegemony, Relations of Force, Historical Bloc. In *The Antonio Gramsci Reader, Selected Writings 1916–1935*, New York: New York University Press, 189–221.

Grossman, H. (1992 [1929]). *The Law of Accumulation and the Breakdown of the Capitalist System*. London: Pluto Press.

Harootunian, H. (2015). *Marx After Marx*. New York: Columbia University Press.

Hilferding, R. (2006 [1911]). *Finance Capital: A Study in the Latest Phase of Capitalism*. London: Routledge.

Hobson, J. A. (2011 [1902]). *Imperialism: A Study*. Cambridge: Cambridge University Press.

Horn, G.-R. (2008). *The Spirit of '68: Rebellion in Western Europe and North America, 1956–1976*. Oxford: Oxford University Press.

Lebowitz, M. (1992). *Beyond Capital*. Basingstoke: Palgrave Macmillan.

Lenin (2004 [1899]). *The Development of Capitalism in Russia*. Honolulu: University of the Pacific Press.

Lenin (2010 [1916]). *Imperialism: The Highest Stage of Capitalism*. London: Penguin.

Luxemburg, R. (2003 [1913]). *The Accumulation of Capital*. London: Routledge.

Luxemburg, R. (2011 [1916]). The Junius Pamphlet: The Crisis of German Social Democracy. In *Rosa Luxemburg Speaks*. New York: Pathfinder Press, 342–439.

Marx, K. (1976 [1867]). *Capital, Volume 1*. London: Penguin.

Marx, K. (1978 [1885]). *Capital, Volume 2*. London: Penguin.

Marx, K. (1980 [1844]). *Economic and Philosophical Manuscripts*. New York: International Publishers.

Marx, K. (1981 [1894]). *Capital, Volume 3*. London: Penguin.

Marx, K. (1993 [1857–58]). *Grundrisse*. London: Penguin.

Marx, K. and Engels, F. (1998 [1848]). *The Communist Manifesto*. New York: Monthly Review Press.

Menon, U. (1982). Women and Household Labour. *Social Scientist*, 10(7): 30–42.

O'Connor, J. (1973). *The Fiscal Crisis of the State*. New York: St. Martin's Press.

O'Connor, J. (1988). Capitalism, Nature, Socialism: A Theoretical Introduction. *Capitalism, Nature, Socialism*, 1(1): 11–38.

Rosdolsky, R. (1977). *The Making of Marx's Capital*. London: Pluto Press.

Schmidt, I. (2011). There Were Alternatives: Lessons From Efforts to Advance Beyond Neoliberal Economic Policies in the 1970s. *Working USA*, 14(4): 473–98.

Schmidt, I. (2014). Capital Accumulation and Class Struggles from the 'Long 19th Century' to the Present – A Luxemburgian Interpretation. *International Critical Thought*, 4(4): 457–73.

Smaldone, W. (1988). Rudolf Hilferding and the Theoretical Foundations of German Social Democracy, 1902–33. *Central European History*, 21(3): 267–99.

Steenson, G. P. (1991). *After Marx, Before Lenin: Marxism and Socialist Working Class Parties in Europe, 1884–1914*. Pittsburgh: Pittsburgh University Press.

Varga, E. (1935). *The Great Crisis and its Political Consequences*. London: Modern Books.

2

Capital and the First International

William A. Pelz

It is common knowledge that Karl Marx wrote *Das Kapital.* Anyone who has studied his life and work is also doubtlessly aware of his involvement in the International Working Men's Association (IWMA), later known as the First International. Although these two aspects of Marx's life activity overlapped in time, few have stressed the significance of the inter-relationship between *Capital* and the International. Unlike his more personally motivated polemics like *Herr Vogt*, *Capital* was always meant to serve the aims of the workers' movement. This essay emphasizes the *importance of both Capital and the International in winning some workers to the idea of internationalism and labour activism.* That the two activities were intertwined was certainly how Marx saw matters. As early as a letter to Friedrich Engels on 14 November 1864, Marx argued the need for a Berlin outlet, 'especially for the sake of the association I was involved in founding in London [IWMA], and for the sake of the book [*Capital*] I am planning to publish' (Marx and Engels 1987: 22).

From its start in 1864, the Provisional Rules of the IWMA argued that 'The emancipation of the working classes must be conquered by the working classes themselves ... [and] that all efforts aimed at that great end have hitherto failed from want of solidarity.' This absence of solidarity was seen not only within the working classes of any one specific nation but also 'from the absence of a fraternal bond of union between the working classes of different countries'. (Institute of Marxism-Leninism 1962: 288). This will develop, according to Marx, not merely by political agitation but because of the laws of capitalism. The capitalist mode of appropriation transforms scattered private property based on personal labour into capitalist private property. This is a more protracted, violent and difficult process than the transformation of capitalist private property, which in fact already rests on the carrying on of production by society, into social property. In the former case, it was a matter of the expropriation of the mass of the people by a few usurpers; but in this case, we have the expropriation of a few usurpers by the mass of the people. (Marx 1976: 929–30)

It is certain Marx never intended *Capital* or any of his other works to be purely academic exercises. Note the excitement he expressed to Engels when the *Miner and Workman's Advocate* published his 'Address' to the IWMA while the English Bricklayers announced they were joining the IWMA (Marx and Engels 1987: 54). In another private correspondence, dated 1 May 1865, with his co-thinker, Marx excuses his tardiness in writing on overwork. He notes he really has been busy with 'completing my book [*Capital*], on the one hand, and the "INTERNATIONAL ASSOCIATION" on the other' (Marx and Engels 1987: 149). That the two projects, one intellectual and literary and the other political and practical, were bonded together in his mind is repeatedly stressed in his writings. Note how his research for *Capital* gave him the intellectual weapons to defeat what he saw as erroneous theories within the IWMA. On 20 May 1865, Marx wrote to Engels explaining that a special meeting of the IWMA was taking place and that he would debate a man favourable to the theories of Robert Owen. Marx notes that he should have worked more on his response but 'thought it more important to get on with writing my book'. So, Marx decided to use examples from his research. He ends the letter with 'YOU CAN'T COMPRESS A COURSE OF POLITICAL ECONOMY INTO 1 HOUR BUT WE SHALL DO OUR BEST' (Marx and Engels 1987: 159–60). In fact, the resulting text, which became known as *Value, Price and Profit*, reads much like a shortened draft of *Capital* Vol. I (Marx and Engels 1985: 101–60).

So, the insights that Marx gained from his research for *Capital* were transmitted to the IWMA. On the flip side, the activity of the IWMA influenced the thinking of Marx and entered into *Capital*. For example, the IWMA minutes from 23 May 1865 included a letter from Lyon explaining how wages were being cut using the argument of cheaper English production. It was resolved that the actual costs and price of labour in England would be researched and the facts sent to the French workers (Institute of Marxism-Leninism 1962: 99). When London employers sought to import German tailors to break the strike action of their workers, the International warned off many unwitting strike-breakers through the German labour press (Institute of Marxism-Leninism 1962: 186). When boot makers in Geneva planned to fight for higher wages, they requested and received help from the IWMA who alerted workers in other nations (Institute of Marxism-Leninism 1962: 193). In his discussion of tailors in *Capital*, Marx rails against the 'barbarous laws against combinations of workers' that partially disappeared in 1825 (1976: 903). It is clear throughout his discourse on the repressive nature of bourgeois law that he understands in a practical, not just theoretical, way the importance of worker solidarity against employer resistance.

Despite it commonly being lampooned as a dry economic work, Marx's *Capital* is actually filled with the passion he absorbed from, and imparted to, the International. He writes in his great work that the 'misery of the agricultural population forms the pedestal for gigantic shirt-factories [with] its own systematic means of rendering workers "redundant" in the form of under-payment and over-work' (1976: 863). As he notes shortly thereafter, the 'misery of Ireland is once again a daily theme of discussion in England' (1976: 867). Here the author of *Das Kapital* overlaps with the member of the General Council of the IWMA. The International was extremely sensitive to the plight of the Irish workers. For example, the plight of Irish political prisoners led to a demand for 'better treatment for these unfortunate men' (Institute of Marxism-Leninism 1962: 166–7). The organization made a class analysis of the Irish situation. As one Council member noted, 'It was our business to show the Irish that it was only a class of the English that wrongs them and that the same class of Irish were as bad' (Institute of Marxism-Leninism 1964: 173). Later in April 1872, the General Council issued a declaration against 'Police Terrorism in Ireland' (Institute of Marxism-Leninism 1965: 149–50).

Ireland's relation to England was said to be the same as Poland's to Tsarist Russia. In other words, both nations were 'oppressed nationalities' (Institute of Marxism-Leninism 1965: 298). At the risk of stating the obvious, the IWMA believed in independence and freedom for both. Marx expresses the same in *Capital*. He argues that it is at heart a search for surplus value. As he wryly notes, if 'the *Reglement organique* of the Danubian Principalities was a positive expression of the appetite for surplus value which every paragraph legalized, the English Factory Acts are the negative expression of the same appetite' (1976: 348). The only human resistance of note, that which would be assisted by the IWMA, was 'the daily more threatening advance of the working-class movement' (1976: 348).

At the same time, Marx's *Capital* was appreciated by, and had influence on, the IWMA members and their milieu when it came out in German in 1867 (Hogsbjerg 2014: 81). Furthermore, Marx aimed his new work at members of the IWMA. So, when the first edition was published in 1867 it carried two imprints on its title page – first was the name of his Hamburg publisher Otto Meissner, but the other was L. W. Schmidt of New York. This may well have been an attempt to appeal to 'the many German Socialists in this city who formed the American sections of the First International' (Foner 1967: 461). Rather than look for praise from academic specialists, Marx desired his *Capital* would be read by workers. On 18 October 1867, Engels writes to Hermann Meyer and says: 'I hope you will be able to bring Marx's book to the attention of the German-American Press and of the workers' (Marx and Engels 1987: 451). A month later, in a letter to Ludwig Kugelmann, Marx asks him to pressure German socialist leader, Wilhelm Liebknecht, to do 'his duty to draw attention to my book at *workers' meetings*' (Marx and Engels 1987: 489, emphasis in original).

Marx sounds so often like the other members of the International in *Capital* that it is difficult to say how much the IWMA influenced him versus the other way around. It surely must have been the proverbial two-way street with each having an effect on the other. It has been argued rather forcefully that no separation is truly possible. Some see the work Marx put into *Capital* as strengthening his work as a leader of the International. At a Council Meeting of the International on 11 August 1868, there was a debate regarding the reduction of the hours of work. During the debate, Marx listened while a member referred to as 'Citizen Eccarius' approvingly and directly quoted 'a statement from Dr. Marx's work on political economy [*Capital*]' (Institute of Marxism-Leninism 1963: 242). This was far from a sterile tribute as a vigorous debate ensued with not all agreeing with either Eccarius or Marx.

Time and time again we read Marx decry an injustice under industrial capitalism only to find that there could be a means to struggle against that wrong within the IWMA. When Marx discusses machinery's effect on workers in large-scale industry he raises gender issues. The new machinery required less skill and strength leading to the discharge of male workers. The result is the 'new machine-minders are exclusively girls and young women ... The overpowering competition crushes the weakest manual workers. The fearful increase in death from starvation during the last ten years in London runs parallel with the extension of machine sewing' (Marx 1976: 601). Many activists in the International had clear if not prophetic vision, evident in the example of Harriet Law, a member of the IWMA General Council from Manchester, who remarked that machines 'made women less dependent on men than they were before and would ultimately emancipate them from domestic slavery' (Institute of Marxism-Leninism 1963: 239). Although all but written out of history, Law had an important career as a public speaker advocating secularism and women's rights. For the better part of a decade, she was editor of *Secular Chronicle* in whose pages she fought for free thought and the liberation of women.

It is noteworthy that the IWMA gave Law a platform for her views and that although an ally of Marx and Engels, she certainly appears to have considered herself their equal (Morgan 2013: 3). Nor was Law a lone female voice crying out in a male wilderness. At the Congress of Lausanne in 1867, a report 'On Woman's Emancipation and Independence' puts forward very advanced views and concludes the IWMA should promote the organization among women so that men and women can 'fight together for the emancipation of labour, which alone will be able to assure independence for everyone' (Musto 2014:102).

The International also had a research aspect to it that fitted very well with Marx's research for *Capital*. For instance, at Marx's suggestion, the IWMA urged sections to survey their working class as to industry, age, sex of those employed, number of workers, salaries and wages, hours of work, meal times, conditions of work (overcrowding, want of sunlight and so on), effect of employment on health, moral condition, education and the state of the trade (Institute of Marxism-Leninism 1962: 342). Research would play handmaiden to political action.

In *Capital*, Marx studied the impact of the industrial revolution in the textile industry on American slaves. Once the export of cotton became of vital interest to slave owners, the overworking of the slave and 'sometimes the consumption of his life in seven years of labour, became a factor in a calculated and calculating system' (Marx 1976: 345). This is because the slave owner buys a slave the same way one would buy a horse. For the slave owner, 'the most effective economy is that which takes out of the human chattel in the shortest space of time the utmost amount of exertion it is capable of putting forth ... [thus] life is most recklessly sacrificed' (1976: 377). Going beyond mere description of the slave system, he went on to explain how it shaped an entire nation. 'In the United States of America', Marx notes, 'every independent workers' movement was paralyzed as long as slavery disfigured a part of the republic.' Marx then proceeded to pen one of his most famous lines, 'Labour in a white skin cannot emancipate itself where it is branded in a black skin' (1976: 414).

This statement was more than noble words. It has been persuasively argued that support for the North during the American Civil War became central to Marx's efforts to build the IWMA (Blackburn 2011: 8). Moreover, the IWMA was not wholly without influence in the American Republic. Many former German radicals, including Marx's friend Joseph Wedemeyer, were prominent in the war effort on behalf of the Union. In fact, one does well to remember that close to a quarter of a million German-Americans fought for the North, including 36,000 who served in German-speaking units (Blackburn 2011: 25).

The International's influence was not lost on the Lincoln administration. When the IWMA had Marx draft a letter to President Lincoln, the American Ambassador to Great Britain gave a public, and very positive, response. At Lincoln's request, the American diplomat said the Union derived 'new encouragement to persevere from the testimony of the workingmen of Europe' (Blackburn 2011: 49). Later, in an open letter to the people of the United States, the Association warned that unless all Americans were free and equal, 'there will yet remain a struggle for the future which may again stain your country with your people's blood' (Institute of Marxism-Leninism 1962: 311). This sensible advice was ignored, with the result that racial bloodletting, mob lynching, riots and strife have continued into the present century.

From the very beginnings of the IWMA, their rules and regulations stressed the need for labour solidarity between workers regardless of the nation-state of residency. This theme consistently appears within *Capital* as well. Neither was the United States an exception nor was solidarity extended only to those in Europe. In his masterwork, Marx wrote bitterly of how the first president of Mexico, Juarez, abolished the bondage of peonage while 'the so-called Emperor Maximilian re-established it by a decree which was aptly denounced ... as a decree for the re-introduction of slavery into Mexico' (1976: 272). Likewise, in 1867, the General Council discussed the French occupation of Mexico and condemned the official press of Europe for attempting to gloss over the crimes committed by Maximilian in his desire to destroy those Mexicans fighting for their country (Institute of Marxism-Leninism 1963: 139).

Recognizing that one solution would not apply exactly the same everywhere, the General Rules of the IWMA allowed for local autonomy. Based in Europe, the organization often could only give advice rather than concrete assistance to radical supporters outside their mainly West European base of support. Although the International had success in mobilizing against European attempts to aid the Confederacy during the American Civil War, other attempts to influence events in the United States were limited by the vastness of the Atlantic Ocean. Even further afield were the communications the IWMA received from New Zealand. More surprising still was the support by artisans in Buenos Aires and early workers' groups in India (Institute of Marxism-Leninism 1965: 126–8). Though the latter was perhaps not quite as surprising given the impact there of English industry. *Capital* cites one British government official in India as admitting horrors that resulted from English cotton machinery being introduced in the 1830s, 'The bones of the cotton weavers are bleaching the plains of India' (Marx 1976: 558).

The same problems facing the IWMA also impacted Marx's *Capital*. That is to say, both were encouraged yet also limited by notoriety, rumour and word of mouth. The first edition of *Capital* was accessible only to people who read German. Although this German first volume was published in 1867, it was not to appear in French until the following decade. In fact, during Marx's lifetime, he was not even able to get an English translation published. For this reason, in

Great Britain and the United States, the text was often criticized for things that it was falsely purported to say. This continued until the fall of 1886 when the English translation appeared (Marx 1976: 109). For much of the world, it would only be decades later that they would have access to the book in their native language. If the International at times became a myth, *Capital* often became a totem to be respected rather than a text to be read and debated. Still, it can be argued that the 1860s saw the fundamental political economy of the working class take shape. This found theoretical expression with Marx's *Capital* and organizational expression in the founding of the First International.

There was a very material problem that held back both the IWMA and the spread of Marx's *Capital* – concretely limiting for the First International and for *Capital*'s translation and propagation was lack of funds. Karl Marx, as even the most cursory glance at his letters to Engels would reveal, lived a life often spent in debt, with all the family's valuables resting safely in the pawn shop for long periods of time. Even Engels, who kept the Marx family afloat for considerable periods of time and lived a comfortable life himself, was not a person with endless financial resources. With few funds to pay for translations or to advertise the book, it would take a great deal of time for the sales of *Capital* to reach significant levels. Perhaps Marx's mother had a reasonable complaint that he should have made capital instead of just writing about it. Though Marx discussed moving from London to Geneva with his family and Engels, where he believed they could live for half the cost as the expensive English capital, in a 17 March 1868 letter to Ludwig Kugelmann he remarked on the impossibility due to the resources he needed for his continued *Capital* research. Further, he lamented leaving the IWMA and the working-class movement, both of which he thought were in a particularly important period (Marx and Engels 1987: 551–2).

Likewise, a study of the financial records contained in the *Documents of the First International* reveal that the organization lived literally from hand to mouth. Despite constant rumours spread by police agents and political opponents that the leaders of the organization lived on the workers' money, the evidence suggests that being an International activist often meant spending one's own funds. Add to this the additional cost of arrests, police attacks, confiscation of newspapers and other publications, and the facts underlying the poverty of the organization are clear. It is important to remember that neither the IWMA nor the original editions of *Capital* had the resources that would later be at the disposal of the mass-based Second International, let alone the state-financed Communist International.

Despite all these limitations, the IWMA directly promoted international class solidarity. This was not always easy as the particular nature of each local struggle might obscure the global essence of the situation. Even when the organizational position was thoughtful and far-sighted, that did not automatically change reality. Thus, no amount of enthusiastic thanks to the International from Polish exiles who agreed with the IWMA stance towards their nation could solve the incredible complexity of the problems facing partitioned Poland (Institute of Marxism-Leninism 1963: 103). Likewise, the problems facing the newly united Italy often defied easy solutions even though national hero Garibaldi was an enthusiastic member of the International.

The organization pushed back against the rising tide of nationalism and racism in a manner that can only be seen as commendable in a world that has witnessed massacres and genocide. Despite personal backsliding or politically incorrect comments, the IWMA was committed to a class-based rather than racially or ethnically based world view. At a time when many, if not most, people accepted racial differences as scientifically proven, the counter-example of the association stands as a sharp exception. In the same way, *Capital* provided an analysis of the world through the prism of class. This was all the more remarkable given the growing nationalism, not to mention the casually accepted racism, of the time.

Another characteristic shared by the International and *Capital* is the amount of venom that has been unleashed on both. Always spied on and subject to police intimidation, after the rising of the Parisian workers who formed the Commune in 1871, it became open season on the IWMA. Police in Leipzig warned taverns that their licences would be in danger if IWMA members were seen gathering within. One chief of police attempted to found an IWMA section so that his agents could intervene as delegates in congresses (Institute of Marxism-Leninism 1978: 74).

Even 'liberal' Great Britain was thrown into the frenzy with Prime Minister Gladstone reportedly thinking of expelling Marx and others from the country. One Member of Parliament claimed that the Commune was planned by leaders of the International who had ordered the French Communards to execute the Paris Archbishop. The mainstream press bayed like a pack of hounds thirsty for the blood of the International. A Swiss watch manufacturer felt it necessary to publicly announce he would not hire IWMA members (Institute of Marxism-Leninism 1964: 68). The Pope even weighed in, joining the attacks on the IWMA, claiming it would subvert all order and all law. Meanwhile, the Roman Catholic Church placed *Capital* on the index of forbidden books. Of course, more enlightened liberal nations and institutions did not ban *Capital*. They did, however, alternately distort its contents beyond recognition and pretend it didn't exist. Each generation of liberals, of all hues of ideological feathers, in turn pronounce *Capital*, like its author Marx, dead.

When making up a balance sheet of the IWMA and *Capital*, one finds aspects that are negative, positive and sometimes, paradoxically, both positive and negative at the same time. On the minus side of the ledger, one must put the difficulty the International had in reconciling various ideological positions. *Capital* was always a work in progress that Marx never truly finished in his lifetime nor Engels in his. Further, both faced the problem of having an international orientation in an age of growing nationalism as the world had so many differing levels of economic development. This led easily to troubles coordinating competing national-based workers' movements. As an open organization, the IWMA had a fluid membership with a wide range of levels of activity.

That being said, the IWMA made significant contributions in two areas. First, it was an example of a group that was rooted in firm but non-sectarian principles. Second, it established an organizational form that allowed competing, if not hostile, ideological groupings to combine for united action. With regard to the former, the IWMA actively and successfully promoted the concept of workers' internationalism. *Capital* was the main theoretical underpinning to this internationalist project. The self-activity of the working class was always made a primary objective from the Provisional Rule of 1864, and through *Capital*, till the end.

When reconsidering the history, success and failures of the International Working Men's Association, one should be careful not to accept the prevailing wisdom without reflection or to make snap judgements about how it should have functioned or what it could have done. The same courtesy needs to be extended to *Capital*. As one delegate from Switzerland at The Hague Congress in 1872 noted, with what might have been a touch of irony, 'why should the International alone be exempt from all the defects and shortcomings of the present generation and as immaculate as befits only the Virgin Mary?' (Institute of Marxism-Leninism 1978: 191).

One could say the same, in the same ironic tone, of Marx's greatest book. After his death, did it not become – in the words of Engels in his Preface to the English Edition – 'the Bible of the working class?' (Marx 1976: 112). It was certainly like the Bible when it was later welded to serve ends that would have shocked the author. And, like the Bible itself, *Capital* was to have a global impact ... and still does.

References

Blackburn, R. ed. (2011). *An Unfinished Revolution: Karl Marx and Abraham Lincoln*. London: Verso.

Foner, P. S. (1967). Marx's Capital in the United States. *Science and Society*, 31(4): 462–6.

Hogsbjerg, C. (2014). Karl Marx and the First International. *Socialist Review*, 81–91.

Institute of Marxism-Leninism (1962). *Documents of the First International, 1864–1866, Vol. I*. London: Lawrence and Wishart.

Institute of Marxism-Leninism (1963). *Documents of the First International, 1866–1868, Vol. II*. London: Lawrence and Wishart.

Institute of Marxism-Leninism (1964). *Documents of the First International, 1868–1870, Vol. III*. London: Lawrence and Wishart.

Institute of Marxism-Leninism (1965). *Documents of the First International, 1871–1872, Vol. V*. London: Lawrence and Wishart.

Institute of Marxism-Leninism (1978). *The Hague Congress of the First International, September 2–7, 1872 – Reports and Letters*. Moscow: Progress Publishers.

Marx, K. (1976). *Capital, Volume 1*. London: Penguin Books.

Marx, K. and Engels, F. (1985). *Collected Works, Vol. 20.* New York: International Publishers.

Marx, K. and Engels, F. (1987). *Collected Works, Vol. 42.* New York: International Publishers.

Morgan, D. (2013). A Law Unto Herself. *Socialist History Society Newsletter,* 3(2): 3–4.

Musto, M., ed. (2014). *Workers Unite! The International 150 Years Later.* London: Bloomsbury.

3

Capital and Soviet Communism

Anej Korsika

When Karl Marx first published *Capital* in 1867, its reception was, well, very non-receptive to say the least. So much so, that in a letter to Ludwig Kugelmann, German social democrat and his confidant, Marx complained about '*the conspiracy of silence*' (Marx 1869) that accompanied his magnum opus. Perhaps one of the reasons why the initial reception was so weak lies in the principle that German censors used after the murder of August von Kotzebue. When the conservative dramatist Kotzebue was murdered by Karl Ludwig Sand, a militant liberal student, Metternich used this as a pretext for a crackdown on liberal press and academic freedom. Among the provisions of the Carlsbad Decrees that ensued, the first determined the length of the publications that were allowed to be in circulation. It stated that no publication of less than 20 sheets of printed matter was allowed to go into circulation without the prior approval of a state official. The obvious underlying assumption being that texts longer than 20 sheets of paper were 'safe', as nobody would actually read them.

Perhaps this is the reason why *Capital* initially suffered a 'conspiracy of silence'. One could also draw an ironic parallel between the labour Marx invested in *Capital* and general wage labour in capitalism: the first being a work of immense self-exploitation, the second representing a much less fulfilling and more alienating systemic exploitation. However, in both cases there is a fate even worse than the sheer fact of exploitation – being ignored. A fate suffered by an increasing number of workers, for whom being superfluous was perhaps the worst condition of all. Marx's *Capital*, his greatest labour of love, and the culmination of almost two decades of continuous devotion to the critique of political economy, thus suffered a fate ironically similar to that of workers unable to sell their labour power. To continue with our (obviously limited) metaphor, the critics market simply ignored the new commodity on the block, thus depriving it of the very possibility of having a meaningful existence. In other words, the only fate worse for a work than being harshly criticized, even torn to pieces, is for it to be simply ignored.

The extent to which we can talk about an actual conspiracy of silence is questionable; a more satisfying explanation would be that Marx's language of the critique of political economy was simply not comprehensible to proponents of political economy as such. Althusser quite rightly compared its radical novelty to the discovery of a whole new continent:

> Marx founded a new science: the science of history. Let me use an image. The sciences we are familiar with have been installed in a number of great 'continents'. Before Marx, two such continents had been opened up to scientific knowledge: the continent of Mathematics and the continent of Physics. The first by the Greeks (Thales), the second by Galileo. Marx opened up a third continent to scientific knowledge: the continent of History. (Althusser 1971: 16)

To truly understand it one would have to leave the old world and embark on a journey that would ultimately put into question that very world. That (political) economists are as unwilling to embark on this journey today as they were a century and a half ago is understandable. In the terms of another French theorist, Jacques Lacan, Marx invented the symptom (Žižek 2008). If one is blind to and in denial of symptoms (economic and ecological crisis) one is bound to fail to see them as mere expressions of deeper structures (global capitalism). Fredric Jameson once remarked that in the capitalist world it is easier to imagine the end of the world than the end of capitalism. The gospel of the end times is not just a purview of religious sects and science fiction; it is literally interwoven into the contemporary political imagination, or rather the lack of it. The world may very well end in an apocalypse, but there will be time to rebuild it and start all over again. Ending capitalism, on the other hand, from the viewpoint of modern liberal democracy, poses a much more ontological threat. One where not only the world but also perhaps time itself are destroyed. It is therefore no accident that the very issue of time was at the heart of debates in the early Soviet Union and its attempts to transcend the time of capitalism.

This Time is Out of Joint

Before delving into practical attempts to employ the conceptual apparatus of Marx's *Capital* in concrete struggle against actually existing capital, let us first devote some time to its theoretical reception. As we've seen, this was rather poor, but interestingly one of the most elaborate assessments of *Capital* came from a somewhat surprising corner of the world: Tsarist Russia. Rather than an English, French or German critic giving it the first review, it came from I. I. Kaufman (1848–1916), a Russian economist and professor of political economy at the University of St Petersburg and author of numerous works on money and credit. Marx felt so satisfied with Kaufman's critique that he quoted it at length in the preface of the next edition of Capital. Kaufman grasped the very core of Marx's argument and presented it in a way that is as valid today, after a century and a half of Marxist debates, as it was at the time of its publication. To illustrate just how well he synthesized Marx's view, we can highlight a passage that Marx himself cites in the preface to the second edition of *Capital*:

> Marx treats the social movement as a process of natural history, governed by laws not only independent of human will, consciousness and intelligence, but rather, on the contrary, determining that will, consciousness and intelligence ... If in the history of civilisation the conscious element plays a part so subordinate, then it is self-evident that a critical inquiry whose subject-matter is civilisation, can, less than anything else, have for its basis any form of, or any result of, consciousness. (Kaufman, quoted in Marx 1990: 100)

Translating this methodology into political practice was the ultimate challenge facing those who refused to be silent about capital. Their revolution in the name of *Capital* against capital occurred in Russia, a place where Marx and the socialist intelligentsia had not imagined it would or could. So it happens that Soviet receptions of *Capital* substantially mark today's view of both *Capital* and capitalism, in theoretical, political and economic senses. Let us take a closer look at these three and try to put them into historical perspective. Our hypothesis is that in all three fields Soviet (theoretical) reception, (political) articulation and (economic) implementation had a decisive and lasting impact on the general apprehension of *Capital*, both in leftist circles and among the general public.

Antonio Gramsci, in the immediate aftermath of the October Revolution, wrote a short yet powerful essay called 'Revolution against *Capital*'. The Bolshevik Revolution, according to Gramsci, was a revolution against Marx's *Capital*, in so far as *Capital* in Russia wasn't the book of the proletariat, but a book of the bourgeoisie. Through sheer political will, enthusiasm and immense organizational ingenuity, the Bolsheviks spearheaded a revolution that should not have been possible – at least according to the 'iron laws of history', supposedly independent, superior and even 'determining' of human will, consciousness and intelligence. What a dramatic change it is, then, when Gramsci writes that:

This thought sees as the dominant factor in history, not raw economic facts, but man, men in societies, men in relation to one another, reaching agreements with one another, developing through these contacts (civilisation) a collective, social will: men coming to understand economic facts, judging them and adapting them to their will until this becomes the driving force of the economy and moulds objective reality, which lives and moves and comes to resemble a current of volcanic lava that can be channelled wherever and in whatever way men's will determines. (Gramsci 1977: 34–5)

The October Revolution was therefore much more than just another event in the unfolding of history; it was an event against history as it was, and that began history as it will be. In his autobiography *Record of a Life*, György Lukács shares a fascinating insight he had during the First World War. At the time, after reflecting critically on the political situation, he came to the following conclusions: In Russia the dynasty of the Romanovs probably won't survive the war, the Hohenzollern family will cause its downfall, which is good. In Germany and Austria, in turn, the Hohenzollern and Hapsburg dynasties will be defeated by British and French liberal democracies, which is also good. However, the question remains, who will defend us against the British and

French capitalist democracies? The answer came in the form of the October Revolution, a solution to the historical and political riddle (Lukács 1983: 44).

The October Revolution represented an immense political opening and a window of freedom and potentiality. The turbulent period between 1917 and Stalin's consolidation of power detonated powerful and transformative ideas, not least in the field of Marxist theory, and social and political practices. The immediate protagonists and their contemporaries, such as Isaac Illich Rubin, Yevgeny Pashukanis and Lukács himself, among others, paved the way for a fundamental renewal and reinvigoration of Marxist thought. The themes of commodity and legal form, class consciousness, abstract labour, etc., were not only conceptualized but intensely discussed, both theoretically as well as politically. In fact, these issues were rarely separated, which makes this period and these authors that much more fascinating. It is hard to imagine how dilemmas about abstract labour and commodity form were at the very centre of political and theoretical life after the revolution, yet they were. To make matters worse, and as Gramsci already foresaw, the Bolsheviks had to face the difficulties of the socialist revolution happening in a country that was not yet a highly advanced capitalist society. On the contrary, it was an economically undeveloped and culturally (relatively) backward country. Before analysing these concrete attempts at implementing the theory of *Capital* against capital in the case of the Soviet Union, let us first look at some of the fundamental concepts Marx developed that played a central role in Soviet debates about economic measures and their implementation.

Abstract Time

Shortly after the first volume of *Capital* saw the light of day, Marx wrote to Engels stressing what he saw as the two most important contributions of his book:

The best points in my book are: 1. (this is fundamental to all understanding of the facts) the two-fold character of labour according to whether it is expressed in use-value or exchange-value, which is brought out in the very First Chapter; 2. The treatment of surplus-value regardless of its particular forms as profit, interest, ground rent, etc. This will be made clear in the second volume especially. The treatment of the particular forms in classical political economy, where they are for ever being jumbled up together with the general form, is an olla podrida. (Marx 1867)

We can show this through an example from Ancient Greek society. In the first chapter of *Capital*, Marx considers the case of Aristotle. Despite his immense intellect and lasting insights into human society, it was objectively and materially impossible for Aristotle to fully grasp the phenomenon of the value form. The Greek philosopher was able to develop the simple value form and came to the conclusion that it is, by its essence, not fundamentally different from the money form. In other words, for example, 5 beds equals 1 house is a relation that is the same as saying that 5 beds equals a certain amount of money. Such equalization, though, is only possible thanks to a common substance through which such empirically diverse things as beds, houses and money find a common expression. Just a step before going straight to the value form itself, Aristotle halted and said that such a substance perhaps aids one in thinking but is otherwise artificial and does not have anything to do with concrete reality.

This substance, of course, is human labour, or, more precisely, abstract human labour. Only through this is it possible to give a common denominator for the whole diversity of concrete expressions of the world of commodities. For human labour to be able to occupy such a structural position, its universal exchangeability must be presupposed. This is exactly the attribute that human labour did not have in Aristotle's slave-owning society. The forms of labour of free citizens and of slaves were by their nature inherently different; they were differently regulated and by no means freely and universally exchangeable (Marx 1990: 151–2).

Abstract time as we understand it and use it today, i.e. the linear progress of identical time units measured with clock and calendar, has taken primacy over the cyclical understanding of time only in the last couple of centuries. Before then, time was 'concrete' and reliant on external events. In the Judaeo-Christian tradition and view of history, events did not happen *inside* time, but rather events themselves *defined* time (Postone 1993: 201). The division of time into inter-commensurable units, freely interchangeable, thus led to the invention of an abstract time that has its own 'life' independent of external circumstances and events is a historically specific social invention. As such it is, like abstract labour, something completely foreign to Ancient societies.

In those societies, time was cyclical and mostly subordinated to agrarian production (the changing of seasons, day and night, natural phenomena, religious traditions), thus making it impossible to talk about abstract exchangeability. The invention of the clock clearly separated time as an abstract entity from concrete human events. That being said it is important to bear in mind that it was not techno-logical innovation that caused social change, but rather social change that gave meaning to already existing technological means. The mechanical clock was present long before the invention of the notion of abstract time. Water clocks that preceded mechanical clocks and were used by many ancient civilizations (Egypt, Syria, Mesopotamia, China, Greece, Rome, etc.) were already in use a couple of thousand years ago. Although the fundamental principle of measuring time with water was relatively simple, there were a number of challenges. Some had to do with the physical properties of water, others with the changing seasons and the length of day. While water clocks were more reliable and practical than sun clocks, they still needed to be constantly adapted to correspond to the changing length of day and night. These devices thus had to be regularly calibrated to ensure their correspond-ence with the changing of the seasons and of the length of day and night, which entailed ever more elaborate mechanisms. In comparison to modern time-measuring devices, where the abstract and universal time frame is the basis on which natural cycles are measured, they were certainly much more complex (Postone 1993: 200–4).

Measuring abstract time and having the notion of abstract labour thus only make sense in a society that is based on capitalist production. These two, however, are not the only forms of abstraction needed and presupposed in capitalism. The Soviet legal scholar Evgeny Pashukanis (1891–1937), renowned in the history of Marxist theory for his *General Theory of Law and Marxism*, saw how the process of capitalist abstraction is complemented through legal abstractions. The notion of the citizen, with its universal rights, freedoms and laws and blindness to concrete individuality, represents one of the conceptual breaks with feudal society wherein most people were born into social roles with pre-assigned rights and duties. In other words, if one was born a peasant, one would most likely die a peasant. In capitalism by contrast, as John Steinbeck once sardonically remarked: 'The poor see themselves not as an exploited proletariat but as temporarily embarrassed millionaires.'

Despite the supposedly abstract universality each concrete individual is legally granted in capitalist society, this very abstraction is also the basis for capitalist exploitation. Pashukanis realized that the legal form is no less crucial for the capitalist production system than the commodity form. Just as individual commodities present themselves as bearers of value by their nature (through their use value), so do the individuals that participate in commodity exchange present themselves as bearers of will and subjectivity (through the liberal concept of abstract citizenship and notions such as human rights). Just as there is a fetish character to commodities, there is also a fetish character to individuals; ultimately they are both one and the same fetishism, in so far as legal contracts are only the other side of exchange and they mutually presuppose one another. In other words, commodity form and legal form are complementary, and the world we experience as an expression of value is actually the commodity-legal world (Pashukanis 2007). Although these themes and problems seem very far removed from the concrete political and economic practice of the early Soviet Union, they are much more related to it than would at first appear. In the next section we will look at how the very perception and understanding of time played a fundamental role in creating a number of different Soviet economic policies.

Rational-Charismatic Time

In a fascinating and somehow overlooked study (the reason most likely being the timing of its publication: 1997), *Time and Revolution: Marxism and the Design of Soviet Institutions*, Stephen E. Hanson offers an original take on the complex interplay between time and revolution in the Soviet Union. Hanson's hypothesis is that Marx, Lenin and Stalin all shared a common view regarding the perception and role of time. They all rejected the 'rational' conception of time, i.e., time as an abstract substance independent of concrete events, rather than determining them. Employing Max Weber's distinction (originally in relation to leadership) between rational, traditional and charismatic, Hanson claims that they also rejected a purely 'charismatic' conception of time. Rather, their understanding was that 'effective revolutionary praxis depends upon utilising rational time discipline to master time itself' (Hanson 1997: 8–9). We will now look how this synthesis of rational and charismatic time has developed throughout the history of Marxism and the attempts at implementing socialist policies.

We begin at the time of Marx's death in the late nineteenth century, when German social democracy became a force to be reckoned with. As the prospect of taking power became ever more realistic, tactics and strategies on how to implement a socialist vision through concrete political practice became ever more burning issues. Three different camps emerged that all gave different answers on how to go about such implementation. The right-wing answer was given by Eduard Bernstein, who argued that revolution was not imminent and that for better or worse a certain kind of truce would have to be achieved with the bourgeoisie. His, according to Hanson, was the 'rational' perception of time, one with which our contemporary, liberal democratic societies are so thoroughly impregnated. All revolutionary voluntarism and fervour is futile, counter-productive, even harmful. In other words, as Bernstein would have it, 'the ultimate aim of socialism is nothing, but the movement is everything'.

Contrary to this, the left-wing answer, represented by Rosa Luxemburg, was that the aim is everything, but the movement, without achieving its aim, is nothing. Faith in the proletarian masses and their capability for self-emancipation were defining traits of this 'charismatic' perception of time. The centrist position, adopted by Karl Kautsky, the 'Pope of Marxism', was an orthodox synthesis, i.e. rational-charismatic view. The centre, despite not offering any genuine political or theoretical contribution, offered a faith in orthodoxy and was, on those grounds, able to both criticize right and left while also keeping the party together. The same dramaturgy played out with different actors when the Bolsheviks took power; now the Mensheviks were the right-wing, saying that conditions were not mature enough and that Russia should first undergo a bourgeois revolution. Leftist forces, still most powerfully represented by Rosa Luxemburg, despite being generally quite welcoming, were very critical of the rising party elite and of the dangers of bureaucratization. Again, Hanson sees the former as an expression of the rational view of time, while the latter expresses the charismatic perception. The centre again combines the two in a rational-charismatic view of time, one embodied in Lenin's views and policies.

In 1914, the Second International disgraced itself when several of its most prominent members voted for war credits. Lenin was one of the few who were profoundly aware what a disastrous decision this was. But instead of immediately turning his attention to organizational issues he spent three months devoting himself to an in-depth study of Hegel's *Logic*. We should bear in mind that at this point Lenin had already devoted more than 20 years of his life to the revolutionary cause, and in spite of that, at the age of 44 and in the midst of war, he devoted himself to one of the most complex philosophers of all time. Ernst Bloch later argued that it was Lenin himself who renewed authentic Marxism by returning to the core of the Hegelian dialectic. He goes on to say that: 'it was precisely orthodox Marxism, as restored by Lenin, that presupposed knowledge of Hegel, as against a vulgar, schematic, and tradition-less Marxism, which, like a shot out of a pistol, isolated Marx from Hegel, thus isolating itself from Marx' (Quote in Anderson 2007: 123). Indeed it was Lenin who after more than half a century of neglect once again shed light on the connection between Hegel and Marx. *History and Class Consciousness* and *Marxism and Philosophy* by György Lukács and Karl Korsch, respectively, were both published in 1923. These two works are usually seen as inaugurating the current of Western Marxism that distanced itself from Soviet philosophy. However, it is rather ironic that the true originator of this current actually appears to be Lenin!

The Central Institute of Labour Versus the Time League

The above two stages in the development of Marxism are well known, however the third one, the field of economics, where Hanson deals with the dialectics of charisma and rationality in the realm of time, offers lesser known insights. These are especially interesting from the point of view of Soviet receptions of *Capital* and the creation of a specific developmental political economy that always tried to maintain a balance between rational progress and economic growth as well as charismatic enthusiasm and the revolutionary abolishment of the old order, i.e. capitalism. Hanson argues that the 'right-wing' interpretation of socialist time discipline was described and prescribed in the works of Aleksei Gastev; on the other side was Platon Kerzhentsev with his charismatic 'left-wing' interpretation. The middle ground, the centre that brought about a synthesis, was developed by Stanislav Strumilin and later adopted by Stalin during the first five-year plan (Hanson 1997: 123–4). Following Hanson's analysis, we will now take a closer look at all three of these developmental models.

In 1920, with the support of Lenin, Gastev founded the Central Institute of Labour (Tsentralnyi Institut Truda, or TsIT). Like Lenin, Gastev was a great admirer of Frederick Winslow Taylor, the American mechanical engineer who was one of the pioneers of productivity studies, time management, and work optimization in general. Taylor's methods included meticulous studies of workers' movements during their working hours. Based on the analysis of such data, Taylor could then suggest 'optimizations', which worked as a kind of capitalist Ockham's razor. Any unnecessary moves were to be eliminated; unproductive time spent, say, waiting for the machines, was to be utilized, etc. In other words, through such improvements the labour force was to become more productive and competitive, able to do more in less time and with fewer resources. Such scientific management is by no means a thing of the past; on the contrary, time management and productivity are at the very heart of present-day capitalism. There is a whole industry dealing with it, including facilitators that help to solve collective problems, motivators that foster team building, and social scientists who develop different productivity techniques. There is also a whole new class of consultants who specialize in the above-mentioned problems and claim that they can boost workers' productivity. Ultimately they only boost their bank accounts, and productivity is increased mainly by heightening the levels of stress and pressure the workers are under.

Gastev, in his fascination with productivity optimization, even went so far as to compare Karl Marx and Henry Ford as, admittedly completely opposite, but nonetheless agreeing in their views and analytical approach towards the production process. The path towards abolishing capitalism and reaching the classless society was thus one of ever more rational capitalist production. Such views are in fact completely opposed to those Marx develops in *Capital*; for Marx, capitalism is a system based on the production of profit for profit's sake, and this basic drive is both tautological as well as teleological as it has nothing outside its own logic on which it could be based. Of course the precondition for the realization of profits is the extraction of surplus value, and in accordance with the law of value, labour is the source of all value. As Marx stressed in his *Critique of Gotha Programme*, labour is not the only source of all wealth, nature being another source as well, but labour alone is capable of producing value. As Marx showed in his critique of political economy, surplus value is produced in the production process, when workers produce more than they are paid for. In essence, the labour time of an individual worker actually consists of the time in which he earns his wage and of the time when he produces surplus value, which is appropriated by the capitalist.

The interest of the capitalist class is to enlarge this surplus as much as possible and consequently realize greater profits. However, in this mindless and eternal race for profit the capitalist is not alone but is always in competition with other capitalists. In gaining an advantage over their competitors, every capitalist relies on science, and all the talk about the necessity of investing in research and development and introducing innovations basically amounts to increasing the productivity of labour. At the end of the day this means producing more in less time and with less labour power, which is just another euphemism for laying off workers and intensifying the exploitation of those remaining.

Platon Kerzhentsev was on the completely opposite end of the production process dilemma. Participating in Bogdanov's Proletkult movement, his vision of revolutionary social transformation was on the 'charismatic side' (Hanson 1997: 116). Kerzhentsev founded the so-called 'Time League' and called upon those with a proper communist consciousness to organize themselves on the basis of 'spontaneous time discipline'. Their actions must have been a sight to behold:

Under Kerzhentsev's leadership, groups of Time League enthusiasts periodically burst into the meetings of party bureaucrats and factory managers, exposing whatever wastage of time they encountered and generally wasting quite a bit of time themselves in the process. In collaboration with the Young Pioneers, Time League propaganda was drummed into the heads of Communist Party youth, who were in this way supposed to absorb the norms of continuous revolutionary time discipline that would become universal under socialism. (Hanson 1997: 125)

Despite Kerzhentsev's charismatic approach and the fact that at its height the Time League included around 25,000 members, like Gastev, Kerzhentsev was not particularly successful. Both were faced with workers who were less than impressed by their rational scientific analysis of the production process or charismatic enthusiasm and encouragement to voluntarily submit themselves to spontaneous time discipline.

The synthesis came in the work of Stanislav Strumilin, who played a central role in designing the first five-year plan. Strumilin came to realize that there is a certain limit to what the human body is capable of, and driving it beyond that limit will result in *less* productive work. He maintained that a person can only work one-third of the day at one-third of his/her full capacity, and that such qualitative and quantitative input brought about the best results. Attempts to amplify the duration or intensity of the work inevitably came at the cost of the other two-thirds of the workers' day and ultimately resulted in lower productivity (Hanson 1997: 123). In a way Strumilin reaffirmed the old triad of eight hours of work, eight hours of free time and eight hours of rest. However, this did not mean that the other two-thirds were not subject to certain regulations in the service of the privileged 'work' third. It was not only important that workers were given enough rest; even more important was that rest and free time were effectively used. Free time was by no means to be used in idleness, but rather in creative pursuit, recreation, etc. Such a positive programme of leisure time would then in turn benefit the work process as such. Leisure time is thus mainly seen as a time in which the worker 'reproduces' (rests, eats, socializes, sleeps) himself so his labour power can then be used again the next day.

New Revolutions on the Horizon

Ultimately none of these three management strategies really succeeded in transcending capitalism at its very core. They were all just variations on how to optimally extract surplus value from the labour force. Be it through revolutionary optimism, meticulous production control or a mixture of both, at the end of the day all three are just varieties of policies governed by the value form. Interestingly enough, the Soviet leadership seemed very conscious of this contradictory task – superseding capitalism by employing its very means. In other words, being better at capitalist production seemed to be a necessary step in abolishing capitalism. Lenin made the concession of introducing the New Economic Policy that significantly liberalized domestic trade, and to some extent even allowed foreign trade. After his death, the party leadership was faced with the pressing issue of abolishing this policy as it threatened to undermine its political sovereignty.

However, in the 1930s, during the time of five-year plans, Stalin famously remarked that the Soviet Union was lagging 50 to 100 years behind the developed capitalist countries. Either this gap had to be made up, or the whole socialist experiment was doomed. Gargantuan efforts and immense human exploitation succeeded in positioning the Soviet Union among the world's leading industrial super powers. Suffice to say, even Stalin's greatest nemesis, Leon Trotsky, was impressed by these achievements, even though such an industrial blitzkrieg was very different from the proposals he made about industrial armies while he was still a member of the party leadership. Even Nikita Khrushchev, despite his proclaimed de-Stalinization, repeated this logic when he felt confident enough to say to the US that 'we will bury you'. History had it the other way around, but not before actually existing socialism pretty much imploded of its own accord. Its fall nonetheless had dramatic consequences and a very detrimental effect on leftist projects in general, the welfare state, trade union power, etc.

In his *Critique of Political Economy*, Marx writes that humanity only asks of itself such tasks as it is already capable of achieving. Nonetheless, wasn't twentieth-century socialism the very question asked before it could be sufficiently answered? In a way it surely was, but then again, there is no one who will make history other than humanity itself. It is possible to see the history of socialist projects, even in their state form, as counter-tendencies to the dynamics of global capitalism. In such a negative perspective these states and societies were, usually with a great deal of economic autarky, able to protect themselves – from, that is, becoming semi- or completely dependent global peripheries, as most of the former Eastern bloc nowadays actually is. Positively speaking, twentieth-century socialisms, as a counter-tendency, were able to provide a much needed space and independence to undertake the projects of industrialization and modernization. It appears that when these projects were successful and eventually brought about specifically capitalist problems (inflation, public and foreign debt), socialism as a global counter-tendency became more and more undermined. Ultimately, submitting to the pressures of capitalist globalization simply would not allow for such economic autarky: one that actually existed only as a kind of anachronism (closed borders, limited human rights and freedoms, etc.) that served no one but the autocratic party leadership clinging to power. The fall of the Berlin Wall opened up vast territories that had become frozen, at least from capital's point of view. Some such spaces exist even today, like North Korea, but generally speaking, capitalist globalization really did its job thoroughly. So much so that capitalism, in order to thrive, is in urgent need of further commodifying social life. This involves unprecedented attempts at international cooperation: Contemporary trade and service agreements such as TTIP (Transatlantic Trade and Investment Partnership), CETA (Comprehensive Economic and Trade Agreement) and TiSA (Trade in Services Agreement) are very much responses of the Western world to the rising global economies usually lumped together under the acronym BRICS. However, they are not merely geopolitical rearrangements but suggest a profound qualitative change of social relations. By transferring a great deal of authority from nation-states to supra-national authorities, usually backed by representatives of corporations and by diminishing states' political sovereignty, these agreements are actually effecting the withering away of the state, only under capitalist conditions. The aim is to abolish the nation-state as the highest sovereign political body in the global system, and demote it to a mere administrative unit.

As joint-stock companies already presented a form that effectively abolished private and introduced collective ownership, all while still inside the capitalist production system, perhaps an analogous process is about to happen to nation-states. While trade and service agreements aim at abolishing any meaningful social, health, education, pension or environmental policy – basically *any* kind of policy making that is not in the direct interest of profit making – it seems that the nation-state is on its way to being fused into regional states and eventually a global state. Left to its own devices, this global state will surely become a highly exploitative and unequal society. Here the counter-tendency project, like that of the socialisms of the twentieth century, once again becomes urgently needed. As broad strata of civil society join in their opposition to the above mentioned processes, a real alternative, at least in fragments, is already opening up. Once this alternative begins to develop in a more organized way, it will be necessary to closely study and learn from the mistakes and achievements of the first attempts at abolishing capitalism.

References

Althusser, L. (1971). *Lenin and Philosophy and Other Essays*. New York: Monthly Review Press.

Anderson, K. B. (2007). The Rediscovery and Persistence of the Dialectic in Philosophy and in World Politics. In S. Budgen, S. Kouvelakis and S. Žižek, eds., *Lenin Reloaded*. Durham, NC: Duke University Press, 123–47.

Gramsci, A. (1977). *Selections from Political Writings: 1910–1920*. London: Lawrence and Wishart.

Hanson, S. E. (1997). *Time and Revolution: Marxism and the Design of Soviet Institutions*. Chapel Hill: University of North Carolina Press.

Lukács, G. (1983). *Record of a Life*. London: Verso.

Marx, K. (1867). Karl Marx to Engels in Manchester. http://marxists.anu.edu.au/archive/marx/works/1867/letters/67_08_24.htm

Marx, K. (1869). Karl Marx to Ludwig Kugelmann. https://www.marxists.org/archive/marx/works/1869/letters/69_02_11.htm

Marx, K. (1990). *Capital, Volume 1*. London: Penguin.

Marx, K. (1991). *Capital, Volume 3*. London: Penguin.

Marx, K. (1993). *Grundrisse*. London: Penguin.

Pashukanis, E. B. (2007). *The General Theory of Law and Marxism*. New Jersey: Transaction Publishers.

Postone, M. (1993). *Time, Labor, and Social Domination*. Cambridge: Cambridge University Press.

Žižek, S. (2008). *The Sublime Object of Ideology*, London: Verso.

4

Capital and the Labour Theory of Value

Prabhat Patnaik

The Labour Theory of Value is often taken as constituting an explanation of the relative prices between the numerous commodities that are produced, or, what is assumed to be the same thing, of the *money prices of the commodities*, i.e. the relative prices of the numerous non-money commodities in terms of the money commodity. This, however, is erroneous. The Labour Theory of Value never claimed to be an explanation of the relative prices of commodities, or of the money price of *any particular* commodity, except at best as a 'first approximation' (whose meaning itself was never unambiguous). The Labour Theory of Value, in my view, is concerned basically with the relative exchange ratio between the money commodity on the one hand and *the world of non-money commodities taken together*, on the other. The Labour Theory of Value presumes that unless this fundamental ratio is specified, in a money-using economy like capitalism, where wages are paid in money, neither the money prices of particular non-money commodities, nor therefore the relative prices of these commodities vis-à-vis one another, can be determined.

In other words, the Labour Theory of Value holds that there is a price-determining meta-rule without which even the relative prices of commodities cannot be determined. Unlike, say, in the Walrasian system, where all commodities, including the money commodity, stand on a par, where symmetry characterizes all commodities, and commodity markets, the Labour Theory of Value holds that the relative prices *between* even non-money commodities cannot be determined without a meta-rule regarding the exchange ratio between the money commodity on the one hand and the entire world of non-money commodities on the other. In other words, the 'money-versus-commodity relationship' and the 'commodity-versus-commodity relationship' are not symmetrical. *The Labour Theory of Value is concerned primarily with the investigation of this meta-rule.*

The meta-rule it postulates of course is that the relative exchange ratio between a unit of the money commodity and a unit of the aggregate of non-money commodities produced is determined by the relative magnitudes of total labour embodied, both directly and indirectly, in a unit of each.[1] But while that is the specific solution it offers, the question it poses, to which it offers this solution, is something that no other theoretical system poses, or even takes cognizance of. And what is more, since the examination of the 'money-versus-commodity relationship', if it is taken to be *sui generis* and asymmetric in comparison with the 'commodity-versus-commodity relationship', falls within the domain of macroeconomics, the Labour Theory of Value is necessarily a macroeconomic theory; it has a perspective on macroeconomics which no other theoretical tradition has. It is concerned with making a number of statements, which in their totality constitute a *sui generis* set, about the macroeconomic properties of a capitalist economy.

To be precise, I shall restate the Labour Theory of Value as a theory about the macroeconomics of a capitalist economy that advances the following three propositions:

Proposition 1: Money is held in such an economy not just for circulating commodities but also as a form of wealth, so that the money held on average over any period far exceeds what is needed for circulation.

Proposition 2: Notwithstanding this fact, for any given level of capacity utilization of the fixed capital stock, there is a unique money value of the aggregate output produced, which is independent of the total money supply.

---

1 When the money value of the aggregate produced output equals the quantity of labour embodied in this aggregate relative to that in a unit of the money commodity, with money wages given, the S/(C+V) that prevails for this aggregate of commodities in the value accounting system will be generally different from the rate of profit in the price accounting system (when the rate of profit is equalized across sectors). In other words, the acceptance of the meta-rule mentioned above does not mean that the 'transformation of values into prices' occurs exactly as Marx had suggested. But that is a matter of secondary importance; what is important is the meta-rule itself.

Proposition 3: For any given level of capacity utilization, a rise in the money wage rate lowers the maximum realizable rate of profit.

These propositions, it should be noted, could also be part of some other theoretical system that provided a different meta-rule, i.e. where the relative exchange ratio between money and the world of non-money commodities was determined by something other than the relative quantities of labour embodied. But since the necessity of the meta-rule itself is recognized only within the problematic of the Labour Theory of Value approach, and none other, these propositions have to be seen as an integral part of the approach to macroeconomics defined by the Labour Theory of Value.

Besides, given this problematic of the necessity of having a meta-rule that determines the money-versus-commodities exchange ratio, a necessity that is emphasized by the Labour Theory of value approach, any answer other than relative labour embodied to the question of what determines this exchange ratio, is inapposite for at least three reasons.

The first is that any such different explanation can always be subsumed under a relative labour embodied explanation anyway, as a variation of it, by bringing in, say, the monopoly rent of gold-mine owners (which may explain why the gold-versus-commodity ratio is not exactly identical with the relative labour embodied). In other words, a fixed ratio between money and the world of commodities, even if it does not empirically correspond to the relative quantities of labour embodied, can still be explained as being based upon it.

Secondly, the explanation in terms of the relative quantities of labour embodied, as is well-known, has profound implications in terms of the analysis of the commodity form. It not only recognizes the centrality of labour as an ontological category under capitalism, but also draws attention to the twofold nature of labour, as concrete and abstract labour, which follows from the twofold nature of commodities: as use value and exchange value.

The third reason is more directly analytical. Take for instance the sixteenth-century inflation which according to Keynes (1979) marked the genesis of modern capitalism. Keynes' own explanation of it was in terms of the inflow of Spanish gold into Europe, which had very different effects in two different segments of the continent.

In countries like England it increased the demand for *goods*, causing a profit-inflation (since money wages were sticky) which improved investment opportunities. But in the more 'feudal' societies like Spain and Portugal this inflow increased the demand for labour services, causing a rise in money wages, and hence squeezing profits and discouraging investment.

But Marx's explanation of the sixteenth-century inflation, derived from the Labour Theory approach, was completely different. It was not the inflow of gold adding to the quantity of the precious metal available in Europe that caused the inflation but the fact that the new mines worked in the Spanish colonies reduced the quantity of labour embodied in a unit of gold. The point here is not to enter into a debate on this particular issue, but merely to underscore the fact that the Labour Theory explanation of inflation is fundamentally analytically different from any version of monetarism (of which arguably there is a trace in Keynes's explanation). Hence the Labour Theory explanation does not relate only to the *level* of the exchange ratio between money and commodities; it relates, even more importantly, to *changes* in it. It represents an alternative perspective on inflation compared to monetarism.

Two caveats must be immediately entered in the context of the above three propositions. One, money here refers to commodity money, like gold (which also includes paper money that is exchangeable freely against such commodity money at a fixed ratio), but not non-convertible paper money (on this more later). Two, the second and third of the above propositions hold for any given level of capacity utilization; they do not claim *per se* that some particular level of capacity utilization will necessarily obtain in the economy 'in equilibrium'. The third proposition for instance must not be interpreted as saying that between equilibrium 1 with a certain level of money wages and equilibrium 2 with a higher level of money wages, the latter must be characterized by a lower rate of profit. The Labour Theory of Value in short is not making any claims on its own on what sort of equilibrium will come about if the money wages rise. It is simply saying that at a given level of capacity utilization, *for instance with a given level of output produced by a given level of capital stock*, if the money wages rise then the rate of profit must fall. The r in the downward-sloping w-r frontier which the

Labour Theory of Value is supposed to postulate refers therefore to a 'given-output-rate-of-profit'.

It is clear that the Labour Theory of Value, interpreted as embodying the three propositions above, is exclusively a theory of Marx. One generally talks of the Labour Theory of Value as having underlain classical political economy, especially the Ricardian system, from whom Marx is supposed to have borrowed it. But the three propositions mentioned above are true only of Marx and not of Ricardo or Smith or anyone else. *So, the Labour Theory of Value as stated by us is not something that is common between Ricardo and Marx. It is exclusively Marxian.* And if one uses the Labour Theory of Value to characterize Ricardo as well, then one should be clear that that theory is an altogether different one from what is outlined above in the form of the three propositions. (In fact one would be better off using some other name altogether for Ricardo's theory.)

It is equally clear that the three propositions mentioned above *do not characterize any other theoretical system in economics, neither the Keynesian, nor the Walrasian, nor the Marshallian, nor, as already mentioned, the Ricardian.* Since I take the Labour Theory to be synonymous with an approach to macroeconomics defined by these three propositions, it follows from my argument that the validity of the Labour Theory approach is dependent on the validity of the three propositions. If the three propositions are valid then the Labour Theory, as a *sui generis* approach to macroeconomics, also gets validated. Moreover, the validation of the Labour Theory approach entails *ipso facto* its scientific superiority over other approaches to macroeconomics; it testifies *ipso facto* in other words to the limitations of these other macroeconomic approaches.

The best way to clarify the gamut of issues involved here is perhaps to see how the three propositions do get conjointly satisfied under the Labour Theory meta-rule on price, but do not get satisfied under any other theoretical system. If this can be established, then the *sui generis* nature of the Labour Theory approach can be established, and also the rationale behind categorizing these propositions as the 'Labour Theory of Value' approach. In what follows I shall be concerned with showing why these three propositions can hold only under the Labour Theory meta-rule and cannot hold, all of them taken together, under any other theoretical system.

In view of the commonly held belief that the Ricardian and Marxian value theories are identical, it may be best to begin with Ricardo and underscore the basic differences between his theory and that of Marx. In Ricardo the money commodity is not on a different footing compared to the non-money commodities. In other words, the same symmetry between money and non-money commodities that characterizes the Walrasian system also characterizes the Ricardian system, notwithstanding the very different price theories they have. In Ricardo for instance, the money commodity enters alongside every other commodity into the wage-rate and profit-rate equalization rule. The money price of any commodity is simply its relative price vis-à-vis money in a situation of equilibrium where all sectors, including the money commodity sector, are earning the same rate of profit and paying the same wage rate per unit of labour; it is determined by the conditions of production and the exogenously given wage rate.

Since, at this equilibrium price configuration, demand equals supply in every sector, it follows that the amount of money supply must also equal the amount of money demand; and if, starting from this equilibrium situation where the 'natural price of money' prevails vis-à-vis the non-money commodities, money supply happens to increase for some reason, then the 'market price' of money must fall below the 'natural price', as in standard Ricardian theory, which means that *all commodity prices in terms of money must rise*.

The proposition that an increase in money supply must raise money prices of commodities, which is an integral part of Ricardo's theory, is nothing else but pure monetarism. Ricardo was a monetarist in the short-run. To use Joan Robinson's striking expression, he read the quantity equation $MV=PQ$ 'from the left to the right' in the short-run (when 'market prices' prevail), but 'from the right to the left' in the long-run (when 'natural prices' or 'prices of production' prevail). The Quantity equation, however, can be read from the left to the right only if the demand for money arises exclusively for circulating commodities, i.e. as a means of circulation, and not as a form of holding wealth, for in the latter case an increase in money supply can simply increase the amount of money held as wealth without any impact whatsoever on the money prices of non-money commodities.

The inclusion of money within the charmed circle of commodities across which the rate of profit and the wage rate are equalized in equilibrium[2] logically entails, therefore, that money must function only as a means of circulation and not as a form of wealth; and Ricardo, as well as his interpreter James Mill, explicitly say so in any case.[3] Indeed, Ricardo's denial of the possibility of generalized *ex ante* over-production and acceptance of Say's Law presupposes that money cannot be a form of holding wealth.

But this denial, that money cannot be a form of holding wealth, is not only empirically untrue under capitalism in an obvious sense, but also logically untenable: even to function as a means of circulation, money must, for a fleeting moment at least, constitute the form in which wealth is held; and if wealth is held in the form of money for a fleeting moment, then there is absolutely no reason why it cannot be held in this form for more than a fleeting moment. And if it is held for a longer or a shorter period, then its velocity of circulation ceases to be a constant, and a situation of *ex ante* generalized over-production becomes possible.

The Ricardian theory of the determination of money prices is thus both empirically and logically untenable and is certainly in contrast to the Marxian theory, in which, as our first of the three propositions makes clear, money is a form of wealth-holding, and in which, therefore, Say's Law does not hold. The exchange ratio between the money commodity and the world of non-money commodities therefore cannot be determined in the same way that relative prices of production are determined across the world of non-money commodities, as in Ricardo (or Sraffa (1960)), *but has to be separately specified*. The Labour Theory of Value does precisely that: it states that this exchange ratio is given by the relative magnitudes of labour embodied in a unit of the money commodity and a unit of the aggregate non-money commodity, which means that the *money commodity does not enter the equalization-of-the-rate-of-profit rule*.

The *sui generis* nature of the Labour Theory of Value approach to the value of money, and hence to macroeconomics in general, in contrast to that of Ricardo therefore, is obvious. A whole gamut of conclusions

---

2   For a discussion of this issue and the analytical difference between Smith and Ricardo over it, see Dobb 1973.

3   For a critique of James Mill's defence of Ricardo about money being only a medium of circulation, and hence having a constant velocity of circulation, see Marx 1971. This entire issue is discussed in Patnaik 2009.

emerges from this approach that are in contrast to Ricardian theory. And these are: money as a form of wealth-holding; the perpetual existence of a hoard of money in excess of what is required for the purpose of circulating commodities alone; the possibility of *ex ante* generalized over-production of produced non-money commodities and hence a denial of Say's Law; and the denial, whether in the short or in the long-run, of monetarism. Marx was implacably opposed to monetarism, a fact that those who see him as only following in Ricardo's footsteps forget for some intriguing reason.

The Walrasian system of course accepts monetarism, so much so that Frank Hahn (1984) has defined monetarism as the belief that the real world is characterized by a Walrasian equilibrium. This essentially precludes the holding of money as a form of wealth. Attempts to incorporate into the Walrasian system the holding of cash balances that bear not just a fixed relationship with the magnitude of money income, as in Marshall, but a variable relationship suggestive of a wealth demand for money, are so beset with logical contradictions that they cannot tell any coherent story: the proposition that all markets clear through price flexibility simply cannot be established in a Walrasian universe, if economic agents hold money as a form of wealth.[4] It follows that the first and the second of our three propositions defining the Labour Theory of Value approach to macroeconomics are violated under the Walrasian system.

But while this is obvious and indisputable, the comparison between the Keynesian and the Labour Theory approaches is far more instructive, since both accept the first proposition, of money being a form in which wealth is held in a capitalist economy, which opens up the possibility of *ex ante* generalized over-production of non-money commodities. The second proposition too holds in the Keynesian system, *but by virtue of the fact that the money wage rate is given.* At any given level of capacity utilization of the fixed capital stock, or, what comes to the same thing, at any given level of output (given the conditions of production), the level of money prices of the produced commodities is determined by the given money wage rate. *It is the third proposition of the Labour Theory approach that does not hold in the Keynesian system.*

---

4   This issue is extensively discussed in Patnaik 2009.

In Keynes, given the level of investment and hence, via the multiplier, the level of aggregate demand, the level of employment gets determined and hence the level of real wages (since Keynes believed in the equality between the real wage rate and the marginal product of labour in equilibrium). The real wage rate in short is endogenously determined from within the system by the level of aggregate demand. A rise in the money wage rate, it follows, *cannot change the real wage rate* unless it causes some change in the level of aggregate demand. For any given level of output, therefore, a rise in the money wage rate does not lower the rate of profit, unlike what the Labour Theory of Value approach believes.

A rise in money wages for any given output has the effect of raising money prices, leaving real wages and the rate of profit unchanged. This, it is obvious, can happen only in a paper money or a credit money world but not in a commodity money world. Indeed the Keynesian theory of money price determination which makes money prices dependent upon the level of money wages, presupposes a paper money or a credit money world, where money itself is not a produced commodity, employs no wage labour, and hence has no cost of production to be compared to the cost of production of non-money commodities.

While the difference between the Labour Theory approach and the Keynesian approach therefore is directly attributable to their respective concepts of money, viz. the fact that the former works in terms of commodity money and the latter in terms of fiat or credit money, it raises an important issue with regard to the Keynesian approach. If money is to be a form of holding wealth, then the prices of commodities must not be expected to rise at a rate higher than their carrying cost, for in such a case commodities would supplant money as the form in which wealth is held. Of course, not all commodities can possibly play such a role but the one with perhaps the least carrying cost, e.g. gold, can supplant money as the form of holding wealth, if its price in terms of money is expected to increase sufficiently. There is therefore a paradox at the heart of Keynesian theory: the *raison d'être* of the theory arises from the fact that wealth is held in the form of money (for otherwise there can be no *ex ante* generalized over-production), but if money is purely fiat or credit money in terms of which commodity prices, including the price of gold, can increase, then it cannot possibly continue to constitute a form of holding wealth.

Of course, if money wages do not increase at all, then the prices of commodities in terms of money will not increase and hence the role of money as a form of wealth-holding will not get threatened (except in situations of *ex ante* excess demand at full capacity output which are exceptional under capitalism). A perceptive Keynesian like Joan Robinson (1956) recognized the problem and sought to resolve it theoretically by postulating an 'inflationary barrier', that is, by postulating that as long as the unemployment rate exceeded a certain threshold, the wage-unit would remain stable, and hence the role of money as a form in which wealth is held would not be threatened. Her argument was confined to a single period; but since the Phillips Curve suggested *on the basis of historical evidence* that the assumption of static price expectation (i.e. that everyone expects the current period's *price-level* to prevail in the next one, even in the midst of inflation) was a realistic one, this contradiction at the heart of Keynesian theory could be quietly tolerated.[5] There was however little theoretical reason for doing so, which is why Keynesianism could get undermined by the subsequent development of the NAIRU theory.

But even leaving aside the NAIRU theory, the basic argument remained: if money that is not commodity money is to serve as a form of wealth-holding, then there must be something in the system that ensures the stability of commodity prices in terms of this money; in a world where all commodities are produced commodities (i.e. there are no 'rent goods'), this required either that a rise in money wages should result in a rise in real wages without any change in prices (or with only a small enough change in prices), or that there should be no rise in money wages at all, for which it was essential to maintain a level of the unemployment rate that was sufficiently high.

Keynesianism, however, postulated neither. (Joan Robinson's 'inflationary barrier' was visualized only as a theoretical possibility with little practical importance.) It used instead, at least in Keynes' original formulation, the tenuous concept of a 'money illusion' to suggest that the workers were so focused on money wages that as long

---

5   Phillips (1958) did not of course directly test for static price expectations. But the relationship he did obtain between the unemployment rate and the rate of change of the money wage rate (or prices in later versions) was tenable only on the basis of static price expectations. See Patnaik 1997, for an elaborate discussion.

as the latter did not decrease, they made no higher wage demands even in a situation of falling *real wages*. It thus swept the problem under the carpet: the role of money as a form of wealth-holding was not undermined even as aggregate demand increased, because there was no reason for money wages to rise, as workers suffered from 'money illusion'. In the process however the Keynesian system retained a serious contradiction.

Let us now examine the Labour Theory of Value approach from this particular point. The Labour Theory of Value approach holds that a rise in money wages leads to a rise in real wages and a fall in the given-output-rate-of-profit, a proposition first explicated by Marx in his speech to a meeting of the First International, subsequently published as *Value, Price and Profit* (and claimed by Marx himself as anticipating the argument of the as yet unpublished *Capital*). Marx's argument was directed against the position of Citizen Weston who was a follower of John Stuart Mill and had argued on the basis of Mill's Wages Fund theory that trade union action could not make all workers simultaneously better off.

Of course both the Ricardian and the Walrasian strands also hold that a rise in money wages increases real wages, but these latter strands do so on the assumption that Say's Law holds and, by inference, that money does not constitute a form of holding wealth. *The specificity of the Labour Theory approach consists in arguing that even in a world where Say's Law does not hold (and hence monetarism is untenable), a rise in money wages nonetheless has the effect of increasing real wages.*

This is where the Labour Theory approach differs from that of both Keynes and Kalecki. In Keynes, as we have seen, real wages are endogenously determined, by the level of aggregate demand; and an increase in money wages, unless it affects aggregate demand, merely increases prices. Kalecki dealt with a world of oligopoly, where prices were the result of firms' decisions. In such a world, while it was true that *if* a money wage increase led to a rise in real wages then profits would not fall but output would increase instead, through a rise in aggregate demand, in point of fact a rise in money wages would not actually raise real wages: the rise in firms' cost of production owing to such a rise in money wages would simply be 'passed on' in the form of higher prices.

This however immediately raises a piquant question: since the wage bargain is in money terms, if a rise in money wages, which is all that successful trade union action can enforce, does not raise real wages, then what explains all the hullabaloo against trade unions under capitalism? This question, which had been at the core of Ashok Mitra's (1980) rejoinder to Kalecki, *The Share of Wages in National Income*, has continued to haunt economists, who reject the view that the labour market 'clears' under capitalism, to this day.

Kalecki himself was haunted by it till the very end. He kept coming back to the problem of reconciling his theory of effective demand with his view that trade unions could raise the share of wages, through a rise in money wages leading to a rise in real wages, without which, after all, there would be no *raison d'être* for them. One of his last articles, 'Class Struggle and the Distribution of Income' (Kalecki 1971), was devoted precisely to this question. But his answer, namely that a rise in money wages would somehow reduce the average 'mark-up', remained, it would not be unfair to add, rather unclear with regard to its *modus operandi*.

The basic problem arose from the fact that if money was not commodity money but fiat or credit money, whose supply for circulation purposes could be augmented (or whose overall supply itself could be augmented in a world of 'endogenous' money), then there was no obvious restraint on the rise in money prices as a result of a rise in money wages. If that which links the two worlds of money and commodities, in the Kaleckian (or Keynesian) universe, and provides the anchorage to money prices, namely the money wage rate, itself changes, then there is nothing obvious to prevent money prices from changing as well.

Marx himself was not unaware of the possibility of inflation through a rise in the wage rate in terms of money that was not convertible to precious metals. But he distinguished between two kinds of inflation: inflation in commodity prices in terms of the money commodity, and inflation in commodity prices in terms of non-convertible money but not in terms of the money commodity. He referred to the latter as a depreciation in the value of non-convertible paper money in terms of commodity money, which was different from a depreciation in the value of commodity money in terms of non-money commodities. While the former could arise because of excessive supply of non-convertible paper money, the latter could arise only because of a change in the condition of production of the money commodity compared to non-money commodities, resulting in a change in the relative quantities of labour embodied in a unit of each. Marx reconciled in this manner his rejection of monetarism with the observation that excessive supply of paper notes could lead to a depreciation of the value of such currency in terms of commodities (even when the conditions of production of all commodities, money and non-money, remained unchanged).

The crucial point however is this. The Labour Theory of Value approach to macroeconomics, ignoring for the moment minor modifications arising because of carrying costs, can be stated as follows: *whatever the concept of money in terms of which wealth is held, a rise in money wages in terms of that concept of money must lead to a fall in the given-output-rate-of-profit, and hence a rise in real wages.* But precisely for this reason there is a constant effort under capitalism to *prevent* money wages from rising; and this effort occurs both spontaneously through the maintenance of 'adequate' unemployment, or, if spontaneity fails, then through the intervention by the state in different ways. The hullabaloo against trade unions then becomes easily explicable: it is to prevent a rise in money wages because such a rise either causes a fall in the given-output-rate-of-profit, or, in the absence of such a fall, a threat to the value of the wealth held in the form of money through inflation. Enfeebling trade unions nips the entire problem in the bud.

All this does not of course mean that a rise in money wages *over time* will necessarily lead to a fall in the rate of profit. We have so far ignored labour productivity increases, and obviously as long as the rise in money wages *over time* does not exceed the rise in labour productivity, there is no reason for a fall in the rate of profit for an unchanged capital-output ratio (i.e. if the Marxian reason for the falling tendency for the rate of profit does not obtain). But the Labour Theory of Value approach that I have been talking about is not defined in terms of what happens to the capitalist economy *over time*. It is a statement not about the *dynamics* of a capitalist economy but about its macroeconomic *properties*, namely that a rise in money wages leads to a rise in real wages with a given output, not despite the fact of money being a form of holding wealth (and hence the economy being vulnerable to *ex ante* over-production crises), but precisely because of this fact.

Capitalist economies, at least of late, have been functioning with non-convertible money. What the foregoing says, however, is that, as long as wealth is held in the form of such money, *it cannot be any different from commodity money in the sense that a rise in the wage rate in terms of such money cannot but raise the real wage rate to the detriment of the given-output-rate-of-profit.* Precisely for this reason, however, capitalist economies operate in a manner that ensures that the given-output-rate-of-profit does not go secularly below a certain threshold of an 'acceptable rate of profit' to the capitalists. This requires *inter alia* the maintenance of a perennial reserve army of labour of at least a certain requisite size.

Such a *denouement*, of a certain size of the reserve army being perennially maintained, may be 'spontaneously' ensured through the functioning of the system as Goodwin (1967) had demonstrated in his 'growth cycle'; or it may be ensured by the intervention of the state in a manner that is the very opposite of what Keynes had advocated, i.e. though fiscal and monetary policies causing an 'adequate' level of *unemployment.*

State intervention operates not just through the maintenance of unemployment but also through denting the strength of trade unions, so that at any given level of the unemployment rate their capacity to bargain for a higher wage is impaired. The extreme case of such a direct attack on trade unions is fascism, which attains 'full employment' but smashes trade unions altogether.

So far we have assumed that all goods are produced by labour acting on means of production, with the help of instruments of production, and that these means and instruments of production themselves are also similarly produced, and so on; in short we have assumed that there are no 'rent goods'. If, as is obviously the case, there are such 'rent goods' (in the form of scarce raw materials like oil), then an increase in the prices of such 'rent goods' can either lower the rate of profit, or destabilize the value of money by causing inflation, and hence undermine its wealth-holding role, even for a given level of real wages. It is essential therefore for the wealth-holding role of money that not only should there always be an 'adequate' level of unemployment within capitalism, but also that the prices of scarce raw materials should not be allowed to increase to the detriment of the value of money. For if the latter happens then again either the given-output-rate-of-profit would fall, or the value of money will depreciate in a manner prejudicial to its role as a form of wealth-holding. The stability in the relative price of scarce raw materials, which largely exist outside of the capitalist sector proper (and even if they did exist within the capitalist sector itself to start with, soon such internal supplies get exhausted and capitalism seeks supplies from outside), is usually ensured by political control by the capitalist state (or by the leading capitalist state) over such outside resources.

The phenomenon of imperialism therefore is immanent, though never theoretically recognized as such, to the Labour Theory of Value approach to macroeconomics, which, to recapitulate, holds that since money is necessarily a form in which wealth is held under capitalism, a rise in money wages or in the money prices of scarce raw materials, must lower the given-output-rate-of-profit of the system to keep alive this form-of-wealth role of money.

References

Dobb, M. H. (1973). *Theories of Value and Distribution Since Adam Smith.* Cambridge: Cambridge University Press.

Goodwin, R. M. (1967). The Growth Cycle. In C. H. Feinstein, ed., *Capitalism, Socialism and Economic Growth: Essays Presented to Maurice Dobb.* Cambridge: Cambridge University Press, 54–8.

Hahn, F. (1984). *Equilibrium and Macroeconomics.* Oxford: Oxford University Press.

Kalecki, M. (1971). Class Struggle and the Distribution of Income. In M. Kalecki, *Selected Essays on the Dynamics of the Capitalist Economy.* Cambridge: Cambridge University Press, 1–9.

Keynes, J. M. (1979). *The Collected Writings of J. M. Keynes,* Vol. VI. London: Macmillan.

Marx, K. (1971). *A Contribution to a Critique of Political Economy.* London: Lawrence and Wishart.

Mitra, A. (1980). *The Share of Wages in National Income.* Delhi: Oxford University Press.

Patnaik, P. (1997). *Accumulation and Stability Under Capitalism.* Oxford: Clarendon Press.

Patnaik, P. (2009). *The Value of Money.* New York: Columbia University Press.

Phillips, A. W. (1958). The Relation Between Unemployment and the Rate of Change of Money Wage Rates in the United Kingdom, 1861–1957. *Economica,* 25(4): 283–99.

Robinson, J. (1956). *The Accumulation of Capital.* London: Macmillan.

Sraffa, P. (1960). *Production of Commodities by Means of Commodities.* Cambridge: Cambridge University Press.

5

Capital and Gender

Silvia Federici

As interest in Marxism and feminism is reviving and Marx's views on 'gender' are receiving a new attention, some areas of agreement among feminists are emerging that also shape my own approach to the subject.[1] First, while denunciations of gender inequalities and patriarchal control in the family and society can be found in Marx's work from an early stage, it is agreed that Marx 'did not have much to say on gender and the family' (Brown 2012: 143) and, even in *Capital*, his views on the subject must be reconstructed from scattered observations.

Nevertheless, Marx's work has made a significant contribution to the development of feminist theory, although not primarily based on his direct pronouncements on the subject. Not only has his historical materialist method helped demonstrate the constructed character of gender hierarchies and identities (Holmstrom 2002: 360–76), his analyses of capitalist accumulation and value creation have also given feminists of my generation powerful tools to rethink the specific forms of exploitation to which women have been subjected in capitalist society and the relation between 'sex, race, and class'. However, the use that feminists have made of Marx has at best taken them in a different direction from the one he traced.

Writing about gender in *Capital*, then, means coming to terms with two different Marxes and two different viewpoints on gender and the class struggle. Accordingly, what follows is divided into two parts. In the first part, I examine Marx's view of gender as articulated in Volume

---

[1] Signs of the new interest in Marx's theory of gender include the recent publications of Heather A. Brown's *Marx on Gender and the Family* (2012), and Shahrzad Mojabed's *Marxism and Feminism* (2015), this last published in concomitance with the conference organized on the subject by Rosa Luxemburg Foundation in Berlin in the same year.

1 of *Capital* in his analysis of women's employment in industrial labour. I also comment on his silences, especially about domestic work, as they are eloquent about the concerns that structured his thought at the time of his writing. My main argument here is that Marx left the question of gender untheorized partly because 'women's emancipation' had a peripheral importance in his political work; moreover he naturalized domestic work and, like the European socialist movement as a whole, idealized industrial labour as the normative form of social production and a potential leveller of social inequalities. Thus, he believed that, in time, distinctions based on gender and age would dissipate, and he failed to see the strategic importance, both for capitalist development and for the struggle against it, of the sphere of activities and relations by which our lives and labour power are reproduced, beginning with sexuality, procreation and, first and foremost, women's unpaid domestic labour.

These 'oversights' concerning the importance of women's reproductive work have meant that, despite his condemnation of patriarchal relations, Marx has left us an analysis of capital and class that is conducted from a masculine viewpoint – that of the 'working man', the industrial waged worker in whose name the International was formed, assumed to be the carrier of a universal aspiration to human liberation. It has further meant that many Marxists have felt justified in treating gender (and race) as cultural matters, dissociating them from class, and that the feminist movement had to start with a critique of Marx.

Thus, while this chapter focuses on the treatment of gender in Marx's major text, in the second part I briefly revisit the reconstruction of Marx's categories developed by feminists in the 1970s, especially in the *Wages For Housework* movement of which I was part. I argue that *Wages For Housework* feminists found in Marx the foundation for a feminist theory centred on women's struggle against unpaid domestic labour because we read his analysis of capitalism politically, coming from a direct personal experience, looking for answers to our refusal of domestic relations. We could then take Marx's theory to places that had remained concealed in Marx's own work. At the same time, reading Marx politically revealed the limitations of his theoretical framework, demonstrating that while a feminist anti-capitalist perspective cannot ignore Marx's work, at least as long as capitalism remains the dominant mode of production (Gimenez 2005: 11–12), it must nevertheless go beyond it.

Marx and Gender on the Industrial Shop Floor

The limits of Marx's theory stand out most clearly in *Capital* Volume 1, as it is in this work that Marx for the first time examined the question of 'gender', not in relation to the subordination of women within the bourgeois family, but with regard to the conditions of women's factory work in the industrial revolution. This was the 'woman's question' of the time (Scott 1988: 139–60) on both sides of the Channel, as economists, politicians and philanthropists clamoured against the destruction of family life it produced, the new independence it gave women, and its contribution to workers' protest, manifested in the rise of trade unions and Chartism. Thus, by the time Marx began his writing, reforms were underway, and he could count on a copious literature on the subject, mainly consisting of reports by the factory inspectors that, by the 1840s, the British government was employing to ensure that the limits imposed on the hours worked by women and children would be observed.

Whole pages from these reports are cited in Volume 1, especially in the chapters on the 'Working Day' and 'Machinery and Large Scale Industry', serving to illustrate the structural tendencies of capitalist production (the tendency to extend the working day to the limit of the workers' physical resistance, to devalue labour power, to extract the maximum of labour from the minimum number of workers) and to denounce the horrors women and children were subjected to at each stage of industrial development.

From these reports we learn of needlewomen dying of over-work and lack of air and food (Marx 1990: 365), of young girls working without meals, 14 hours a day or crawling half-naked in mines to bring coal to the surface, of children dragged from their beds in the middle of the night 'compelled to work for bare subsistence', 'slaughtered' by a vampire-like machine, consuming their lives until 'there remains a single muscle, sinew or drop of blood to be exploited' (Marx 1990: 365, 353, 416).

Few political writers have described as uncompromisingly the brutality of capitalist work – outside of slavery – as Marx has done and he must be praised for it. Particularly impressive is his denunciation of the barbaric exploitation of child labour, which is unmatched in Marxist literature. But despite its eloquence, his account is generally more descriptive than analytic and is remarkable for the absence of a discussion of the gender issues it raises.

We are not told, for instance, how the employment of women and children in the factories affected workers' struggles, what debates it prompted in workers' organizations, or how it affected women's relations with men. We have instead various moralistic comments to the effect that factory labour degraded women's 'moral character' by encouraging 'promiscuous' behaviour, and made them neglect their maternal duties. Almost never are women portrayed as actors capable of fighting on their own behalf. Mostly they appear as victims, although their contemporaries noted their independence, their boisterous behaviour, and their capacity to defend their interests against the factory owners' attempts to reform their ways (Seccombe 1993: 121).

Missing in Marx's account of gender on the shop floor is also an analysis of the crisis that the near extinction of domestic work in proletarian communities caused for the expansion of capitalist relations, and the dilemma that capital faced – then as now – with regard to the optimal place and use of women's labour. These silences are especially significant as the chapters I mentioned are the only ones in which issues concerning gender relations have any presence.

Gender issues have a marginal place in *Capital*. In a three-volume text of thousands of pages, only in about a 100 we find any references to family, sexuality or women's work, and these are often passing observations. References to gender are missing even where they would be most expected, as in the chapters on the social division of labour or the one on wages. Only at the end of the chapter on machinery and large-scale industry we find clues to the gender politics that we know Marx advocated in his political work, as secretary of the First International, in which capacity he opposed attempts to exclude women from factory employment (Brown 2012: 115). These are consistent with his life-long belief that – for all its violence and brutality – capitalism was a necessary evil and even a progressive force, since by developing the productive forces capitalism creates the material conditions of production that alone can form the real basis of a higher form of society, a society in which the full and free development of every individual is the ruling principle (Marx 1990: 739).

Applied to gender this meant that, by 'liberating' labour from the constraints of specialization and from the need for physical strength, and by drawing women and children into social production, capitalist development and industrialization in particular paved the way to more egalitarian gender relations. For on one side they freed women and children from personal dependence and parental exploitation of their labour – the trademarks of domestic industry – and on the other enabled them to participate on an equal basis with men in social production.

As Marx put it, while discussing the introduction of elementary education for child factory workers:

> However terrible and disgusting the dissolution of the old family within the capitalist system may appear, large scale industry, by assigning an important part in socially organized processes of production, outside the sphere of the domestic economy, to women, young persons and children of both sexes, does nevertheless create a new economic foundation for a higher form of the family and of relations between the sexes. (1990: 620–1)

What this new family would look like, how it would reconcile 'production and reproduction', is not something Marx investigates. He only cautiously added that: 'the fact that the collective working group is composed of individuals of both sexes and all ages must under appropriate conditions turn into a source of humane development, although in its spontaneously developed, brutal, capitalist form, the system works in the opposite direction' (1990: 621).

Though not explicitly articulated, the key to Marx's assumption that the displacement of domestic by large-scale industry would produce a more humane society was undoubtedly also the idea (to which he returned in several sections of *Capital*) that industrial work is more than a multiplier of the power of production and a guarantor (presumably) of social abundance. It is – potentially – the creator of a different type of cooperative association and a different type of human being, freed from personal dependence and not 'fixed' in any particular set of skills, thus capable of engaging in a broad range of activities and the regular type of behaviour required by a 'rational' organization of the labour process.

Continuous with his conception of communism as the end of the division of labour, and with his vision in *The German Ideology* (Marx and Engels 1988) of a society where one would fish and hunt in the morning and write poems in the evening, the idea of an industrial, cooperative, egalitarian society, where (paraphrasing a provocative pronouncement in the *Communist Manifesto* (Marx and Engels 1967)) gender differences would have lost all 'social validity' in the working class, may seem enticing, and not surprisingly it has inspired generations of socialist activists, feminist included.

Yet, as feminists in the 1970s discovered, there are major limits to this perspective. Four are worth noting, all with implications beyond gender, relating to Marx's conception of industrialization and capitalist development as emancipating forces and conditions for human liberation. By praising modern industry for both liberating women from the fetters of domestic work and patriarchal rule and for making possible their participation in social production, Marx assumed that: (i) women had never before been involved in social production, that is, reproductive work should not be considered socially necessary labour; (ii) what in the past had limited their work participation was lack of physical strength; (iii) essential to gender equality is a technological leap and; (iv) most important, anticipating the argument that Marxists would repeat for generations, factory work is the paradigmatic form of social production, consequently the factory, not the community, is the site of anti-capitalist struggle. Questions must be raised on all these counts.

We can quickly dispose of the argument about 'physical strength' as an explanation for gender-based discrimination. Suffice to say that Marx's own description of women's and children's conditions of industrial employment is a counter argument to it, and the factory reports he cited make it clear that women were recruited in industrial work not because automation lessened the burden of their labour (Marx 1990: 527), but because they could be paid less, and were considered more docile and more prone to give all their energies to the job. We should also dispel the idea of women's confinement to home-work prior to the advent of industrialization. For the domestic industry from which women were liberated employed only a small part of the female proletariat, and was itself a fairly recent innovation resulting from the collapse of the artisan guilds (Henninger 2014: 296–7). In reality, prior to and during the industrial revolution, women worked in many different jobs, from agricultural work, to trading, domestic service and domestic work. Thus – as Bock and Duden have documented – there is no historical basis for the idea – to which Marx and other socialists subscribed – that 'the development of capitalism, with its increasingly industrial (productive) work of women, freed and frees them from the age-old feudal reigns of housework and tutelage by men' (Bock and Duden 1980: 157).

Marx also underplayed in his conception of large-scale industry as a leveller of social and biological distinctions the weight of inherited and reconstructed sexual hierarchies ensuring that women would experience factory work in specific ways, different from men's. He noted that gender assumptions continued to be prominent in industrial work, used, for example, to justify keeping women's wages lower than men's, and that 'promiscuous' work conditions could mean vulnerability to sexual abuse, often resulting in pregnancy at a very early age (Marx 1990: 852). But, as we have seen above, he assumed that these abuses would be overcome when workers would take political power and redirect industry's objectives towards their well-being. However, after two centuries of industrialization we can see that, while the end of capitalism is nowhere in sight, wherever it has been achieved or approximated, equality in the workplace has been a product of women's struggles not a gift of the machine.

More crucial is that Marx's identification of industrial labour as the normative form of work and privileged site of social production leaves no space for any consideration of domestic reproductive activities, which, as Fortunati (1997) has pointed out, Marx only mentioned to note that capital destroys them by appropriating all of women's time.[2] There is an interesting contrast here with the approach to the factory-home relation in the work of Alfred Marshall, the father of neo-classical economics. Marx's view of industrial labour as a more rational type of work recalls Marshall's 'general ability to work', which he described as

---

2   Fortunati adds that Marx saw women's reproductive work 'through reading government's reports which had realized the problem posed by [factory work's] usurpation of housework much earlier' (1997: 169).

a new capacity, possessed (at the time) by few workers in the world: 'not peculiar to any occupation' but 'wanted by all, enabling workers to keep at any kind of work for a long time', 'bear in mind many things at a time ... accommodate quickly to changes in detail of the work done, to be steady and trustworthy' (Marshall 1938: 206–7).

Marshall, however, in line with contemporary reformers, believed that the prime contributor to the production of this 'general ability' was home-life and especially the influence of the mother (Marshall 1938: 207), so that he strongly opposed women's external employment. Marx, by contrast, gives little attention to domestic work. No discussion of it appears in his analysis of the social division of labour, where he only states that the division of work in the family has a physiological basis.[3] Even more remarkable is his silence on women's domestic work in his analysis of the reproduction of labour power, in the chapter entitled 'Simple Reproduction'.

Here he turned to a theme that is crucial for understanding the process of value-creation in capitalism. That is: labour power, our capacity to work, is not a given. Daily consumed in the work process, it must be continuously (re)produced, and this (re)production is as essential to the valorization of capital as 'the cleaning of machinery', for '[i]t is the production of the capitalists' most precious means of production: the worker itself' (Marx 1990: 718).

In other words, as he also suggested in the notes later published as *Theories of Surplus Value* (Marx 1969), in *Capital* as well, Marx indicates that the reproduction of the worker is an essential part and condition of capital accumulation. However, he conceives it only under the aspect of 'consumption' and places its realization solely within the circuit of commodity production. The workers – Marx imagines – use the wage to buy the necessities of life – and by consuming them reproduce themselves. It is literally production of waged workers by means of commodities produced by waged workers. Thus, 'the value of labour-power is the value of the means of subsistence necessary for the maintenance of its owner', and it is determined by the labour time

---

3 'Within a family ... there springs up naturally a division of labour caused by differences of sex and age, and therefore based upon a pure physiological foundation' (Marx 1990: 471).

necessary for the production of the commodities the workers consume (Marx 1990: 274).

At no point in *Capital* does Marx recognize that the reproduction of labour power entails women's unpaid domestic work – to prepare food, wash clothes, raise children, make love. On the contrary, he insists on portraying the waged worker as self-reproducing. Even when considering the needs the worker must satisfy, he portrays him as a self-sufficient commodity-buyer, listing among his necessities for life food, housing, clothing but awkwardly omitting sex, whether obtained in a familial set-up or purchased, suggesting an immaculate male workers' life, with only women being morally tainted by industrial labour (Marx 1990: 275). The prostitute is thus negated as a worker, and relegated to an example of women's degradation, being pictured as belonging to 'the lowest sediment of the surplus population', that *lumpen*-proletariat (Marx 1990: 797) that in *The 18th Brumaire* he had described as 'the refusal of all classes' (Marx 1968).

There are a few passages where Marx comes close to breaking this silence and implicitly admitting that what appears as 'consumption' to the waged worker may be reproductive work from the viewpoint of his female counterparts. In a footnote to a discussion on the determination of the value of labour power, in 'Machine and Large Scale Industry', he writes: 'from this we see how capital for the purpose of its self-valorization, has usurped the family labour necessary for consumption', adding that:

[s]ince certain family functions, such as nursing and suckling children, cannot be entirely suppressed, the mothers who have been confiscated by capital must try substitutes of some sort. Domestic work, such as sewing and mending, must be replaced by the purchase of ready-made articles. Hence the diminished expenditure of labour in the house is accompanied by an increased expenditure of money outside. The cost of production of the working class therefore increases and balances its greater income. In addition to this, economy and judgment in the consumption and preparation of the means of subsistence becomes impossible. (1990: 518)

However, of this domestic work 'that cannot be entirely suppressed' and has to be replaced by purchased goods nothing more is said, and we are also left to wonder if the cost of production only increases for the worker or increases for the capitalist as well, presumably through the struggles workers make to gain higher wages.

Even when referring to the generational reproduction of the workforce, Marx makes no mention of women's contribution to it, and rules out the possibility of any autonomous decision making on their part with regard to procreation, referring to it as the 'natural increase of the population', commenting that 'the capitalist may safely leave this to the workers' drives for self-preservation and propagation' (Marx 1990: 718) – a contradiction with the previously cited comment that female factory workers' neglect of their maternal duties practically amounted to infanticide. He also implied that capitalism does not depend on women's procreative capacity for its self-expansion, given its constant creation of a 'surplus population' through its technological revolutions.

Attempting to account for Marx's blindness to such ubiquitous work as reproductive work, that must have unfolded daily under his eyes in his own household, in earlier essays I have stressed its near absence in proletarian homes at the time of Marx's writing, given that the entire family was employed in the factories from sun-up to sun-down (Federici 2012: 94). Marx himself invites this conclusion when, quoting a doctor sent by the British government to assess the state of health of the industrial districts, he noted that the shutting down of the cotton mills, caused by the American Civil War, had at least one beneficiary effect. For the women now 'had sufficient leisure to give their infants the breast instead of poisoning them with Godfrey's Cordial (an opiate). They also had the time to learn to cook. Unfortunately, the acquisition of this art occurred at a time when they had nothing to cook ... This crisis was also utilized to teach sewing to the daughters of the workers in sewing schools' (Marx 1990: 517–18). An American revolution, he concluded, and a universal crisis were needed in order that working girls, who spin for the whole world, might learn to sew!

But the abysmal reduction of the time and resources necessary for the workers' reproduction which Marx documents was not a universal condition. Factory workers made up only 20 to 30 per cent of the female working population. Even among them, many women abandoned factory work once they had a child. In addition, as we have seen, the conflict between factory work and women's 'reproductive duties' was a key issue in Marx's time, as the factory reports he quoted and the reforms they produced demonstrate. Why, then, this systematic exclusion? And why could Marx not realize that the parliamentary drive to reduce women's and children's factory work harboured a new class strategy that would change the path of class struggle?

No doubt part of the answer is that, like classical political economists, Marx viewed housework not as a historically determined type of work with a specific social history, but as a natural force and female vocation, one of the products of that great 'larder' that for us (he argued) is the earth. When, for instance, he commented that overwork and fatigue produced an 'unnatural estrangement' between female factory workers and their children (Marx 1990: 521), he appealed to an image of maternity in tune with a naturalized conception of gender roles. That in the first phase of capitalist development women's reproductive work was only (in his terminology) 'formally subsumed' to capitalist production,[4] i.e., it was not yet reshaped to fit the specific needs of the labour market, possibly contributed to it. Yet, such an historically minded and powerful theoretician as Marx was should have realized that though domestic work *appeared* as an age-old activity, purely satisfying 'natural needs', its form was actually a very historically specific form of work, the product of a separation between production and reproduction, paid and unpaid labour, that had never existed in pre-capitalist societies or generally societies not governed by the law of exchange value. Having warned us against the mystification produced by the wage relation, he should have seen that, from its inception, capitalism has subordinated reproductive activities, in the form of women's unpaid labour, to the production of labour power and, therefore, the unpaid labour the capitalists extract from workers is far more conspicuous than that extracted during the waged work day, as it includes women's unpaid housework, even if reduced to a minimum.

---

4 Marx uses the concept of 'formal' (versus 'real') subsumption to describe the process whereby in the first phase of capitalist accumulation capital appropriates labour 'as it finds it', 'without any modification in the real nature of the labour process' (Marx 1990: 1021). By contrast, we have 'real subsumption' when capital shapes the labour/production process directly for its own ends.

Was Marx silent on domestic work because, as previously suggested, he 'did not see social forces capable of transforming domestic labor in a revolutionary direction'? This is a legitimate question if we 'read Marx politically'(Cleaver 2000), and take into account that his theorizing was always concerned with its organizational implications and potential (Negri 1991: 182). It opens the possibility that he was guarded on the question of housework because he feared that attention to it might play into the hand of workers' organizations and bourgeois reformers glorifying domestic labour to exclude women from factory work.[5] But by the 1850s and '60s housework and family had been for decades at the centre of a lively discussion between socialists, anarchists and a rising feminist movement, and reforms of the home and housework were also being experimented with (Scott 1988; Hayden 1985).

We must conclude then that Marx's disinterest in domestic work had deeper roots, stemming both from its naturalization and its devaluation that made it appear, in comparison with industrial labour, as an archaic form soon to be superseded by the progress of industrialization. Be this as it may, the consequence of Marx's under-theorization of domestic work is that *his account of capitalist exploitation and his conception of communism ignore the largest activity on this planet, and a major ground of divisions within the working class.*

There is a parallel here with the place of 'race' in Marx's work. Though he recognized that 'labour in a white skin cannot emancipate itself where it is branded in a black skin'(Marx 1990: 414), he did not give much space in his analysis to slave labour and the use of racism to enforce and naturalize a more intense form of exploitation. His work, therefore, could not challenge the illusion – dominant in the socialist movement – that the interest of the white male waged worker represented the interest of the entire working class – a mystification that in the twentieth century led anti-colonial fighters to conclude that Marxism was irrelevant to their struggle.

Closer to home, Marx did not anticipate that the brutal forms of exploitation that he so powerfully described would be soon a thing of the past, at least in much of Europe. For threatened by class warfare

---

5   As Wally Seccombe, among others, documents, even among trade unions the demand for higher workers' wages was often fought with the argument that their wives could return to their proper role (1993: 114–19).

and the possible extinction of the workforce, the capitalist class, with the collusion of some workers' organizations, would embark on a new strategic course, increasing investment in the reproduction of labour power and male workers' wages, sending women back home to do more housework, and in this process changing the course of the class struggle.

Though aware of the immense waste of life the capitalist system produced, and convinced that the factory reform movement did not proceed from humanitarian inclinations, Marx did not realize that what was at stake in the passing of 'protective legislation' was more than a reform of factory work. Reducing the hours of female labour was the path to a new class strategy that reassigned proletarian women to the home, to produce not physical commodities but workers.

Through this move, capital was able to dispel the threat of working-class insurgency and create a new type of worker: stronger, more disciplined, more resilient, more apt to make the goals of the system his own – indeed the type of worker that would look at the requirements of capitalist production 'as self-evident natural laws' (Marx 1990: 899). This was the kind of worker that enabled end-of the-century British and US capitalism to make a technological and social shift from light to heavy industry, from textile to steel, from exploitation based upon the extension of the working day to one based upon the intensification of exploitation. This is to say that the creation of the working-class family and the full-time proletarian housewife were an essential part and condition of the transition from absolute to relative surplus. In this process, housework itself underwent a process of 'real subsumption', for the first time becoming the object of a specific state initiative binding it more tightly to the needs of the labour market and the capitalist discipline of work.

Coinciding with the heyday of British imperial expansion (which brought immense riches to the country, boosting workers' pay checks), this innovation cannot be solely credited with the pacification of the workforce. But it was an epochal event, inaugurating the strategy that later culminated in Fordism and the New Deal, whereby the capitalist class would invest in the reproduction of the workers in order to acquire a more disciplined and productive workforce. This was the 'deal' that lasted until the 1970s, when the rise of the feminist movement and women's struggles internationally put an end to it.

Feminism, Marxism and the Question of 'Reproduction'

While Marx, as a proponent of 'women's emancipation' through participation in social production mostly understood as industrial labour, inspired generations of socialists, a different Marx was discovered in the 1970s by feminists who, in revolt against housework, domesticity and economic dependence on men turned to his work in search of a theory capable of explaining the roots of women's oppression from a class viewpoint. The result has been a theoretical revolution that changed both Marxism and feminism.

Mariarosa Dalla Costa's analysis of domestic work as the key element in the production of labour power (Dalla Costa 1975: 31), Selma James's location of the housewife on a continuum with the 'wageless of the world' (James 1975) who nevertheless have been central to the process of capital accumulation, the redefinition by other activists of the movement of the wage relation as an instrument for the naturalization of entire areas of exploitation, and the creation of new hierarchies within the proletariat: all these theoretical developments and the discussions they generated have at times been described as the 'household debate', presumably centring on the question of whether housework is or is not productive. But this is a gross distortion. What was redefined by the realization of the centrality of women's unpaid labour in the home to the production of the workforce was not domestic work alone but the nature of capitalism itself and the struggle against it.

It is not surprising that Marx's discussion of 'simple reproduction' was a theoretical illumination in this process, as the confirmation of our suspicion that the capitalist class never would have allowed so much domestic work to survive if it had not seen the possibility of exploiting it. Finding in Marx that the activities that reproduce labour power are essential to capitalist accumulation brought out the class dimension of our refusal. It showed that this much-despised, always taken for granted work, dismissed by socialists as backward, has been in reality the pillar of the capitalist organization of work. This resolved the vexed question of the relation between gender and class, and gave us the tools to conceptualize not only the function of the family, but the depth of the class antagonism at the roots of capitalist society.

From a practical viewpoint, it confirmed that, as women, we did not have to join men in the factories to be part of the working class and make an anti-capitalist struggle. We could struggle autonomously, starting from our own work in the home, as the 'nerve centre' of the production of the workforce (Fortunati 1997: 125). And our struggle had to be waged first against the men of our own families, since through the male wage, marriage and the ideology of love, capitalism has empowered men to command our unpaid labour and discipline our time and space. Ironically, then, our encounter and appropriation of Marx's theory of the reproduction of labour power, in a way consecrating Marx's importance for feminism, also provided us with the conclusive evidence that we had to turn Marx upside down and begin our analysis and struggle precisely from that part of the 'social factory' that he had excluded from his work.

Discovering the centrality of reproductive work for capital accumulation also raised the question of what a history of capitalist development would be like if seen not from the viewpoint of the formation of the waged proletariat but from the viewpoint of the kitchens and bedrooms in which labour power is daily and generationally produced. The need of a gendered perspective on the history of capitalism – beyond 'women's history' or the history of waged labour – is what led me, among others, to rethink Marx's account of primitive accumulation and discover the witch-hunts of the sixteenth and seventeenth centuries as foundational moments in the devaluation of women's labour and the rise of a specifically capitalist sexual division of work (Federici 2004: 92–102). The simultaneous realization that, contrary to Marx's anticipation, primitive accumulation has become a permanent process also put into question Marx's conception of the necessary relation between capitalism and communism. It invalidated Marx's stadial view of history, with capitalism depicted as the purgatory we need to inhabit on the way to a world of freedom and the liberating role of industrialization.

The rise of eco-feminism, which connected Marx's devaluation of women and reproduction with his view that humanity's historic mission is the domination of nature, strengthened our stand. Especially important have been the works of Maria Mies and Ariel Salleh, which have demonstrated that Marx's effacement of reproductive activities is not an accidental element, contingent to the tasks he assigned to

Capital, but a systemic one. As Salleh put it, everything in Marx establishes that what is created by man and technology has a higher value: history begins with the first act of production, human beings realize themselves through work, a measure of their self-realization is their capacity to dominate nature and adapt it to human needs, and all positive transformative activities are thought in the masculine: labour is described as the father, nature as the mother (Salleh 1997: 72–6), the earth too is seen as feminine – *Madame la Terre*, Marx calls it, against *Monsieur le Capital*. Eco-feminists have shown that there is a profound connection between the dismissal of housework, the devaluation of nature, and the idealization of what is produced by human industry and technology.

Here is not the place to reflect on the roots of this anthropocentric view. Suffice to say that the immense miscalculation Marx and generations of Marxist socialists made with regard to the liberating effects of industrialization are today all too obvious. No one today would dare to dream – as August Bebel did in *Woman Under Socialism* (1903) – of the day when food would be all chemically produced and everyone would carry with him a little box of chemicals wherewith to provide his food supply of albumen, fat and hydrates of carbon, regardless of the hour of the day or the season of the year. As industrialization is eating the earth and scientists at the service of capitalist development are tinkering with the production of life outside of the bodies of women, the idea of extending industrialization to all our reproductive activities is a nightmare worse than the one we are experiencing with the industrialization of agriculture.

Not surprisingly, in radical circles we have been witnessing a 'paradigm shift', as hope in the machine as a driving force of 'historical progress' is being displaced by a refocusing of political work on the issues, values and relations attached to the reproduction of our lives and the life of the ecosystems in which we live. We are told that Marx too in the last years of his life reconsidered his historical perspective and, on reading about the egalitarian, matrilineal communities of the American North East, began to reconsider his idealization of capitalist, industrial development and to appreciate the power of women.[6]

---

6   See on this topic Marx's *Ethnological Notebooks*, as discussed in Brown 2012, chapters 6 and 7.

Nevertheless, the Promethean view of technological development that Marx and the entire Marxist tradition have promoted, far from losing its attraction, is making a comeback, with digital technology playing for some the same emancipatory role that Marx assigned to automation, so that the world of reproduction and care work – valorized by feminists as the terrain of transformation and struggle – is at risk once again of being overshadowed by it. This is why, though Marx devoted limited space to gender theories in his work, and may have changed some of his views in later years, it remains important to discuss them and stress, as I have tried to do in this chapter, that his silences on this matter are not oversights, but the sign of a limit his theoretical and political work could not overcome, but that ours must.

References

Bock, G. and Duden, B. (1980). Labor of Love – Love as Labor: On the Genesis of Housework in Capitalism. In E. H. Altback, ed., *From Feminism to Liberation*. Revised edition. Cambridge, MA: Schenkman Publishing Company, Inc., 153–92.

Brown, H. B. (2012). *Marx On Gender and the Family: A Critical Study*. Leiden-Boston: Brill. Historical Materialism Book Series, Vol. 39.

Cleaver, H. (2000). *Reading Capital Politically*. Leeds: Anti/Theses.

Dalla Costa, M. (1975). Women and the Subversion of the Community. In M. Dalla Costa and S. James, *The Power of Women and the Subversion of the Community*. Bristol: Falling Wall Press.

Federici, S. (2004). *Caliban and the Witch: Women, the Body and Primitive Accumulation*. Brooklyn: Autonomedia.

Federici, S. (2012). *Revolution at Point Zero: Housework, Reproduction and Feminist Struggle*. Oakland: PM Press.

Fortunati, L. (1997). *The Arcane of Reproduction: Housework, Prostitution, Labor and Capital*. Brooklyn: Autonomedia.

Gimenez, M. E. (2005). Capitalism and the Oppression of Women: Marx Revisited. *Science and Society*, 69(1): 11–32.

Hayden, D. (1985). *The Grand Domestic Revolution*. Cambridge, MA: MIT Press.

Henninger, M. (2014). Poverty, Labour, Development: Toward a Critique of Marx's Conceptualizations. In M. Van der Linden and K.-H. Roth, eds., *Beyond Marx: Theorising the Global Labour Relations of the Twenty-First Century*. Leiden-Boston: Brill, 281–304.

Holmstrom, N. (2002). A Marxist Theory of Women's Nature. In N. Holmstrom, ed., *The Socialist Feminist Project: A Contemporary Reader in Theory and Politics*. New York: Monthly Review, 360–76.

James, S. (1975). *Sex, Race and Class*. Bristol: Falling Wall Press.

Marshall, A. (1938). *Principles of Economics: An Introductory Volume*. London: Macmillan.

Marx, K. (1968). *The 18th Brumaire of Louis Bonaparte*. New York: International Publishers.

Marx, K. (1969). *Theories of Surplus Value, Part 1*. Moscow: Progress Publishers.

Marx, K. (1990). *Capital, Volume 1*. London: Penguin.

Marx, K. and Engels, F. (1967). *The Communist Manifesto*. London: Penguin Classics.

Marx, K. and Engels, F. (1988). *The German Ideology*. New York: International Publishers.

Mojabed, S. (2015). *Marxism and Feminism*. London: Zed Books.

Negri, A. (1991). *Marx Beyond Marx: Lesson on the Grundrisse*. Brooklyn: Autonomedia.

Salleh, A. (1997). *Ecofeminism as Politics: Nature, Marx and the Postmodern*. London: Zed Books.

Scott, J. W. (1988). *Gender and the Politics of History*. New York: Columbia University Press.

Seccombe, W. (1993). *Weathering the Storm: Working-Class Families from the Industrial Revolution to the Fertility Decline*. London: Verso.

conditions, Marx deliberately invoked notions of predictive law, determination and science. Exactly what he meant by those terms and how they can be reconciled with the anti-determinism of his work therefore becomes a genuine hermeneutical problem. This chapter accepts that challenge by closely examining how Marx actually deploys the notion of law in *Capital*, distinguishing the various meanings he gives to it, tracing their interrelations and how they implement the book's larger arguments. We uphold an anti-determinist reading of *Capital* not by skating over its language, but by working through Marx's analyses to the point where their praxis-based historical contingency emerges.

Superficially, the determinism problem in Marx can appear as one of inexact translation. 'Science' in nineteenth-century German had a broader meaning of systematic inquiry than the mechanistic, natural science prototype the word evokes in modern English. Similarly, 'determination' in Marx often has a Hegelian meaning of specification, the concretization of an abstract category through its conceptual-historical implementation (Marx 1973b: 83–111). Thus it is much closer to the dialectical notion of mediation than it is to any billiard-ball model of causality. The rich polysemy of 'laws' in *Capital*, however, defies any simple characterization. In addition to their shared characteristic of making the most sense 'as an approximation, a tendency, an average' (Engels 2010; cf. Thompson 1978: 75–6), we distinguish no fewer than six meanings: causal, ironic, logical, historical, phenomenological and dialectical. Exploring their distinctiveness, respective argumentative purposes, and interrelations forms the heart of this chapter.

An inquiry into the nature of socio-economic laws in *Capital* is timely at an early twenty-first-century moment when the separate constitution of the human from the natural sciences has fallen into disrepute. Between Marx and the current horizons of, e.g., ecosocialism, actor network theory, new materialism, political ontology and critical animal studies lay a period of relative stability in which the natural sciences, allegedly based on causal explanation, were thought to be separated from the human sciences, allegedly based on interpretive understanding. Dilthey (1989) influentially articulated this distinction in the year of Marx's death, and except for ongoing positivist attempts to make the human sciences conform methodologically to the natural sciences, it largely held throughout the twentieth century. Underlying this distinction was an implicit ontological divide of being-in-itself, defined by classic realist assumptions and susceptibility to external causal determination, from being-for-itself, defined by reflexivity and therefore capable of praxis and self-determination. Although Marx wrote before this split became institutionalized in the disciplines, he deeply understood the issues it turned on, and even nodded in *Capital* (1976: 493) to Vico's (1984) pioneering formulation of them. Marx's own position was that human and natural science are destined to merge, but only under communism – since capitalism's internal antagonisms and instrumentalization of nature preclude any practical reconciliation (1975a: 355; see also Foster et al. 2010).

On one hand, Marx rejected quite early the mechanistic tendencies of natural science. His doctoral thesis of 1841 compares Democritus' atomic physics to that of Epicurus, who in contrast allows that atoms are not entirely subject to deterministic laws, but may swerve of their own accord when possessed of their concept. Marx's argument is remarkable for its will to impose the capacity for praxis on matter at the atomic level via an unreconstructed Hegelian idealism (Hegel 1977; McCarthy 1990: 21, 31). Yet even as he shifted towards materialism, Marx continued an essentially humanist polemic against its mechanistic or passive variants for their deterministic foreclosure of self-activity (Marx and Engels 2010: 124–34; Marx 1975b), a critique that continues into *Capital* (1976: 494).

On the other hand, Marx saw the human sciences of his day, still firmly subordinated to philosophy, as speculative, prone to idealism, and marginalized practically (Marx and Engels 2010, 1970). Praxis as a humanist ideal permeated the Young Hegelian milieu from which Marx emerged (Lobkowicz 1967: ch. 13) but, following Feuerbach, he felt the need to ground it in naturalistic criticism (1975a: 281). The result was a discovery of capitalism as an alienating disruption of human praxis and relations with nature. If the conditions for praxis do not yet fully exist, and required communism for their realization, then Marx could not endorse any attempt to confer an autonomous status on the human sciences that put them comfortably beyond questions of necessity. Alienation creates a space where laws, be they natural, social or hybrid in character, emerge as real limits to human self-determination that praxis must overcome. Freedom, in other words, must be won from necessity concretely and historically, not by ontological decrees but by establishing enabling material conditions

(Marx and Engels 1970: 38). Labour is key in this process; it not only mediates nature and society but concretely embodies human limitation and possibility.

Law's sense of compulsion and external imposition readily applies to relations of exploitation, servitude, over-work, poverty, isolation, dependency and powerlessness in class societies. That such relations may operate quasi-deterministically does not mean that they themselves are inevitable. Praxis can alter the real conditions from which they spring, but it must always work through them, and can never simply evade them. The process of making any particular laws real is therefore always a process of struggle: we have to know them to understand the structuring of social life, the structures and limits applied to struggle, and how struggle is itself about changing the parameters of these laws. This combination of specific historical constraint and general open-endedness is, we argue, key to the resolution of the apparent economism paradox in Marx and the related question of laws in *Capital*.

Laws in *Capital*

The first meaning of law in *Capital* can be characterized as *simple causality*: a process that, given a set of existing conditions, must proceed in a particular way. In the Preface, Marx begins by comparing his analysis of capitalism to the task of a physicist who must secure the proper conditions of observation. In privileging England as capitalism's 'classic ground', he continues: 'Intrinsically, it is not a question of the higher or lower degree of development of the social antagonisms that result from the natural laws of capitalist production. It is a question of these laws themselves, of these tendencies winning their way through and working themselves out with iron necessity' (1976: 90–1). This, and the related claim 'to lay bare the economic law of motion of modern society' (92) in *Capital*'s Introduction (92), have encouraged a physical rather than historical reading of Marx's materialism. Indeed, Marx often invokes law as objective necessity that is indifferent to subjective understandings and intentions. Thus, he argues that workers' or horses' need for rest (341, 375–6, 419, 498, 638) or the soil's need for replenishment (637–8) stem from natural laws that are independent of capitalism's wishes, and may ultimately manifest themselves within and against it.

Marx also argues that human purpose in productive activity takes on the quality of a law, a compulsion that arises internally as consciousness within labourers but seizes and subordinates them as an external force while they, in turn, impose it on the natural world (1976: 284). *The German Ideology* identifies the source of this compelling ideality when it holds that 'it is not consciousness that determines life, but life that determines consciousness' (Marx and Engels 1970: 37), a claim later rephrased as 'it is not the consciousness of men that determines their existence, but their social existence that determines their consciousness' (Marx 1970: 21). These expressions of base and superstructure have long enabled vulgar materialist readings of Marx. But they need mean only that human thought presupposes, is shaped by, and so is always indirectly and inadvertently 'about' the social conditions out of which it arises: a form of determination to be sure but hardly a determinism. Nonetheless, Marx's polemic with idealism required the assertion that mind is 'burdened' with matter (Marx and Engels 1970: 43–4), that humanity does not transcend but must realize itself within nature (Marx 1975a: 327–8), and so ultimately is subject to laws in a naturalistic sense. Thus, there is a notion of law as naturalistic causal compulsion, and it extends into the human domain.

More frequently, Marx invokes causal, natural law as an analogy for capitalism's compulsions. He observes that capital imposes its necessities upon both workers and capitalists as a social compulsion so thoroughly comparable to that of law that he designates it as such: 'with the authority of a law of nature' (1976: 479) and 'with the rigidity of a law' (284) are typical formulations. Examples include fluctuating exchange rates between commodities, the determination of value by socially necessary labour time, competitive pressures among capitalist producers, the rising minimum amount of capital needed to enter or remain in production, the imperative to extract profits, of capitals to centralize, of workers to sell their labour power, to sell it below its value and retrain when capital's demand for them shifts, and for the social distribution of wealth to become progressively more skewed (101, 168, 180, 381, 433, 436, 465, 476, 480, 618, 739, 769, 777, 793, 798, 800, 899). Yet, as we will discuss below, no sooner does Marx assert the causal sense of law within the social than it begins to assume historical and phenomenological inflections. This movement is fundamental to Marx's sense of law and contrasts sharply with both a mechanistic materialism and the pretence to natural law of classical political economy. So the paradox embodied by these causal uses of 'law' is that their social and historical qualities are masked in a naturalistic guise. It is, however, a mask that reflects how they actually appear to those being compelled by them.

A second meaning of law that we distinguish in *Capital* is *ironic:* critical, often satirical, and above all meant to counter the reduction of social relations to natural law suggested in the first meaning. Throughout Volume 1, Marx mocks classical political economists for finding 'eternal laws of Nature' in capitalism and its epiphenomena – such as the apparent determination of prices by supply and demand (1976: 301, 666, 705, 759, 771, 925, 929; 1894: 282–297) – when such laws are in fact socially contingent and of recent origin. At first glance, this critique might seem to contradict Marx's naturalist materialism announced in the first understanding of law above, but in fact it largely presupposes it, implying only that there are situations to which naturalistic understandings of law do not apply. Here we run up against the limits of law, and the further implication that reality may be shaped by forces of a different order, even if they sometimes masquerade as laws. Marx was acutely aware that the whole field is an ideological battle ground:

> In France and England the bourgeoisie had conquered political power. From that time on, the class struggle took on more and more explicit and threatening forms, both in practice and in theory. It sounded the death knell of scientific bourgeois economics. It was thenceforth no longer a question whether this or that theorem was true, but whether it was useful to capital or harmful, expedient or inexpedient, in accordance with police regulations or contrary to them. (1976: 97)

Here, Marx asks us to entertain a different kind of efficacy, one that is not based on causality, does not operate independently of human consciousness in a classic realist manner, but is effective instead because of its rhetorical ability to convince or orient independently of whether or not it is objectively correct. The very idea of such efficacy implies the subjectivist notion that agents' orientations matter because they shape reality at some level instead of merely registering or responding to it.

This is praxis: conscious and strategic interventions that alter the objective conditions that shape actors and their actions. It is not a moment that entirely escapes law and its orderings but is instead thoroughly intertwined with them. Yet it does amount to a reciprocal subjective action back on its formative objective conditions, one that may be more or less inadvertent or strategic, reproductive or transformative, but is always saturated with unintended consequences and necessarily produces indeterminacy. Thus without ceasing to act compulsively, law opens out into something else: struggle over objective conditions instead of a simple causal determination of subjectivities by them. Behind this ironic usage of law therefore lies a serious theoretical point. Taken together, then, the causal and the ironic meanings of law in *Capital* amount to the reciprocal determinations of base and superstructure. Their interaction may be asymmetric and still dominated by the weight of objective conditions, but those conditions themselves are also in play.

A third meaning of law in *Capital* is that of *logical necessity*. Marx consistently resorts to definitions and algebraic formulas to present the workings of capital as analytically as possible. On this basis, he advances arguments of a purely logical sort, calling them laws because they are true by definition. Examples include that money in circulation equals the total price of commodities in circulation divided by the average velocity at which money circulates (1976: 216), that the mass of surplus value produced equals the mass of variable capital advanced multiplied by the rate of surplus value (418), and that the efficiency of labour power is in inverse proportion to its duration (535). Such laws are tautologies, and if they are to be rescued from triviality, they must serve as the logical apparatus of a larger substantive argument that insightfully identifies the inner workings of empirical phenomena. Consider, for example, a further set of laws true by definition: that (a) a working day of the same length always produces the same amount of value regardless of its productivity; (b) the value of labour power and surplus value are inversely related; and (c), the value of labour power drives fluctuations in its inverse relation with surplus value, not the other way around (656–60). These laws identify important dynamics in the capitalist system only because they embody one of its foundational premises: what Dunayevskaya (1975: 138) and Elson (1979) have called the 'value theory of labour', the reduction of labour to a source of valorization by making the worker provide surplus labour as the basic condition of employment (Marx 1976: 650–1).

Capital is overwhelmingly an account of the capitalist system's immanent logic, so this logical sense of law pervades the entire study. Commodities must express their value through a universal equivalent (Marx 1976: 180, 294), value must underwrite rates of commodity exchange (301, 342–3), value must derive from production as socially necessary labour time (168), whose reduction ceaselessly spurs capitalist competition and innovation (381, 436), which leads the organic composition of capital to rise (570, 773) and capital to centralize (777): all are laws that contribute to our understanding of the workings of capitalism. To count as immanent, the logic in question cannot be entirely abstract but rather must embody capitalist premises and capitalism's historical preconditions – a dispossessed working class, a capitalist class compelled to maintain competitive profitability, and a social division of labour mediated by commodity exchange – none of which can be established by formal logic alone. Thus, logical and historical necessity turn out to be intimately related in *Capital*. The materialist critique that founded the Marx-Engels partnership from *The Holy Family* onward clearly and consistently indicates, however, that substantive historical conditions are the point of departure for social logics and not the reverse. Marx may have kept a mathematical notebook, but he was no Platonist and never tried to equate mathematics and ontology as Badiou (2005) has recently done.

Marx's order of exposition is potentially a source of confusion here. By starting with commodities, the laws of value by which they exchange, and the social division of labour they presuppose, Volume I establishes capitalism's preconditions in terms that are simultaneously logical, historical and experiential for a subject enmeshed in market relations. Only after Marx has thoroughly unpacked these preconditions and posed the mystery of how profits are possible under conditions of equal exchange does he introduce wage labour into the discussion, a specifically capitalist determination that shifts the focus from exchange to production. A lengthy exploration of surplus value ensues in terms that are historically inflected but primarily logical until the exposition is complete. Then Marx dives into the historical creation of a dispossessed working class obliged to sell its labour power as a commodity, the fundamental precondition of the entire preceding discussion of surplus value's logic that comprises the bulk of Volume 1. This concluding dramatic flourish, with the laws of capital having to *be made*, 'dripping ... with blood and dirt' (1976: 926), subordinates the logical analysis to the historical, by revealing its contingent basis. By so thoroughly giving itself over to a systematic logical exploration of capitalism's premises, *Capital* distils and finally reveals their fundamental historicity.

We thus arrive at a fourth and decisively central meaning of law in *Capital*, that of *historically conditional necessity*. Even a critical review of an early edition noted (Marx 1976: 100–2) that laws do not appear as abstract or universal necessities in *Capital*, but rather as relative to specific historical conditions themselves subject to change and succession. For instance, capitalism absolutely requires workers to sell their labour power, capitalists to produce surplus value, and all classes to buy and sell commodities that mediate the social division of labour. Yet these necessities are predicated on capitalism's foundational conditions noted above. When they are absent, as in the mid-nineteenth-century colonial situations Marx mentions at the end of Volume 1 (931, 936, 939), no such compulsions apply – much to the chagrin of earnest administrators like Wakefield, who assumed the universal applicability of laws developed under English conditions. Only when those foundational conditions are present, and 'real subsumption' exists (1034–8, 1064–5), does capital's immanent logic take form.

We see this clearly in Chapter 25 of Volume 1, in which Marx builds up the general law of capitalist accumulation through a series of lower-level laws. First, accumulation requires a growing use of labour power if the organic composition of capital remains constant, since only thus can more surplus value be produced. Second, as capitalist accumulation advances, the organic composition of capital rises such that the proportion of constant to variable capital increases. The productivity of labour rises and so overcompensates for the relative diminution of variable capital as a proportion of total capital outlay. This efficiency spurs capitalist competition and, through it, the centralization of capital. Third, as capital employs progressively less labour in the course of its accumulation, a surplus population or industrial reserve army takes form. Thus, Marx posits laws of population specific to capitalism and its working class (1976: 783–97). One part of the working class lies idle while the other part is subjected to over-work and pressures to sell its labour power below its value. Fourth, the working class is constantly reshaped and divided according to the needs of capital as it cyclically enters and is expelled from production, passing through destitution, criminality and other abject states. Thus, the stunted human development of the worker and 'multiplication of the proletariat' must accompany the accumulation of capital, and this – also a somewhat ironic twist on the laws of accumulation and population posited by classical political economy – is '*the absolute general law of capitalist accumulation*' (764, 798). It explains relationships and chains of events that are necessary, yet dependent on a mode of production's historical conditions for the regularity of their effects and their ability to compel.

All other meanings of law in Marx's oeuvre revolve around this one of historically conditional necessity. It retains the senses of physical and natural compulsion and those of logical entailment, but radically limits their applicability from a universal to a specific horizon and launches an anti-deterministic counter-tendency that finds contingency and subjectivity beneath law. The first indication of this larger anti-determinism is Marx's consistent argument that class struggle establishes the historical conditions within which epochally limited forms of necessity arise. This is one central meaning of the *Manifesto*'s slogan that 'the history of all hitherto existing societies is the history of class struggle' (Marx and Engels 1973: 67). At several points in *Capital*, Marx interrupts his exposition of capitalism's immanent logic or 'laws of motion' with lengthy interludes that reveal how class struggle established capitalism's basic preconditions and developmental tendencies. This is particularly true of Chapters 10 and 15 of Volume 1, which narrate how struggles over the working day and the deployment of machinery in the labour process underwrite the shift from absolute to relative surplus-value extraction presented in adjacent chapters. Far from spiriting itself into being of its own accord, relative surplus-value extraction is the outcome of struggles for control over the labour process. Chapters 27 and 28 go further, describing the expropriation of the peasantry in England and its legislated conversion into a dispossessed working class obliged to sell its labour power to capitalists. These developments were anything but automatic. They presupposed capitalism as an emergent but not yet dominant social logic, agents capable of extending it aggressively into rural domains where it previously did not apply, and the resistance of the dispossessed. Taken together, these chapters show that capitalism and its impersonal 'laws of motion' depend on human agency and humanly induced processes and events. These interludes in *Capital*, and Marx's vast but neglected political writings that share much with them in tone, are therefore not just sentimental, Dickensian window-dressing on an otherwise scientific analysis but are, on the contrary, central to it.

A fifth or *phenomenological* meaning of law in *Capital* denotes the many instances in which Marx explains fetishistic appearances, illusions or subjective experiences as a consequence of underlying material-historical conditions. Marx was systematically concerned with how capitalism's fundamental dynamics do and do not manifest themselves to the various classes and class fractions it produces. That they fail to do so transparently was the premise of *Capital*'s vast labour:

> While it is not our intention here to consider the ways the immanent laws of capitalist production ... enter into the consciousness of the individual capitalist as the motives which drive him forward, this much is clear: a scientific analysis of competition is possible only if we can grasp the inner nature of capital, just as the apparent motions of the heavenly bodies are intelligible only to someone who is acquainted with their real motions, which are not perceptible to the senses. (Marx 1976: 433, see also 421, 436)

Capital in all of its three volumes systematically addresses the incongruities between appearances and underlying relations. Capitalist practices generate different subject positions and points of view experientially, all of which are still the outgrowth of, and to that extent, still 'about' those practices. This is the phenomenological notion of intentionality, that is, a pre-reflective orientation or disposition towards an underlying state of affairs. Thus an important reason that Volume 1 begins with commodity exchange and commodity fetishism is that they are the form in which capitalism immediately presents itself to most people. Only by drilling down into the social division of labour, the value form, the labour theory of value and the relationship between wage labour and capital can Marx establish its underlying relations. One of the most central arguments of Volume 1 is Marx's exposition of the contradiction suggested by the law of commodity exchange: how are profits possible, if commodities exchange at their value? Marx revels at some length (1976: ch. 5) in this paradox, the solution to which is that labour power, as institutionalized under capitalism, is the one commodity capable of producing more value than it itself possesses, such that a capitalist can purchase it at its value and still realize from it an additional increment, surplus value (301–2, 650–1). But to notice this, one has to distinguish the valorization process that occurs exclusively in production from the circulation process which occurs outside of it (268), something that practising capitalists have little reason to do.

Similarly, Volume 2's tracing of capital's circuits from various points of departure within them is more than an obsessive accounting exercise. It shows how these circuits, and related questions such as the distinction of 'productive' from 'unproductive' labour, can appear differently from the standpoint of labour or capital, or even different fractions among them. The infamous 'transformation problem' of how relations of value underwrite prices – but are seldom directly manifest in them due to accidents of supply and demand (itself another fetishistic appearance of law), and other superficial 'noise' in the system – is another example of this kind of treatment. Announced in Volume 1 (1976: 196, cf. 261) and given extended treatment in Volume 3, Marx proceeds through an inquiry into how underlying social relations of value both reveal and conceal themselves in their outward appearances.

Phenomenological determination (cf. Hegel 1977), with its depth-surface dynamic, imparts a distinctive emphasis on mediation to the causal, logical and historical senses of law with which it interacts heavily. For example, capitalism's historical preconditions become the pre-reflective and largely taken-for-granted premises of its immanent logic, which tend to be more manifest and accessible to consciousness as matters of more immediate concern. An interesting consequence is that in contrast to positivist understandings of law as explanatory bedrock, here law operates as a refracting mediation between underlying historical conditions and appearances. *Capital*'s laws do not address those underlying relationships themselves, which are largely assumed to be the indeterminate outcome of class struggle, but rather how those conditions translate into appearances. By introducing refraction in the depth-surface relationship, phenomenological laws both refine and depart from the model of simple causality with which Marx began. Here, the elements organized by underlying relations begin to assert something of their own character even as they are acted upon, thus giving rise to a more complex and interactive form of determination that involves masking, displacement, etc. Such laws are at best limited and conditional explanations operating mid-way up a depth-to-surface hierarchy, and at worst they are ideological illusions (such as circulationist understandings of profit) that themselves require a phenomenological account. Either way, they are not the foundation of an explanatory hierarchy. As with the ironic use of law, the assumption here is that appearances matter because they affect how people act on underlying conditions, whether by disclosing, displacing or outrightly obscuring them.

The sixth and final meaning of law we identify in *Capital*, that of a *dialectical tendency* met by a counter-tendency, is already incipient in several of the examples above, but is perhaps best illustrated in the 'Law of the Tendential Fall in the Rate of Profit' around which much of Volume 3 revolves. Of all the laws discussed in *Capital*, this is probably the one most frequently (mis)read deterministically. The law itself is a fairly simple tautology: as the rate of surplus-value is s/v, while the rate of profit is s/(c+v), it follows that the rate of profit must fall as the volume of c (constant capital) rises, a development equated with increases in the productivity of labour (Marx 1981: 317–48). A deterministic reading of this law thus identifies it as grounds for an eschatology of capitalism, because it seems to indicate that capitalism is doomed by its own development. Yet there are several things to note from the outset: first, the tautological form of the law is merely an implication of the definition of the rate of profit, that tells us little by itself. (It requires all other variables, including the rate of exploitation, to remain the same.) Most crucially, Marx identifies it as a tendency that sets in motion counter-tendencies inherent to the same process. Which ones succeed is not a theoretical question, but an empirical one tied to cycles of accumulation and class struggle. At first glance, this may look like just another instance of phenomenological masking, but the difference is that we are now dealing with a struggle between two opposed dynamics or principles operating on approximately the same horizontal level, not a more vertical tension between superficial appearance and underlying ground. The most deterministic reading possible of this law is that, by establishing limits, it gives us insight into what tendencies are likely in the absence of class struggle from below, and also that class pressures are likely – from above – to prevent a falling rate of profit. This gives the law no less explanatory power, but it means that it explains something rather different than the 'imminent collapse' forecasts so frequently associated with it.

The meaning of law as dialectical tendency has a special relation to the logical meaning of the term explored above. Most obviously, it appears as contradiction within capitalism's immanent logic, revealing it to be composed of conflicting forces or principles, each of which has its own implications, demands and reasons for being which cannot be reduced to the other. For example, in the contradiction between use value and exchange value, Marx attributes to the former a far greater autonomy from capitalist logic than the latter (1976: 126, 198–9, 209, 235–6). To the extent that workers produce only to acquire use values, they maintain a distinctive social orientation, something that overly rigid 'structural' analyses of capitalism overlook at their peril. Similarly, Marx's close attention to production as the site of valorization also reveals a massive development of cooperation, interdependence and centralized planning, all of which form a real basis for challenging capitalist private property and building communism (1976: ch. 32). As Marx puts it, 'this expropriation is accomplished through the action of the immanent laws of capitalist production itself, through the centralization of capitals' (929). Once again, capitalism proves to be a less than homogeneous order. It produces developments that may escape its logic and form a point of departure for a new and potentially opposed social order. Contradiction, then, marks a limit of determinacy where system breaks into possibility, and logic further melds into historicity.

This tension between the centralization and the socialization of capitalist production suggests that class struggle over basic productive conditions is the privileged example of law's dialectical meaning in Marx. At this least deterministic of all moments, when new possibilities are clearly in play, the notion of law does not disappear but takes on a new, enabling sense. Thus the *Manifesto* speaks of laws as strategic possibility in class struggle:

Since the development of class antagonism keeps even pace with the development of industry, the economic situation, as they find it, does not yet offer to them the material conditions for the emancipation of the proletariat. They therefore search after a new social science, after new social laws, that are to create these conditions. (Marx and Engels 1973: 95; cf. Marx 1976: 618; 1974: 254)

Likewise in Volume 1 of *Capital*, Marx argues that capitalism's endless demand that workers retrain can serve as a providential springboard into communism, where full human development guides variation in labour:

But if, at present, variation of labour imposes itself after the manner of an overpowering natural law, and with the blindly destructive action of a natural law that meets with obstacles everywhere, large scale industry, through its very catastrophes, makes the recognition of variation of labour ... into a question of life and death. This possibility of varying labour must become a general law of social production, and the existing relations must be adapted to permit its realization in practice. (1976: 618)

Lastly, 'The Civil War in France' observes of the working class in the Paris Commune that:

They know that this work of regeneration will be again and again relented and impeded by the resistance of vested interests and class egoisms. They know that the present 'spontaneous action of the natural laws of capital and private property' – can only be superseded by the 'spontaneous action of the laws of the social economy of free and associated labour' by a long process of development of new conditions. (Marx 1974: 253–4)

Remarkably, in all these cases law no longer denotes a fixity of present conditions but instead accompanies and consolidates their revolutionary transformation. Only thus can a latent or emergent order realize itself against a dominant one. The result is both an open challenge to and a limited retention of the lingering determinism that the historical and phenomenological understandings of law transmitted from its simple causal meaning. The objective basis of indeterminacy here becomes the active struggle between different tendencies, dynamics and class forces over the shaping of reality. Such struggles necessarily presuppose and develop subjectivity as the differential embodiment and emergent consciousness of contending forces and orientations. Yet subjectivity is not a leap into unfettered freedom and requires a struggle over the objective conditions of its own determination, and hence law must remain a central concern.

If in the above examples class struggle determines the conditions from which new social laws spring, Marx elsewhere proposes a more teleological alternative in which the development of the productive forces drives history forward through periods of revolution and consolidation (Marx and Engels 1970: 38, 44, 48–9, 74–7; Marx 1970: 20–1). The differences in tone between these formulations and those that emphasize class struggle can be stark and shocking, but their real differences are ultimately less than meets the eye. Both give primacy to the determining conditions under which people live, the first as the object of class struggle and the second as a cumulative, trans-historical baseline that new struggles will contest. Each emphasizes one of the reciprocal determinations in the base-superstructure relation but, in so doing, immediately presupposes the other. Basic conditions of association given by the productive forces therefore regularly influence the process of 'becoming a class' in political struggle (Marx and Engels 1970: 76–7; Marx 1973a: 238–9; 1976: ch. 32). Similarly, some of the ostensibly most determinist passages in Marx have voluntaristic conclusions (e.g. Marx 1970: 20–1). It is long past time to move beyond the debilitating antagonism between political economy and the philosophy of praxis within Marxist tradition. We need to rediscover how to read dialectically across both registers.

Conclusion

Our discussion has proceeded from an anti-determinist, philosophy of praxis perspective, which insists that human and natural history are in principle open-ended. It has nonetheless worked through law, determination and the base-superstructure metaphor instead of dismissing them, and striven for a productive relation with this other major strand of the Marxist tradition. The key, as Marx himself argued, is to deploy the materialist impulse historically rather than ontologically, a level at which it would inevitably revert to idealism (1976: 494). Praxis shares with historicized understandings of law a necessary immersion in a horizon defined by specific social conditions. Without these conditions, praxis has nothing to intervene in, and so loses its defining specificity, its artful and strategic character. Whereas law emphasizes the agent's determination by concrete conditions, praxis highlights how action addresses and potentially modifies them. The conditions must themselves be established, as the outcome of ongoing struggle. Each moment presupposes and interpenetrates the other, however, such that they are separable only as distinctions within a unity. Insisting on the dialectical character of base and superstructure means conceding a degree of law-like determination to establish the very ground on which praxis works, even as that ground may change. To speak of laws of capital is thus to speak of processes of contestation and the making of the social world. *Capital*'s discussion of economic laws makes this point admirably.

Marx's use of law in *Capital* transposes a natural scientific notion into the human realm without reducing the latter's defining characteristics. By inflecting this initially mechanistic notion with ironic, logical, historical, phenomenological and dialectical properties, Marx humanizes law but simultaneously uses it to reveal the burden of received and unmastered conditions on social existence. Without naturalizing those conditions, it nonetheless highlights their ability to compel human action involuntarily. Such a determinism-with-immanent-limits is surely worth emphasizing in our individualist age of consumer choice, abstracted democratic illusion and displaced class conflict. At the same time, it is the dialectical Marx who reminds us of the freedom that arises within necessity and shapes how determination plays out in a process whose outcome is not preordained, but which never ceases to struggle against constraint and the horizons of possibility.

References

Badiou, A. (2005). *Being and Event*. New York: Continuum.

Dilthey, W. (1989 [1883]). *Selected Works Volume I: Introduction to the Human Sciences*. Princeton: Princeton University Press.

Dunayevskaya, R. (1975 [1958]). *Marxism and Freedom: From 1776 until Today*. London: Pluto.

Elson, D. (1979). The Value Theory of Labour. In D. Elson, ed., *Value: The Representation of Labour in Capitalism*. London: CSE Books, 115–80.

Engels, F. (2010 [1895]). Letter to Conrad Schmidt. In K. Marx and F. Engels, eds., *Marx and Engels Collected Works*, Vol. 50. London: Lawrence and Wishart.

Foster, J. B., Clark. B. and York, R. (2010). *The Ecological Rift: Capitalism's War on the Earth*. New York: Monthly Review Press.

Hegel, G. W. F. (1977 [1807]). *Phenomenology of Spirit*. Oxford: Oxford University Press.

Lobkowicz, N. (1967). *Theory and Practice: History of a Concept from Aristotle to Marx*. Notre Dame: University of Notre Dame Press.

McCarthy, G. (1990). *Marx and the Ancients*. Savage: Rowman and Littlefield.

Margolis, J. (1989). The Novelty of Marx's Theory of *Praxis. Journal for the Theory of Social Behaviour*, 19(4): 367–88.

Margolis, J. (1992). Praxis and Meaning: Marx's Species Being and Aristotle's Political Animal. In G. McCarthy, ed., *Marx and Aristotle: Nineteenth-Century German Social Theory and Classical Antiquity*. Latham: Rowman and Littlefield, 329–55.

Marx, K. (1970 [1859]). *A Contribution to the Critique of Political Economy*. New York: International Publishers.

Marx, K. (1973a [1852]). The Eighteenth Brumaire of Louis Bonaparte. In K. Marx. *Surveys from Exile*. London: Penguin, 143–249.

Marx, K. (1973b [1857–8]). *Grundrisse*. New York: Penguin.

Marx, K. (1974 [1871]). The Civil War in France. In K. Marx, *The First International and After*. London: Penguin, 187–268.

Marx, K. (1975a [1844]). *The Economic and Philosophical Manuscripts of 1844*. In K. Marx, *Early Writings*. London: Penguin, 279–400.

Marx, K. (1975b [1845]). Concerning Feuerbach. In K. Marx, *Early Writings*. London: Penguin, 421–3.

Marx, K. (1976 [1867]). *Capital, Volume 1*. London: Penguin.

Marx, K. (1978 [1885]). *Capital, Volume 2*. London: Penguin.

Marx, K. (1981 [1894]). *Capital, Volume 3*. London: Penguin.

Marx, K. (2010 [1861–3]). Theories of Surplus Value. In *Marx and Engels Collected Works*, Vols 30–33. London: Lawrence and Wishart.

Marx, K. (2012 [1841]). *Doctoral Dissertation*. Manchester: Michael George.

Marx, K. and Engels, F. (1970 [1845–6]). The German Ideology, Vol. 1. In *Marx-Engels Collected Works*, Vol. 5. Moscow: Progress Publishers, 19–452.

Marx, K. and Engels, F. (1973 [1848]). Manifesto of the Communist Party. In K. Marx, *The Revolutions of 1848*, London: Penguin, 62–98.

Marx, K. and Engels, F. (2010 [1844]). The Holy Family. In *Marx and Engels Collected Works*, Vol. 4. London: Lawrence and Wishart, 5–211.

Mill, J. S. (1848). *Principles of Political Economy*. London: John W. Parker.

Thompson, E. P. (1978). *The Poverty of Theory: or an Orrery of Errors*. London: Merlin 1995.

Vico, G. (1984 [1744]). *The New Science of Giambattista Vico*. Ithaca: Cornell University Press.

7

Capital and the Labour Process

Paul Thompson and Chris Smith

Readings of *Capital* are never innocent let alone uncontentious. Currently making conceptual and political waves are theories of cognitive capitalism, based on claims that 'material production' is no longer a source of value, that labour time is not a significant object of interest for employers, and that the real subordination of labour is reversed (Vercellone 2007; Moulier-Boutang 2012; Hardt and Negri 2000, 2009). Located in the post-*operaismo* tradition, such commentators prefer to focus on Marx's 'Fragment on Machines' from the *Grundrisse* as a blueprint for an end to scarcity and an imminent transition to postcapitalism or communism depending on the degree of optimism (Pitts 2016). These arguments have received a considerable boost with their popularization by Paul Mason. He argues that while *Capital* was an historic achievement full of brilliant insights, it is in essence history. 'Info goods' are corroding value and labour is no longer the ultimate source of profit. Info capitalism is strangled by its own contradictions; hence postcapitalism will be born on a tide of networked, collaborative zero-cost production. One perceived consequence is that antagonism is displaced from the labour process and employment relationship and 'the class struggle in cognitive capitalism increasingly takes the form of a distribution struggle' (Jeon 2010: 19). In slightly different terms, politics shifts from the factory to the social factory, radical demands focusing on a universal basic income and full automation replacing the 'drudgery' of wage labour (Mason 2016; Srnicek and Williams 2015).

In this chapter we make a partial defence of the relevance of Marx's writings on the labour process in *Capital* and the privileging of that terrain for an understanding of contemporary economies, though not necessarily for other social relations. Nothing written a century and a half ago can be entirely timely, for example with respect to the growth of complex managerial and employment systems. However, the tools of analysis of capital-labour relations in the production process and contested terrain around control, science, technology and effort remain a vital source for critical researchers if they are prepared to simultaneously apply and innovate. In the rest of the chapter we explain how this task was undertaken by Braverman, subsequent labour process theory and the research community with which we are associated. We argue that these efforts broadened conceptions of managerial regimes and restored a focus on labour agency, while at the same time they utilized – with benefits and limitations – a 'narrow' reading of *Capital* focused on the transformation of the labour process within different accumulation regimes. The second half of chapter is taken up by an exposition and critique of current claims that production and the labour process are no longer a significant site for the creation of value and for labour-capital contradictions. *Capital* remains a better guide to analysis and action in the present conjuncture than 'The Fragment on Machines'.

Marx's *Capital*: Concepts, Legacy, Tendencies and Relevance

In *Capital* Marx developed a theory of capitalism as a totality, with different spheres – production, circulation and reproduction – that formed an integrated but contradictory system of political economy. Marx's theory of capitalism moved the focus from market relations to production relations as core to the political economy. While waged labourers and capitalists meet in the marketplace as sellers and buyers, it is not through these roles as market transactors that value is produced and reproduced. Rather, value creation occurs in the 'hidden abode' beyond the marketplace, in production, where both actors are transformed into new agents of *worker* and *capitalist*. In *Capital* Marx laid out the architecture of the capitalist labour process. 'The simple elements of the labour process are (1) purposeful activity, that is work itself, (2) the object on which that work is performed, and (3) the instruments of that work' (Marx 1976: 284). These elements exist in all political economies, but it is only in capitalism that production is animated for the purpose of producing exchange value, from which the capitalist derives profit. The components of the labour process are: labour; raw materials or an object of production; and the tools, techniques and technology through which objects are transformed into use values, which under capitalism must serve the purpose of generating surplus value and profit for the capitalist. 'The production process, considered as the unity of the labour process and the process of creating value, is the process of production of commodities; considered as the unity of the labour process and the process of valorization, it is the capitalist process of production, or the capitalist form of the production of commodities' (Marx 1976: 304).

Animation of the components of the labour process requires organization and coordination – an authority structure to bring workers and managers together – and because workers only offer 'labour power' for sale (an *embodied capacity* of the living worker) there is always a control imperative (or authority/power) required to convert this potential into work that is productive of use, and more importantly exchange value. Exchange, for Marx, is unequal but hidden, as workers do not receive a full return on their effort, and the production process disguises the extraction of surplus value from workers. Due to accumulation forces within capitalism, labour power is constantly pressured to enhance its productive power, which typically divides between extending the length of the working day (time in work) to intensifying productivity in the labour process through applying science and technology, including the social technology of organizing the work and workers in more productive patterns.

Marx suggested that the rise of modern industry threatened craft work. A growth of the 'collective labourer', and the rise of detailed labour specialized in a limited range of tasks and dominated by the manufacturer and technology, meant skilled labour declined because of the productivity advantage of 'one-sidedly specialized workers' (Marx 1976: 458). He goes on to argue that 'Machinery does not just act as superior competitor to the worker, always to the point of making him superfluous. It is a power inimical to him, and capital proclaims this fact loudly and deliberately, as well as making use of it' (1976: 562). The move into modern industry reorganized the labour process and technology embodied deskilling and subordination for labour, themes that later labour process theorists, especially Braverman, developed further. With the application of science and technology, Marx suggested that production was no longer the outcome of worker's skill and initiative, but capital, which harnessed the '*general* products of human development, such as mathematics, to the immediate process of production' (1976: 1024). This movement altered the position of labour from formal to real subordination, which we discuss in the next section.

Accumulation depends on expanding controls over labour, employing technology, drive and intensification tools to generate more surplus value. Commentators have critiqued aspects of Marx's formulations of these trends. Too tight a periodization implies set trends, a throwing-off of one type of labour process for another more superior one, say replacing handicraft work with factory-based mechanization. Marx's periodization in *Capital* was rather technologically determinist and linear – over-emphasizing the impact of technology on industrial organization (Lazonick 1990). He also overstated the development of industry, suggesting the decline of sweated trades through the development of modern industry or the move from cooperation to manufacture as somehow inevitable, when these trends have been shown to be historically variable (Lazonick 1990; Littler 1982).

However, Marx's intellectual legacy remains relevant today and concepts such as labour power, surplus value and the social division of labour are recurrent references for understanding work in contemporary capitalism. Take the issue of control. Marx noted that 'the labour process exhibits two characteristics. First, the worker works under the control of the capitalist to whom his labour belongs ... Secondly, the product is the property of the capitalist and not that of the worker, its immediate producer' (1976: 291–2). Control is present due to ownership obligations – the capitalist owns both the labour time of the worker and the product of the labour process. However, labour time for Marx is constantly fought over in *Capital*. He quotes factory inspectors reporting capitalists' 'small thefts' from workers' meal-times and recreation times, described in reports as 'petty pilfering's of minutes', 'snatching a few minutes' or 'in the technical language of workers "nibbling and cribbling at meal-times"' (1976: 352). Sports Direct, a major retailer in the UK, was recently accused of such nibbling, docking 15 minutes pay for being late by one minute, and detaining workers for so long with excessive and intrusive searches that minimum-wage legislation was infringed (Management Today 2015).

Of course, key concepts can still be unpacked and modified in their (re)application. Marx largely operated with a single dominant model of control, what he termed 'despotism in the workshop'. This formulation underplays the variety of control strategies connected to the growth of management as a class of supervision, for example production management differed from personnel or what is now called HR managers, to offer competing ways of relating to and managing workers based on the embodied nature of labour power and technical, managerial expertise. Another example would be the way in which Marx highlighted the embodiment of labour as consisting of male, female and child categories, especially, and today we would extend these to the emotional and aesthetic aspects of labour, for example (Bolton 2004; Warhurst et al. 2000).

Finally, there is the question of labour agency. In *Capital*, the labour process is structured through class struggle between labour and capital, with the role of law taken largely as an expression of class interests – with the factory acts, limitations on the length of the working day, requirements for children's education, protective legislation towards child and female labour: all examples of the legislation that came out of class struggle in production relations (Marx 1976: 517–32). Marx reported on resistance by workers in the labour process, but ultimately displaced this to wider class struggle that would ultimately lead to the overthrow of capitalism in the so-called gravedigger thesis, whereby 'the proletariat would be compelled to challenge and transform class society by virtue of its objective location in the system of production, although the struggle would increasingly shift to a wider terrain and be expressed through a political party' (Thompson 1990: 115). The passage of time has progressively weakened any claim that there is a relationship between the capitalist labour process and wider class identity, but the teleological nature of the thesis left less space for an understanding of the capacity for self-organization and resistance in the workplace, and the development of a more specific and distinctive 'politics of production'.

Origins of the Rediscovery of the Labour Process Debates

The revival of interest in a Marxist analysis of the labour process owes some debt to French and Italian writers. The former were concerned with the consequences of technological change, especially around the broad idea of automation for workers' control in the workplace. Gorz argued that 'the contemporary transition from mechanisation to automation will bring about a crisis in the organisation of work and the technique of domination founded upon it ... Manual and intellectual work will tend to go together and cause the rebirth of humanism of work which was destroyed by Taylorism' (1967: 126, quoted in Smith 1987: 31). Italian theorists saw the development of the Fordist mass worker as equivalent to Marx's idea of 'abstract labour' and as a positive step towards turning wage struggles into a more general struggle against work and wage labour itself (Baldi 1972). Later contributors focused on workers' struggles for autonomy and around *refusal of work*, which was much more consistent with critiques of how capital was transforming the labour process and the emergence of the mass worker. They were dismissive of demands for workers' control mechanically produced through automation. This orientation, we argue below, was eventually abandoned by autonomists through their emphasis on the social factory. Nevertheless, what both traditions offered was an interest in Fordism and the labour process and a critique of the model of work in actual existing socialist societies – most especially the Soviet models, where there was a lack of workers control and a view of technology (and the means of production) as neutral – and not, as Marx had argued, saturated with capitalist social relations, hierarchy and division of labour between mental and manual workers (Sohn-Rethel and Sohn-Rethel 1978).

However, the major contribution to the explosion of interest in Marx's understanding of the labour process came from Harry Braverman, whose *Labor and Monopoly Capital* (1974) ignited interest across the social sciences (and humanities) especially among radical economists, labour historians, industrial relations writers and sociologists of work. We have elsewhere catalogued the reaction of writers to Braverman's reading of Marx and evaluated what had been taken forward, left behind and developed from Braverman's book (Thompson and Smith 2009; Smith 2015). Braverman followed *Capital* in emphasizing production rather than market relations, and with this labour power, technology and the reserve army of labour. But he added a thesis on skill bifurcation between management (and allied technical cadre) and a mass of unskilled workers, through an extended discussion on the role of Taylorism and Scientific Management, which, like Marx's discussion of the work of Andrew Ure or Babbage in *Capital*, can be seen as an *ideal* reading of Taylor's work, rather than examining the actual diffusion of Taylor's practice across American industry and beyond (Merkle 1980; Nelson 1980; Littler 1982; Lazonick 1990). There is some continuity with Marx, as Braverman assumes a certain periodization in the development of the labour process, here with Taylorism very much the apex management control system.

Though Braverman's concern with skill and scientific management has been most critiqued for its focus on a narrow range of phenomena, it did stimulate an important line of inquiry around science and technology. This saw writers like Cooley (1976; 1980) and Noble (1979) expanding Marx's idea of the embodiment of capitalist rationality within the design of technology in capitalism. For them the idea that fixed capital is neutral, and that design is for the general good, ignored the context of design, which incorporated capitalist social relations of production within the forces of production. Braverman was right to focus on management in the workplace, but connecting work to capitalism as political economy is also critically important, and working within an implicitly American context meant this was not always evident in Braverman. He nevertheless provides key points for developing empirically orientated labour process writing, an engagement with the objective materialism of capitalism that goes back to *Capital*, which offered a rich and concrete account of the labour process in particular industries (cotton, wool, potteries, bread and match making, etc.) and occupations, albeit based on secondary analysis from new professions of factory inspectors, parliamentary reports and medical doctors.

The Development of Labour Process Theory, Post-Braverman

The positive aspect of the post-Braverman debate has been workplace-bounded research on working in a whole range of industrial sectors. These detailed case studies of workplaces offer rich accounts of the actuality of work and the subjectively lived experience of capitalist social relations for workers and managers. They offered, in essence, a control–resistance–consent model of labour processes, where all management control strategies produce worker resistance tactics and strategies (Thompson and Ackroyd 1995). This focus on class *at work* went beyond what in the late 1960s and early '70s had been a concern with class as a connection between 'objective' and 'subjective' components within Marxist debates about 'degrees' of class consciousness, which were rightly abandoned as largely dead-ends. Our argument is that the narrowing of the focus away from the idea of the working class as gravedigger and towards the diverse ways in which labour agency is executed in real labour processes, actually emerges from the nature of labour power, and the capitalist labour process, with its structured antagonism creating different ways in which workers exact autonomy and resistance in diverse contexts (Edwards 1986). This research unites labour market and labour process interactions, and is both narrower and broader, highlighting as it does multiple points of resistance in the workplace.

Though this 'narrower' reading of *Capital* had many positives, a focus on the workplace and the dynamics of skill loss and control strategies tended to lose touch with a wider connection to political economy. A key writer trying to reconnect the two is Michael Burawoy (1979; 1985), who theorized typologies of production regimes, and was systematic in connecting the micro-analysis of work (informed through rich, direct ethnographic accounts of working) with macro political economy and state regimes – creating a politics of production, with the workplace at its centre. What Burawoy did through a theoretical and empirical approach was to show the role of managerial agency and the variety of labour control regimes operating under specific socio-economic conditions. But his concept of factory regime was too broadly formulated – identifying long historical periods in which workplace social relations were explained by a particular regime of accumulation. It thus suffered from an absence of meso-level or intermediary concepts that could link regimes of accumulation to workplace dynamics. Examples of more recent attempts to create more active linkages between political economy and workplace relations can be found in Thompson's (2013) work on 'disconnected capitalism', which traces the negative impact of financialization on outcomes for labour in the workplace; Smith's (2003; Liu and Smith 2016) analysis of China's emerging global labour systems and worker mobility; or Taylor et al.'s (2015) work on global value/supply chains and the role of worker agency. Taken together, the intent of such recent work has been to identify new forms of accumulation within the full circuits of capital, while maintaining links to value extraction and labour agency within production. In this writing there is a recognition of the value of labour process research, inspired by Marx's *Capital*. As we discuss in the following sections, this comes into partial conflict with new thinking about the nature of value, forms of capitalism and the material and immaterial nature of labour produced by systemic shifts in the technological foundations of capitalist society created by the internet and social networking.

Capital and Labour Transformed?

Cognitive capitalism theory (CCT) is a successor to (largely discredited) conceptions of post-Fordist accumulation regimes.[1] Though influenced by knowledge economy and informational capitalism perspectives, the specific derivation is from a combination of Italian (post-) *operaismo*[2] and French regulation school influences (see Hardt and Negri 2000, 2009; Vercellone 2007; Moulier-Boutang 2012; Boffo 2012 for lineage and variations).

The core of the theory is that CC is a third type of capitalism (after mercantile and industrial) with a distinctive system of accumulation based on knowledge value (Moulier-Boutang 2012: 57). A new system of accumulation is characterized by a profound transformation of the antagonistic relation of capital and labour, and the conflicts that derive from it. Value extraction is based on knowledge that cannot be measured and is produced by the 'general intellect' through socially cooperative labour or outside the workplace in the 'commons' (notably through the web and online communities) or by biopolitical labour in the production of social life itself (Hardt and Negri 2009; Mason 2016). Because of an abundance of use values and minimal cost of reproduction, scarcity disappears other than that of time and attention

---

1   Parts of this section are drawn from Thompson and Briken 2016.

2   *Operaismo* refers to an intellectual and political tradition that formed in Italy in the 1960s and 1970s and whose contemporary prominence is associated largely with the various works of Hardt and Negri. Post-*operaismo* broadly refers to the development of this tradition in a new era after Fordism and the mass worker.

(Moulier-Boutang 2012: 66, 72), while information 'corrodes value' in general and the price mechanism for digital goods in particular (Mason 2016: 142–3). Any account of value based on labour time in production, material production or commodity-producing labour is held to be in crisis.

CC, with its increase in abstract knowledge and intellectual powers in production is associated with 'a radical change of the subsumption of labour to capital and indicates a third stage of the division of labour' (Vercellone 2007: 15). This tradition is also characterized by seeking to identify an emblematic figure of labour based on a specific 'class composition'. In the contemporary period, it is immaterial labour; defined variously as that which is cerebral, affective, communicative or relational, or that which contributes to the informational or cultural content of a commodity. As a result, there is a (qualitative) hegemony of intellectual labour or 'diffuse intellectuality'.

Vercellone frames this change by using Marx's distinction between formal and real subordination of labour. Marx made this distinction to emphasize the ways in which capital's use of machinery and science in what was then the modern factory enables new and more powerful mechanisms of control and value extraction, overcoming what was previously just the general control of the employer that lacked the means to affect the actual mode of working (Marx 1976: 1011). Thus, three stages of the division of labour are envisaged by Vercellone: formal subsumption of labour in the early factory system; real subsumption beginning in the industrial revolution and reaching its peak in the standardized mass production and 'Smithian' division of labour of the Fordist era; and finally the general intellect under CC in which real subsumption is reversed. Purely physical labour power is consigned to the Fordist and Taylorist era of industrial capitalism. Unlike that era, cognition and conception are now no longer appropriated by capital, and living labour is no longer incorporated into science and machinery (Vercellone 2007: 16).

To the extent that any of these theorists refer concretely to the organization of work – specialization, standardization, codification and managerial interest in individual performance are all said to be decreasing (Moulier-Boutang 2012: 54, 65). Autonomous labour is 'outside measurement' and beyond management (Hardt and Negri 2009: 6). As for any engagement with ideas of managerial hierarchy or the firm, it is largely to repeat post-Fordist and mainstream business notions of the horizontalization of corporate forms and networks displacing markets and hierarchies and prefiguring a postcapitalist future, except with an emphasis on digitalization (Moulier-Boutang 2012: 61–5; Mason 2016: xix).

Despite reference to capitalism in general, much of the argument rests on interpretations of developments within digital industries: 'the new information technologies, of which the digital, the computer, and the Internet are emblematic in the same way in which the coal mine, the steam engine, the loom and the railroad were emblematic of industrial capitalism' (Moulier-Boutang 2012: 57). Mason emphasizes the growth of 'non-market production: horizontally distributed peer-production networks, that are not centrally managed, producing goods that are either completely free, or which – being Open Source – have very limited commercial value', with Wikipedia as the primary example (2016: 143).

Whereas the concept of formal and real subordination was developed by Marx through his analysis of the labour process in Volume 1 of *Capital*, the general intellect is taken from the *Grundrisse* and in particular a series of unfinished notes – 'The Fragment on Machines'. Here it is envisaged that at some time in the future, knowledge developed through science and technology will become the source of real wealth rather than labour expended in production. This would mark the possibility of a transition to communism. For CCT that time has arrived (see Vercellone 2007: 15). However, there is a partial critique of the contradictions of cognitive or info capitalism. This emphasizes the efforts by capital to offset the losses incurred in the law of value in production by enforcing it elsewhere. Capital uses its monopoly position in networks to manufacture scarcity through the extraction of rents based largely on intellectual property (see Vercellone 2007: 33–34), or expropriates value produced in the wider society from the 'general intellect'. The distinction between profit and rent collapses and capital becomes purely 'parasitic' (see Boffo 2012: 261).

Critique 1: The Subordination of Labour

A number of underlying claims associated with the hegemony of the general intellect are clearly at odds with trends in the labour market.

Low-paid, low-skill service jobs have been the engine of growth and there is extensive evidence of under-employment and a decline in graduate-level jobs (CIPD 2015). The best that could be said about job growth is a polarization, with increases in professional and IT work partially offsetting the low-wage service jobs. Given the focus of this chapter, we want to concentrate on the labour process dimension and in particular claims concerning the division of labour. Assertions of spontaneous social cooperation and autonomy bear little relationship to workplace research. Any (uneven) increase in decision latitude over tasks is constrained by decline in employee voice mechanisms, limited wider organizational involvement and higher levels of work intensity (Findlay and Thompson, forthcoming). As developments from call centres to Amazon warehouses and retail indicate, labour time remains a fundamental focus of managerial attention. Indeed, the use of tracking and monitoring software provides tools that F. W. Taylor could only have dreamed of.

Such trends are also connected to a wider increase in performance management in large organizations. In the private sector, it is primarily linked to cascading and often punitive targets, aided in many cases by electronic monitoring and tighter work flow (Taylor 2013: 46–7). What has become fashionably known as knowledge management (KM) is also part of enhanced performance exposure. KM is particularly significant in knowledge-intensive industries, the supposed heartland of creative and cooperative labour. Of course these characteristics *are* present, but alongside the use of IT systems to capture, convert and codify the tacit knowledge of expert labour in order to speed up the innovation or molecule to market process (McKinlay 2005).

The use of IT systems to capture tacit knowledge is now part of a widespread recognition of the emergence of digital or knowledge-based Taylorism that includes the capacity of artificial intelligence to incorporate living labour into machine systems. Brown et al. (2011) refer to digital Taylorism as the extraction, codification and digitaliza-tion of knowledge into software prescripts and working knowledge. In manufacturing this is driven by the development of engineering systems that allow global operating companies to 'calculate, to compare and to standardise processes worldwide' (Westkämpfer 2007: 6).

Finally, the misapprehension of the present is sustained by a misreading of the past – notably the designation of the 'industrial stage' of capitalism as based on physical labour, 'devoid of any intellectual or creative quality' (Vercellone 2007: 24). As Marx noted, labour power is always an 'aggregate of those physical and mental qualities' (1976: 270). Not only were there significant numbers of design, engineering or other conceptual jobs under Fordism, those involved primarily in execution still contained tacit knowledge that employers are now seeking to identify and leverage.

Critique 2: Actually Existing Capital

We are told little or nothing about how capital is actually organized in companies or value chains, or how money is made through particular business models. Of equal importance, CCT overestimates the extent to which capitalism is defined and dominated by internet-based companies. If we look at data about which industries and firms dominate the global economy we find that though Apple is currently the most profitable company in the world, it is far from the largest either by revenue or capitalization, and many of the other 'exemplary' internet firms are marginal. Global capitalism is dominated by energy, finance and telecoms/utilities and sometimes retail or tobacco. An examination of how Exxon Mobil, Wal-Mart or Toyota make their money offers a major corrective to the CCT narrative of immaterial production and zero-cost reproduction at the heart of economic value. The global dimension and the dynamics of value chains are also a key consideration, as cost control through the supply chain (Froud et al. 2014), and, specifically, very low direct labour costs in suppliers (Cleland 2014), are key factors in business models. In his critique of Mason, Fuchs (2016: 232) refutes claims that value has collapsed in the digital sector, pointing to profits made on the basis of product innovation, exploitation of direct and indirect labour and (most significantly) targeted advertising. Capital can and does adapt to technological change and find new ways to monetize and monopolize, precisely in those social media and Web 2.0 sectors (Tyfield 2015). The focus on networks as the central coordinating mechanism is little better than fantasy economics. A key trend across all sectors is the concentration of capital. In contrast to the daydreams of global commons, concentration is particularly marked in virtual and vertical integration internet-based or new media (Fitzgerald 2015; Keen 2015). Peer production and genuine sharing economy projects exist in specialist niches, while digital platforms such as Uber and Air B&B develop hierarchical business models, utilize flexible (self-)employment and seek to dominate more traditional markets. It is telling that it is hard to find any substantive, collaborative peer-production example in Mason other than Wikipedia. The power and resilience of capital is obscured by designating it as purely parasitic and this formulation evades any attempt to analyse its actual workings. It is true that in some sectors, intellectual property is a source of value capture, but rent-seeking through monopoly is not a new feature of capitalism and nor does it exhaust how firms use their power in markets and value chains.

Critique 3: Value Inside and Outside Production

Commentators influenced by autonomism defend the labour theory of value (LTV) or a version of it, but not as envisaged in *Capital*: 'the Autonomist perspective emphasizes the idea that "labour", understood as value-producing activity, has moved outside the workplace and employment relationship, and so is no longer under the direct control of management' (Böhm and Land 2012: 232–3). For this reason, they argue that labour process theory can no longer argue for a 'privileging' of the labour process as site of analysis within the capitalist circuit of production (2012: 218). In contrast, we do not seek to defend the LTV – past or present – but do argue that the labour process remains a central site both for the creation and extraction of value. The organization and productivity of labour are often the focal point of managerial intervention to control costs within corporate operating profit margins and favourable cost ratios. Such interventions are part of complex struggles over claims to the same limited value added fund between lead firms and suppliers, and between labour and capital across and within those firms (Froud et al. 2014).

However, research on the rise of finance-dominated regimes of accumulation shows that there have indeed been shifts in the circuits of capital (Stockhammer 2008; Thompson 2013). Pressures to meet capital-market requirements and service debt influence non-financial firms to focus on leveraging value through financial extractions and assets compared to the rate of return on manufacturing and operational investment. Shareholder value pressures involve and impact on the labour process through 'taking labour out' via headcount reduction, outsourcing and supply chain harmonization; reducing labour share through downward pressure on rewards; and working labour harder through tightened performance management, cascading financial controls and work intensification (Cushen and Thompson 2016).

Nor do these observations exhaust the range of new value-creating practices. Willmott (2010) makes an effective case for a post-Marxian emphasis on the sphere of circulation. In particular, he emphasizes another aspect of financialization – the monetization of intangible assets or 'symbolic artefacts', notably brand equity. Willmott, along with others influenced by Arvidsson's (2006) work (Fuchs 2016), highlights the participation of unwaged user-consumers in the creation of these assets, alongside the labour of waged workers such as product developers, brand managers, advertising specialists and stylists. User consumers or prosumers make their contribution by making assessments of products and services on Web 2.0 sites such as Facebook, Trip Advisor and YouTube.

There can be no doubt that such 'shadow work' contributes indirectly to value production in some sectors. The problem with the wider claims is their over-extended nature. This takes a number of forms, including exaggerating the number of industries where user-consumers play a significant role and overestimating its contribution in value terms. Further unwarranted extension comes from applying the 'value in the totality of social life' perspective to encompass all activities that reproduce labour power such as housework and education (Böhm and Land 2012: 226) and seemingly all consumption activities 'beyond the internet' (Fuchs 2016: 236). Fuchs includes as 'productive consumption' deleting spam, installing software updates, working on the train, time spent on online dating platforms, self-assemblage of IKEA furniture and using ATMs and self-service bars in restaurants. Aside from the difficulty of demonstrating direct or measurable links to value production, neither reproduction nor much of consumption practices are new, therefore telling us little or nothing about contemporary capitalism.

Critique 4: Labour Agency and (not) Reinventing the Gravedigger Thesis

As we indicated earlier, there have been two versions of a politics of production: the gravedigger thesis and the labour process tradition of linking mobilization to more contingent forms of workplace resistance and recalcitrance. The versions of cognitive or post-capitalist political economy examined in this chapter tend to shift the graveyard, while rethinking the digger. Whereas the 'struggle against work' once meant challenging capital inside the workplace, now that struggle is said to have moved outside. Rationales for a politics of postcapitalism and post-work rest on extremely pessimistic readings of the struggles of waged workers. In recent accounts from Mason (2016) and Srnicek and Williams (2015) the *working* class (in both developed and developing economies) is presented as fragmented, divided and in thrall to consumption and debt, while the labour movement is largely defeated, demoralized and sclerotic.

For most influenced by such perspectives, this does not mean abandonment of the gravedigger thesis. The *operaismo* tradition has moved from the mass worker to the socialized worker and more recently the 'multitude' (Hardt and Negri 2009). Mason is sympathetic to the latter formulation and explicitly uses the term gravedigger to identify a 'new social force' and historical 'agent of change' based on the 'educated and networked human beings' (2016: xvii, 212). Their battlefield is 'all aspects of society' and evidence can be found in city squares and streets across the globe. Fuchs (2016) rightly describes these views as naive. The rich and powerful are also (better) networked and a collection of heterogeneous struggles does not add up to an agency with any significant degree of common interest or identity. Unfortunately, the latter point also applied to Fuchs's own gravedigger, whereby a global collective worker is created because 'consumers and users have become part of the working class' (2016: 137).

Capital and the production process do not produce a social force that can act as a universal liberating class. However, the capitalist labour process does continue to produce many of the conditions that shape and stimulate a diversity of labour struggles and forms of organization. Free from the gravedigger thesis and a conflation between the labour movement and the movements of labour, it is possible to have a much more realistic appreciation of that diversity of labour agency and a more grounded understanding of how those grievances can be mobilized and connect to wider struggles and social movements.

Concluding Comments

We have argued that while there have been changes in the circuits of capital and the character of labour, claims that 'value production shifts from the material production of tangible commodities to the immaterial production of social relationships, knowledge and affect' (Böhm and Land 2012: 224) are inconsistent with what is happening with actually existing capital and labour. In *Capital*'s treatment of the labour process, Marx combines brilliant conceptual insights with a sustained empirical observation that lays bare the ideological distortions of contemporary economists and other commentators. It is hard to make an empirically based critique of autonomist and related perspectives. This is not for want of available counter evidence, but because for such perspectives a normative orientation is dominant and there is a 'cavalier attitude' to the validity of facts and numbers (Jeon 2010: 3). Moulier-Boutang (2012: 54, 60), for example, is aware of challenges to his claims, but is dismissive of 'the empirical approach', taking refuge (with others) in supposedly 'exemplary industries' or 'paradigmatic work'.

When it is not driven solely by their own political desires, some of the tendency towards excessive speculation derives, as indicated earlier, from reliance on 'The Fragment on Machines'. Pitts (2015) notes that in his claims such as that automation reduces necessary labour to an amount so small that work would become optional, Mason represents 'peak Fragment' and inherits its weaknesses around value and labour. A series of short, speculative notes constituting a 'thought experiment' (Mason 2016: 188), the Fragment has been the basis of 'endless as well as obscure exegeses' (Turchetto 2008: 306). For this reason, it (and other elements of the *Grundrisse*) should be treated with care and read in context (Choonara 2015). Whatever the validity of Marx's arguments about the development of science, technology and automation as a basis for a transition to a postcapitalist future, it is clear that we are far from this point. As we have shown, not only is much of value capture taking place in traditional ways and through non-digital sectors, capital has been extremely successful in finding new ways to valorize new ICTs and social media, both within and outside the labour process. In this sense, Marx's emphasis on the incessant expansion of the commodity form under capitalism is still pertinent.

Without this recognition, earlier claims from Mason that information 'corrodes value' or 'dissolves markets and ownership' (Mason 2016) or that we have moved to an era of the 'rule of science' (Moulier-Boutang 2012: 54) are susceptible to accusations of techno-logical determinism and utopianism (Fuchs 2016: 237; Pitts 2015). Whichever of these interpretations is dominant, the arguments attribute to (info) technology transformative powers that it does not and cannot independently possess. In abandoning Marx's critique of the social character of science and technology and the consequences for the division of labour, a key aspect of the radical legacy of *Capital* is wrongly consigned to history.

References

Arvidsson, A. (2006). *Brands: Meaning and Value in Media Culture*. Hove: Psychology Press.

Baldi, G. (1972). Theses on Mass Worker and Social Capital. *Radical America*, 6(1): 3–21.

Boffo, M. (2012). Historical Immaterialism: From Immaterial Labour to Cognitive Capitalism. *International Journal of Management Concepts and Philosophy*, 6(4): 256–79.

Böhm, S. and Land, C. (2012). The New 'Hidden Abode': Reflections on Value and Labour in the New Economy. *The Sociological Review*, 60(2): 217–40.

Bolton, S. C. (2004). *Emotion Management in the Workplace*. London: Palgrave Macmillan.

Brown, P., Lauder, H. and Ashton, D. (2010). *The Global Auction: The Broken Promises of Education, Jobs, and Incomes*. Oxford: Oxford University Press.

Burawoy, M. (1979). *Manufacturing Consent: Changes in the Labor Process under Monopoly Capitalism*. Chicago: University of Chicago Press.

Burawoy, M. (1985). *The Politics of Production: Factory Regimes under Capitalism and Socialism*. London: Verso.

Choonara, J. (2015). 'Brand New, You're Retro', *International Socialism*, 48 (autumn), http://isj.org.uk/brand-new-youre-retro

CIPD (2015). Over-qualification and Skills Mismatch in the Graduate Labour Market. Chartered Institute for Personnel and Development, London.

Cleland, D. (2014). The Core of the Apple: Dark Value in Global Commodity Chains. *Journal of World Systems Research*, 20(1): 82–111.

Cooley, M. (1976). Contradictions of Science and Technology in the Productive Process. In H. Rose and S. P. Rose, eds., *The Political Economy of Science: Ideology of/in the Natural Sciences*. London: Macmillan Education, 72–95.

Cooley, M. (1980). *Architect or Bee?* Slough: Langley Technical Services.

Cushen, J. and Thompson, P. (2016). Financialization and Value: Why Labour and the Labour Process Still Matter. *Work, Employment & Society*, 30(2): 352–65.

Edwards, P. K. (1986). *Conflict at Work*. Oxford: Blackwell.

Findlay, T. and Thompson, P. (forthcoming). Work and its Meanings. *Journal of Industrial Relations*.

Fitzgerald, S. (2015). Structure of the Cultural Industries – Global Corporation to SMEs. In K. Oakley and J. O'Connor, eds., *The Routledge Companion to the Cultural Industries*. London: Routledge, 70–85.

Froud, J., Johal, S., Leaver, A. and Williams, K. (2014). Financialization Across the Pacific: Manufacturing Cost Ratios, Supply Chains and Power. *Critical Perspectives on Accounting*, 25(1): 46–57.

Fuchs, C. (2010). Labor in Informational Capitalism and on the Internet. *The Information Society*, 26(3): 179–96.

Fuchs, C. (2016). Henryk Grossmann 2.0: A Critique of Paul Mason's Book 'Postcapitalism: A Guide to Our Future'. *tripleC: Communication, Capitalism & Critique. Open Access Journal for a Global Sustainable Information Society*, 14(1): 232–43.

Gorz, A. (1967). *Strategy for Labour: A Radical Proposal*. Boston: Beacon Press.

Green, F. (2006). *Demanding Work: The Paradox of Job Quality in the Affluent Economy*. Princeton: Princeton University Press.

Hardt, M. and Negri, A. (2000). *Empire*. Cambridge, MA: Harvard University Press.

Hardt, M. and Negri, A. (2009). *Commonwealth*. Cambridge, MA: Harvard University Press.

Jeon, H. (2010). Cognitive Capitalism or Cognition in Capitalism? A Critique of Cognitive Capitalism Theory. *Spectrum: Journal of Global Studies*, 2(3): 89–116.

Keen, A. (2015). *The Internet is Not the Answer*. London: Atlantic Books.

Lazonick, W. (1990). *Competitive Advantage on the Shop Floor*. Cambridge, MA: Harvard University Press.

Littler, C. R. (1982). *The Development of the Labour Process in Capitalist Societies: A Comparative Study of the Transformation of Work organization in Britain, Japan, and the USA*. London: Heinemann Educational Publishers.

Liu, M. and Smith, C. (eds.) (2016). *China at Work: A Labour Process Perspective on the Transformation of Work and Employment in China*. London: Palgrave.

Lucarelli, S. and Vercellone, C. (2013). The Thesis of Cognitive Capitalism. New Research Perspectives. An Introduction. *Knowledge Cultures*, 1(4): 15–27.

McKinlay, A. (2005). Knowledge Management. In S. Ackroyd, R. Batt, P. Thompson and P. Tolbert, eds., *The Oxford Handbook of Work and Organization*. Oxford: Oxford University Press, 242–62.

Management Today (2015). Sports Direct is under fire over working conditions (again). 5 October, http://www.managementtoday.co.uk/news/1367119/sports-direct-fire-working-conditions-again

Marx, K. (1976). *Capital, Volume 1*. London: Penguin Books.

Mason, P. (2016). *Postcapitalism: A Guide to Our Future*. London: Macmillan.

Merkle, J. (1980). *Management and Ideology: The Legacy of the International Scientific Management Movement*. Berkeley: University of California Press.

Moulier-Boutang, Y. (2012). *Cognitive Capitalism*. Cambridge: Polity Press.

Nelson, D. (1980). *Fredrick W. Taylor and the Rise of Scientific Management*. Madison: University of Wisconsin Press.

Noble, D. F. (1979). *America by Design: Science, Technology, and the Rise of Corporate Capitalism*. Oxford: Oxford University Press.

Pitts, F. H. (2015). Review of Paul Mason, *Postcapitalism: A Guide to Our Future. Marx & Philosophy: Review of Books*. 4 September, http://marxandphilosophy.org.uk/reviewofbooks/reviews/2015/2008?searched=paul+mason&advsearch=exactphrase&highlight=ajaxSearch_highlight+ajaxSearch_highlight1

Pitts, F. H. (2016). Beyond the Fragment: The Postoperaist Reception of Marx's Fragment on Machines and its Relevance Today. Working Paper No. 02–16, University of Bristol School of Sociology, Politics and International Studies.

Smith, C. (1987). *Technical Workers: Class, Labour and Trade Unionism*. London: Macmillan.

Smith, C. (2003). Living at Work: Management Control and the Dormitory Labour System in China. *Asia Pacific Journal of Management*, 20(3): 333–58.

Smith, C. (2006). The Double Indeterminacy of Labour Power: Labour Effort and Labour Mobility. *Work, Employment and Society*, 20(2): 401–14.

Smith, C., (2015). Continuity and Change in Labor Process Analysis: Forty Years After *Labor and Monopoly Capital. Labor Studies Journal*, 40(3): 222–42.

Smith, C. and Liu, M. (2016). In Search of the Labour Process Perspective in China. In M. Liu and C. Smith, eds., *China at Work: A Labour Process Perspective on the Transformation of Work and Employment in China.* London: Palgrave, 1–28.

Sohn-Rethel, A. and Sohn-Rethel, M. (1978). *Intellectual and Manual Labour: A Critique of Epistemology.* London: Macmillan.

Srnicek, N. and Williams, A. (2015). *Inventing the Future: Postcapitalism and a World Without Work.* London: Verso.

Stockhammer, E. (2008). Some Stylized Facts on the Finance-dominated Accumulation Regime. *Competition & Change,* 12(2): 184–202.

Taylor, P. (2013). *Performance Management and the New Workplace Tyranny. A Report for the Scottish Trade Union Congress.* Glasgow: University of Strathclyde.

Taylor, P., Newsome, K., Bair, J. and Rainnie, A. (eds.) (2015). *Putting Labour in its Place: Labour Process Analysis and Global Value Chains.* London: Palgrave.

Thompson, P. (1990). Crawling from the Wreckage: The Labour Process and the Politics of Production. In D. Knight and H. Willmott, eds., *Labour Process Theory.* London: Macmillan, 95–124.

Thompson, P. (2013). Financialization and the Workplace: Extending and Applying the Disconnected Capitalism Thesis. *Work, Employment and Society,* 25th Anniversary edition, 27(3): 472–88.

Thompson, P. and Ackroyd, S. (1995). All Quiet on the Workplace Front? A Critique of Recent Trends in British Industrial Sociology. *Sociology,* 29(4): 615–33.

Thompson, P. and Briken, K. (2016). *Kognitiver Kapitalismus. Wider Eine Fragfwürdige Diagnose,* West End, Frankfurt: IFS.

Thompson, P. and Smith, C. (2000). Follow the Redbrick Road: Reflections on Pathways in and out of the Labour Process Debate. *International Studies of Management & Organization,* 30(4): 40–67.

Thompson, P. and Smith, C. (2009). Labour Power and Labour Process: Contesting the Marginality of the Sociology of Work. *Sociology,* 43(5): 913–30.

Turchetto, M. (2008). From 'Mass Worker' to 'Empire': The Disconcerting Trajectory of Italian Operaismo. In J. Bidet and S. Kouvelakis, eds., *Critical Companion to Contemporary Marxism.* Boston: Brill, 285–308.

Tyfield, D. (2015). On Paul Mason's 'Post-Capitalism' – An Extended Review, http://www.lancaster.ac.uk/staff/tyfield/On_Postcapitalism_1.pdf

Vercellone, C. (2007). From Formal Subsumption to General Intellect: Elements for a Marxist Reading of the Thesis of Cognitive Capitalism. *Historical Materialism,* 15(1): 13–36.

Warhurst, C., Nickson, D., Witz, A. and Marie Cullen, A. (2000). Aesthetic Labour in Interactive Service Work: Some Case Study Evidence from the 'New' Glasgow. *Service Industries Journal*, 20(3): 1–18.

Westkämper, E. (2007). Digital Manufacturing in the Global Era. In P. F. Cunha and P. G. Maropoulos, eds., *Digital Enterprise Technology: Perspectives and Future Challenges*. New York: Springer, 3–14.

Willmott, H. (2010). Creating 'Value' Beyond the Point of Production: Branding, Financialization and Market Capitalization. *Organization*, 17(5): 517–42.

8
Capital and Organized Labour

Carlo Fanelli and Jeff Noonan

Capital is dead labour, that, vampire-like, only lives by sucking living labour, and lives the more, the more labour it sucks. The time during which the labourer works, is the time during which the capitalist consumes the labour-power he has purchased of him. (Marx 1986: 163)

Introduction

At the heart of *Capital* is an exploration of an emergent world capitalism, not questions of workers' struggles or trade unions as agents of political transformation. Although trade unions emerged from the working class, they did not come to represent the interests of the class as a whole or the long-term human interest in transforming capitalism into a socialist society. In this chapter we explore these questions scarcely addressed in *Capital*, developing further Marx's critical insights on labour as a transformative social and political force. While organizing workers at the point of production is not only important but necessary, Marx (and Engels) argued that in failing to come to terms with the root sectionalism of trade unionism organized labour risked impeding the formation of an alternative political and class project.[1] Challenging the entrenched power of capital and the state required the development of a class-oriented trade unionism that responded to the undemocratic and alienating structures upon which capitalism depends in ways that built upon the radical potential of the working class as a whole. In doing so, however, trade unionists would need to

---

1 It should be noted that Engels made invaluable contributions not only to Marx's theoretical insights, but also to the study of working-class politics. Here, we will generally use the singular Marx, with the caveat that his ideas were heavily influenced by and, indeed, in some cases a direct outcome of Engels' pathbreaking work. See Engels 1977.

come to terms with the structural constraints of organizing within the political and economic parameters of capitalism, developing a class-oriented counter-culture of resistance that pursued social justice and workplace democracy.

Despite the manifold problems that the history and current leadership of trade unions poses to the formation of a union-informed movement for social transformation, we will argue that it would be a political mistake to turn our backs on the radical potential of unions. Even though labour unions in particular, and the working class in general, have suffered major defeats over the last four decades, it remains the case that millions of workers belong to unions – making them an obvious space in which to build a unified movement for social transformation. But, as Marx argued, unions needed to go beyond depoliticized, economistic struggles – that is, struggles limited to the immediate conditions of work, pay and greater labour market regulation – to building wider solidarities beyond the workplace with the aim of transcending social relations of servitude. Still, even these limited struggles at the point of production implicitly contest the fundamental principle of capital: that capital alone will decide how to use and dispose of the surplus it creates through exploitation and alienation. We will argue that a key task of the left must be to draw out this implicitly radical contestation, and connect success in the struggle to control ever more of the surplus to a long-term struggle for socialism. Since workers' interests and relationships extend beyond the workplace, and paid employment is not the only incubator of struggles between labour and capital, the long-term struggle for socialism is part of the long-term struggle for democracy, a struggle to which Marx's work made an irreplaceable contribution. If direct appeals to class-consciousness sound too nineteenth century today, appeals to democracy continue to resonate. Hence we suggest recasting the goals of trade union and socialist struggle as crucial elements in the struggle for democracy against an increasingly oligarchic and life-destructive moneyed elite.

The Antagonism Between Capital and Labour

Michael Lebowitz opens his influential book, *Beyond Capital: Marx's Political Economy of the Working Class*, by asserting that

Capital is essentially about capital – its goals and its struggles to achieve those goals. Its theme is not workers (except insofar as capital does something to workers), not workers' goals (except to mention that they differ from those of capital) and not workers' class struggle (except insofar as workers react against capital's offensives). Even where Marx made sporadic comments in *Capital* about workers as subjects, those comments hang in mid-air without anything comparable to the systematic logical development he provides for the side of capital. (2003: ix)[2]

Lebowitz here picks up on a theme first explored briefly by Gramsci, in his analysis of the Russian Revolution – a revolution, he claimed, that was 'against *Capital*'. For Gramsci, *Capital* was corrupted by 'positivism and naturalism' and forgot that 'the main determinant of history is not lifeless economics, but man; societies made up of men, men who have something in common, who get along together, and because of this (civility) they develop a collective social will' (Gramsci 1917). The Bolsheviks rejected the 'laws' of capitalist development when they rejected a stagist theory of history and led a revolution in 'backward' Russia (see Schmidt, and Korsika, this volume).

One might respond that it is no surprise that *Capital* displaces class struggle from centre stage. Its focus is the inner process through which labour creates value and the exploitation of labour creates surplus value – hidden truths that workers must understand if their struggles are to be efficacious. Nevertheless, Lebowitz (and Gramsci) are right to argue that the lack of attention to class struggle means that *Capital* is one-sided. In reality, the amount of surplus labour available to capital for conversion to surplus value, as well as the rate at which labour must be paid (which affects profitability), are not a pure function of the inner dynamics of capital itself, but are decisively affected by class struggle. Since the labour power exploited by capital is inseparable from human beings, and human beings react against the harms they suffer, workers are never simply passive objects of economic processes,

---

2 Draper shares this view, noting how 'trade unionism is glancingly mentioned', and that Marx had initially intended to devote a study of labour and trade unionism to planned future volumes of *Capital* (1978: 94).

mere 'personifications' of their functions, but fight back against them as living subjects (Marx 1986: 21).

'There is a critical silence' in *Capital*, Lebowitz argues, 'a silence which permits the appearance that, for the scientist, the only subject … is capital, growing, transcending all barriers, developing – until, finally, it runs out of steam and is replaced by scientists with a more efficient machine' (2003: 25). Unless this analysis is situated within Marx's work as a whole, where the focus is on class struggle and the determination of social conditions by the combined actions of human beings pursuing their interests in determinate circumstances, a mechanistic, deterministic, undialectical and undemocratic Marxism follows. 'Limited to *Capital*', he concludes, 'we have only the mechanical laws of capital, a structure without a subject, a one-sided Marxism' (Lebowitz 1992: 149). The one-sidedness ignores the fact that the struggle for socialism is not in essence a struggle for a different set of economic laws, but a different way of living in which the satisfaction of fundamental natural and social human needs is paramount.

According to Lebowitz (2003: 27–8), Marx intended to explain the role of class struggle on the operations of capitalism in a volume on wage labour that he never wrote. We are not interested here in the Marxiological question of whether Marx ever formally abandoned the original six-volume plan for *Capital*. Rather, we are interested in the practical question of what the struggle for socialism looks like when we take seriously, as Marx typically did in his political work and as Lebowitz does, struggles *within* capitalism for a shorter working day, higher real wages, and universal access through public provision of needed life-goods. When we take those struggles seriously we discover that the struggle for socialism is neither the necessary product of the working out of the endogenous laws of capitalism nor the result of a voluntaristic, all or nothing, once and for all revolutionary movement, but a process arrayed along a continuum of better or worse lives for working people, determined by the degree of democratic control they are able to assert over the production process, the amount of time outside of alienated labour they are able to secure, the extent to which they are able to satisfy their human life-requirements, and the extent to which the private accumulation of capital is redirected towards the public provision of life-requirement satisfiers.

These struggles occur within the dynamics of capitalist society, but react back against them, modifying their impact on real human lives. Lives can be better or worse for working people in capitalism depending on whether or not their struggles are successful. The laws of capitalism that Marx explains in *Capital* are not, in reality, forces that can exist independently of the combined actions of people (if they were, they could never be overthrown but only transform themselves into different laws or exist in perpetuity). The difference between natural laws and social laws is that the latter emerge from human action and interaction and change when those patterns of interaction change (see Gose and Paulson, this volume). As Marx himself notes in *Capital*, 'the economic categories ... bear the stamp of history' (Marx 1986: 120). While Marx himself in *Capital* often fails to follow out consistently the implications of this position, frequently referring to capitalist dynamics as governed by 'iron laws', we must interpret these claims in the philosophical context furnished by historical materialist method, which, as the quotation above reveals, is rooted in the principle that humanity is ultimately a self-determining subject (see, for example, Marx 1986: 7). As such, nothing that the exploited and alienated segments of humanity do to free themselves from alienation and exploitation is irrelevant, nor are the organizations through which those class struggles are expressed irrelevant just in case they are not directed immediately to the overthrow of capitalism. What matters, in our view, is whether the struggles aim at reducing the structural power of capital over human life, and whether they are rooted in explicit recognition of a shared life-interest in reducing that power over human beings, and not whether they are led by trade unions or revolutionary parties, or explicitly aim at revolution in the short term or only at demonstrable improvements in human life within capitalism.

Despite the incomplete picture of the role of class struggle painted by Marx, *Capital* begins to dispel a number of previously taken-for-granted assumptions regarding the capital-labour relationship. First and foremost, Marx shows how:

The directing motive, the end and aim of capitalist production, is to extract the greatest possible amount of surplus-value, and consequently to exploit labour-power to the greatest possible extent. As the number of the co-operating labourers increases, so too does their resistance to the domination of capital, and with it, the necessity for capital to overcome this resistance by counter pressure. The control exercised by the capitalist is not only a special function, due to the nature of the social labour-process, and peculiar to that process, but it is, at the same time, a function of the exploitation of a social labour-process, and is consequently rooted in the unavoidable antagonism between the exploiter and the living and labouring raw material he exploits. (1986: 231)

Like the quotation that opens this chapter, here Marx is drawing attention to the historically specific social relations that govern capital accumulation. Of course, for capitalists the purpose of producing a commodity is to make a profit. Before Marx, much of the classical political economy tradition assumed that profits emanated from the act of buying cheap and selling dear. David Ricardo's, and to a lesser extent Adam Smith's, labour theory of value came closest, but failed to distinguish between labour and labour power (see Patnaik, and Thompson and Smith, this volume). Marx showed how workers are paid for their labour power for a certain period of time, and not for everything their labour produces during that time. Because workers produce (surplus-labour) in excess of what they are paid and what their products or services will realize in the market, and this belongs to the capitalist, Marx demonstrated in *Capital* that profits (surplus-value) derived from this discrepancy.

Second, this class-based structural inequality renders workers 'free' 'in the double sense that neither they themselves form part and parcel of the means of production, as in the case of slaves, bondsmen, &c., nor do the means of production belong to them, as in the case of peasant proprietors; they are, therefore, free from, unencumbered by, any means of production of their own' (Marx 1986: 507). In other words, they are 'free' in the first instance to sell their labour power, that is, unbound from any socio-economic relationships that may constrain the sale of their labour power and, second, of any ownership or control over the means of production in so far as they must sell their labour power in order to survive. Third, this makes labour power also a commodity that can be bought and sold in the market 'converting the working class into a class dependent on wages' (1986: 411) whose value is determined by social subsistence norms. Although 'the value of labour-power is the value of the means of subsistence necessary for the maintenance of the labourer' (1986: 121), market pressures compel capitalists to drive real wages below subsistence levels. Like continuous technological developments that produce mass unemployment and keep real wages down (see Chapter 15 in *Capital*), 'a surplus labouring population is a necessary product of accumulation ... It forms a disposable industrial reserve army that belongs to capital quite as absolutely as if the latter had bred it at its own cost ... it creates, for the changing needs of the self-expansion of capital, a mass of human material always ready for exploitation' (1986: 411).

Capital sought to counter the prevailing orthodoxy of liberal political economy by demonstrating that markets are not governed by opportunity and choice, and that the paired opposition of social classes was the basis for this exploitation. Rather, economic compulsion and political necessity were the driving motifs of capital accumulation. As Wood (2003) has argued, material life and social reproduction in capitalism are universally mediated by the market so that all individuals must enter into market relations in one way or another to gain access to the means of life. Although capitalist class relations give the unique impression that the labourer is a 'free vendor of his labour-power' (Marx 1986: 194), market-dependence is an instituted compulsion: capital has a choice, while wage labour does not.[3] In denaturalizing capitalism, Marx showed how unequal social relations were not trans-historical or unchanging, but rooted in the historically specific imperatives of capitalism – that is, the vampire-like bloodsucking of living labour, cutthroat competition, and labour rationality. To challenge the subordination of labour, it was necessary, in Marx's view, to recognize both the progressive potential and political limitations of unions: 'Instead

---

3 Marx concludes then that: 'The creation of a normal working day is, therefore, the product of a protracted civil war, more or less dissembled, between the capitalist class and the working-class' (1986: 194). He later notes: 'Hence, the historical movement which changes the producers into wage-workers, appears, on the one hand, as their emancipation from serfdom and from the fetters of the guilds, and this side alone exists for our bourgeois historians. But, on the other hand, these new freedmen became sellers of themselves only after they had been robbed of all their own means of production, and of all the guarantees of existence afforded by the old feudal arrangements. And the history of this, their expropriation, is written in the annals of mankind in letters of blood and fire' (1986: 508).

of the conservative motto, "A fair day's wage for a fair day's work!" they ought to inscribe on their banner the revolutionary watchword, "Abolition of the wages system!"" (Marx 1866a).

Beyond Trade Unionism

As capitalist social relations gained greater prominence through the 1800s – that is to say, as more workers left or were forced from the countryside, becoming wage-dependent labourers – traditional craftwork and the putting-out system were replaced by urban concentrations of industrial factories. Considering the unsafe and overall dreadful working conditions, vividly chronicled by Engels in *The Condition of the Working Class in England*, workers increasingly began to organize themselves into unions in an effort to resist unbridled exploitation. This resistance was actively opposed not only by captains of industry who organized militias to violently repress workers, but also by 'those great trade unions of the ruling classes' (i.e. states) who sometimes led and in other instances created the conditions for capital to lead in ensuring conditions favourable to capital accumulation; not to mention radicals of various persuasions who refused to recognize the importance of unions in struggles against capitalism (Marx in Lapides 1987: 112; Draper 1978).

For Marx, the unionization of workers represented an initial attempt on the part of labour to 'organize a regular co-operation between employed and unemployed in order to destroy or to weaken the ruinous effects of this natural law of capitalistic production on their class' (1986: 448).[4] Because trade unions were among the first attempts by workers to constrain competition, Marx recognized in their demands a fundamental potentiality that under definite social conditions embodied an emancipatory force capable of challenging the power of capital. As workers struggled together, unions increasingly

---

4 As Marx (1866b) noted a year earlier: 'The immediate object of trades' unions was therefore confined to everyday necessities, to expediencies for the obstruction of the incessant encroachments of capital, in one word, to questions of wages and time of labor. This activity of the trades' unions is not only legitimate, it is necessary. It cannot be dispensed with so long as the present system of production lasts. On the contrary, it must be generalized by the formation and the combination of trades' unions throughout all countries.'

began developing a counter-culture of resistance that served as a guiding framework for programmatic demands, popular education and collective strategizing. Not only did this open up the possibility for improving immediate life-conditions in the fight for living wages, workplace health and safety standards, a shorter working day, an end to child labour, respect for prison labour, and the collection of workplace statistics and legislative safeguards, it also generated the conditions for unions to act as 'organized agencies for superseding the very system of wage labour and capital rule' (Marx 1866b).

Let us take an example to help illustrate the potential of unions. Not coincidentally, this example is the one exception to the rule of *Capital*'s not focusing on class struggle: Marx's historical analysis of the struggle for a shorter working day, a struggle in which trade unions played a decisive role. We cannot reconstruct the fine detail of Marx's argument but instead want to focus on its general structure, to support the political point about the relevance of trade unions and struggles within capitalism to the ultimate overcoming of capitalism we are making. The *drive* of capitalists to lengthen the working day is forced upon them by the competitive dynamics of capitalism. From the perspective of capital, 'the labourer is nothing else ... than labour-power, ... all his disposable time is by nature and law labour time, to be dedicated to the self-expansion of capital. Time for education, for intellectual development, for fulfilling social functions and for social intercourse – moonshine' (Marx 1986: 179).

For workers as subjects, of course, education and social intercourse are not fantastical luxuries but human necessities, *for which they will fight, regardless of the objective requirements of capitalist accumulation.*

After capital had taken centuries in extending the working day to its normal maximum limit ... there followed on the birth of mechanism and modern industry in the last half of the eighteenth century a violent encroachment like that of an avalanche in its extent and intensity. All bounds of morals and nature, age, sex, day and night, were broken down ... As soon as the working class regained ... its senses, its resistance began. (Marx 1986: 184).

Thus, instead of a mechanical determination of the working day by the system requirements of capitalist accumulation, the actual working day is the product of class struggle, historically led, in this instance, by English trade unions. 'The capitalist maintains his rights as purchaser when he tries to make the working day as long as possible ... On the other hand, the peculiar nature of the commodity sold implies a limit to its consumption ... and the labourer maintains his rights as seller when he wishes to reduce the working day ... There is here, therefore, an antinomy, right against right ... Between equal right, force decides' (Marx 1986: 163–4). What is lacking here is only an unpacking of what is the 'peculiar nature' of the labour-power commodity.

The peculiar nature is of course constituted by the fact that labour power is always connected to a labourer who is not an inert thing (despite capital's construction of it as such) but a living being that can join with fellow labourers to alter their conditions of life. Labourers are human beings that *feel* their exploitation and alienation and react against it as harm that violates their integrity and interests as human beings. In this view, the struggle to limit the working day is not a mechanical reflex against capitalist laws, but a conscious effort to create free time for education, self-development, mutualistic interaction and cultural cultivation.[5] As Lebowitz argues, 'what happens during free time is a process of production, a process in which the nature and the capability of the worker is altered. It is "time for the full production of the individual"' (2003: 68). If the entire point of socialism is to replace a society in which need-satisfaction is subordinate to the accumulation of capital, to ensure that resources and social institutions enable the expression and enjoyment of human life-capacities in forms of activity that are meaningful to the agents and valuable to the lives of others over an open-ended human future, then struggles that free the life-time of mortal individuals from alienated labour, even if they do not lead to the revolutionary overthrow of capitalism, cannot be regarded as irrelevant to that overall project, precisely because they accomplish to a limited extent that which the struggle for a socialist alternative to capitalism hopes to realize absolutely: the satisfaction of the social conditions for all round self-realizing freedom.

Still, it remains true that, as Marx argued, while organizing waged workers at the point of production was necessary, if the trade

---

5   For more on the centrality of free time to the structure of a free human life see Noonan 2009; 2012.

unions failed to carry such political momentum forward beyond the workplace it could potentially impede future gains. This meant at every opportunity turning seemingly 'economic' gains into political openings that could translate advances for a small number of workers into larger ones for the benefit of the class as a whole. But while industrial unions became increasingly larger and more organized, the failure to translate these gains to the non-waged, especially for women and racial/ethnic groups, deepened existing cleavages among the working classes (see Federici, this volume). This played a dual role. First, in fomenting internal working-class resentment aimed at a so-called 'labour aristocracy' that apparently benefitted at the expense of the non-unionized and unpaid and, second, in leading some unions into 'partnerships' with capital (mediated by an allegedly 'neutral' state) in the hopes that such improvements would continue.

The contradictions of trade union struggle are nicely illustrated by the struggle for higher wages. The struggle for higher real wages is not only an 'economistic struggle' to put more money in the pockets of workers as individual consumers, it is a struggle against their dependence on capital for the satisfaction of human life-requirements. In that respect it is, like the struggle for free time, a struggle *within* capitalism *against* the control that capital and capitalists can exert on human life. 'The struggle of workers to satisfy their many-sided needs are thus struggles against the position of capital as mediator within society. They are class struggles ... Rather than directed only against *particular* capitals, they are struggles against capital *as a whole*', even if they are directed in their immediate form against this or that company (Lebowitz 2003: 186). Any success in improving real wages means that economic wealth (produced by the collective labour of workers) is channelled out of the circuits of private capital accumulation towards workers' power to better satisfy their own fundamental human needs (which are typically priced commodities in capital).[6]

---

6 This conclusion assumes that the money is not recaptured by ecologically destructive consumer industries. The coherence of Lebowitz's position (and Marx's for that matter) depends upon making explicit the distinction between mere use value and life-value. Life-value is a term that was first developed by John McMurtry. That which has life-value either a) satisfies a real life-requirement, or b) is the enjoyed expression of a core life-capacity (see McMurtry 2011: 214). To illustrate the relevant point here: cyanide has a use

Lives are good or bad to the extent that they involve the enjoyed expression of life-capacities. The enjoyment and expression of life-capacities presupposes the satisfaction of life-requirements. Capital subordinates the satisfaction of human needs to the conditions of its own reproduction and expansion. Only combined struggle against these forces can ensure that workers are able to better satisfy their needs and realize their life-capacities. Hence, collective struggles for higher real wages can materially improve the life-conditions and lives of workers within capitalism and are thus essential components of the overall struggle against capitalism's control over life-conditions; an essential component of the struggle *towards* socialism.

However, the paradox for Marx, no less than Engels, was that despite radical initiatives like the struggle to free life-time from capital by shortening the working day, overall, rather than developing the capacities of workers as class organizations, unions were integrating the logic of capital into trade union practices (e.g. tying wage gains to increases in productivity and encouraging competition rather than demanding the abolishment of the wage-labour system). In other words, although unions emerged out of the working class, they were not representing the interests of the class as a whole but rather the sectionalist interests of their own members. Even if some legislative and social gains were extended to the non-unionized and unwaged, in the eyes of Marx they would always be conjunctural and under attack. In narrowly devoting their energies to maximizing the value of workers' commodified labour power, unions were increasingly failing to come to terms with the systemic tendencies that progressively undermined the extension of those gains to the non-unionized, un(der)employed and those who work but are not paid (e.g. caregivers and domestic workers responsible for social reproduction).[7]

---

value, but when used against human beings, no life-value, since its only use would be to kill people. For a complete defence of this position, which we do not have time to pursue here, see Noonan 2011.

7 'In the outside department of the factory, of the manufactory, and of the warehouse, the so-called domestic workers, whose employment is at the best irregular, are entirely dependent for their raw material and their orders on the caprice of the capitalist, who, in this industry, is not hampered by any regard for depreciation of his buildings and machinery, and risks nothing by a stoppage of work, but the skin of the worker himself. Here then he sets

Combined, these pressures worked to depoliticize and declass trade unions, while integrating workers into the dependent orbit of capital.[8] This was accompanied by the general integration (and in some cases co-optation) of labour unions across much of North America and Europe with social democratic parties that accepted the logic of capital (see Fanelli 2015), and thereby an electoral landscape that marginalized class-oriented labour struggles that sought to transcend capitalist social relations in favour of incrementalism and trade unionism as an end in itself.[9] For Marx, when unions focused almost exclusively on workplace gains, particularly those economic in nature, exclusion from the benefits of unionization would arouse working-class resentment. And although trade union gains often translated into some concessions from capital or legislative benefits for the non-unionized and non-waged, these would come to be associated with the party in power rather than the class struggles that precipitated their making.

While workplace-based struggles, protective legislation and, much later, the 'welfare state' took the sharp edges off of capitalist exploitation (albeit for an increasingly limited number of workers), it did not put an end to the main thing that had to be eliminated:

The reproduction of a mass of labour power, which must incessantly re-incorporate itself with capital for that capital's self-expansion;

---

himself systematically to work to form an industrial reserve force that shall be ready at a moment's notice; during one part of the year he decimates this force by the most inhuman toil, during the other part, he lets it starve for want of work' (Marx 1986: 315).

8 As Marx put it: 'Too exclusively bent upon the local and immediate struggles with capital, the Trades' Unions have not yet fully understood their power of acting against the system of wages slavery itself. They therefore kept too much aloof from general social and political movements' (1866b).

9 'The trade unions are an aristocratic minority. The poorer workers cannot join them: the great mass of workers, driven daily by economic developments from the villages into the cities, remain outside the trade unions for a long time, and the poorest of all never belong to them. The same goes for the workers born in London's East End, where one out of ten belongs to the trade unions. The farm workers, the day laborers, never belong to these trade unions. The trade unions by standing alone are powerless – they will remain a minority. They do not have the mass of proletarians behind them' (Marx in Lapides 1987: 82).

which cannot get free from capital, and whose enslavement to capital is only concealed by the variety of individual capitalists to whom it sells itself, this reproduction of labour power forms, in fact, an essential of the reproduction of capital itself. Accumulation of capital is, therefore, increase of the proletariat. (Marx 1986: 435)[10]

For Marx, if trade unions were going to have a progressive future they needed to recognize that while they could bargain within the wages system they could not escape the political and economic forces that stymied the continued enhancement of wages and working and living conditions owing to the structural exploitation at the root of capital accumulation. The challenge before unions, then, was to simultaneously improve the working conditions of their members while extending those gains to the non-unionized, un(der)employed and unwaged as part of generating a socialist class consciousness. Unless unions made an effort to broaden their aims and advocate on behalf of and in accordance with all of society's oppressed, unions risked degenerating into almost reactionary enclaves of privilege, upholding the manifest divisions of the working class and stunting its political development. Rather than applying palliatives, trade unions must cure the malady:

Apart from their original purpose, they [unions] must now learn to act deliberately as organizing centers of the working class in the

---

10   As Marx notes in *Capital*: 'A larger part of their own surplus-product, always increasing and continually transformed into additional capital, comes back to them in the shape of means of payment, so that they can extend the circle of their enjoyments; can make some additions to their consumption-fund of clothes, furniture, &c., and can lay by small reserve funds of money. But just as little as better clothing, food, and treatment, and a larger peculium, do away with the exploitation of the slave, so little do they set aside that of the wage worker. A rise in the price of labour, as a consequence of accumulation of capital, only means, in fact, that the length and weight of the golden chain the wage worker has already forged for himself, allow of a relaxation of the tension of it' (1986: 436). The shares earlier parallels with his Economic and Philosophic Manuscripts: 'An enforced increase of wages (disregarding all other difficulties, including the fact that it would only be by force, too, that such an increase, being an anomaly, could be maintained) would therefore be nothing but better payment for the slave, and would not win either for the worker or for labour their human status and dignity' (Marx 1964: 34).

broad interest of its complete emancipation. They must aid every social and political movement tending in that direction. Considering themselves as acting as the champions of the whole working class, they cannot fail to enlist the non-society men [the unorganized and unwaged] into their ranks. They must look carefully after the interests of the worst paid trades, such as agricultural laborers, rendered powerless by exceptional circumstances. They must convince the world at large that their efforts, far from being narrow and selfish, aim at the emancipation of the downtrodden millions. (Marx 1866b)

It is important to note however, as Hal Draper has reminded us, that for Marx 'the trade union movement was not the end of the road for the working class' (1978: 99), that is to say, it was not the revolutionary vanguard of an enlightened segment of the working class, but a crucial element in the building of organizational and political capacities capable of transcending capitalist social relations. As Marx and Engels stressed throughout their lives: 'The emancipation of the working class must be the work of the working class itself. We cannot, therefore, go along with people who openly claim that the workers are too ignorant to emancipate themselves but must first be emancipated from the top down, by the philanthropic big and petty bourgeois' (1879).[11]

---

11   As Marx (1864, with guidance from Engels) wrote a few years earlier: 'Considering, That the emancipation of the working classes must be conquered by the working classes themselves, that the struggle for the emancipation of the working classes means not a struggle for class privileges and monopolies, but for equal rights and duties, and the abolition of all class rule; That the economical subjection of the man of labour to the monopolizer of the means of labour – that is, the source of life – lies at the bottom of servitude in all its forms, of all social misery, mental degradation, and political dependence; That the economical emancipation of the working classes is therefore the great end to which every political movement ought to be subordinate as a means; That all efforts aiming at the great end hitherto failed from the want of solidarity between the manifold divisions of labour in each country, and from the absence of a fraternal bond of union between the working classes of different countries; That the emancipation of labour is neither a local nor a national, but a social problem, embracing all countries in which modern society exists, and depending for its solution on the concurrence, practical and theoretical, of the most advanced countries; That the present revival of the working classes in the most industrious countries of Europe, while it raises a

Although Marx recognized the progressive potential of trade unions, he was sanguine about their political limitations. 'Trades Unions work well as centers of resistance against the encroachments of capital ... They fail generally from limiting themselves to a guerilla war against the effects of the existing system, instead of simultaneously trying to change it, instead of using their organized forces as a lever for the final emancipation of the working class that is to say the ultimate abolition of the wages system' (1866a). Marx recognized full well that the capital-labour relationship extended far beyond the realm of paid employment. And even though class exploitation lay at the core of Marx's analysis, this was an intersectional class approach (albeit imperfect) from the very beginning. 'Marx's mature social theory revolved around a concept of totality that not only offered considerable scope for particularity and difference, but also made those particulars – race, ethnicity or nationality – determinants for the totality' (Anderson 2010: 244; see also Brown 2013).

If organized labour is going to have a progressive future, it would need to be anchored in a politics that oriented its struggles towards the emancipation of the working class as a whole; linking trade union activism with socialism as part of a revolutionary programme. Marx was apprehensive, however, about a politics based on differences alone and sought the means through which the diversity of the working class could be transformed via a class project that recognized how multiple registers of privilege and oppression were socially and politically interconnected. In other words, how to build a working-class social and political formation united in difference.

Conclusion: Socialism and the Continuum of Democratic Struggle

The need, therefore, for workers to go beyond traditional trade union based forms of struggle is unquestionable. At the same time, we exist

---

new hope, gives solemn warning against a relapse into the old errors, and calls for the immediate combination of the still disconnected movements; For these reasons – the International Working Men's Association ... declares: That all societies and individuals adhering to it will acknowledge truth, justice, and morality as the basis of their conduct toward each other and toward all men, without regard to color, creed, or nationality; That it acknowledges no rights without duties, no duties without rights.'

at a moment of history where vanguard revolutionary parties have been discredited, and there is no evidence, in the European and North American contexts, that their fortunes will ever be revived. Thus the question remains: if trade unions and social democracy are incapable of solving the problems they address themselves to because they are not revolutionary, and the historical moment of vanguardist politics seems to have definitively passed, how is the struggle for socialism to be conducted today? The answer to that question lies in the creative intelligence of people in struggle; no theoretical intervention can substitute itself for political practice. What we aim to do in conclusion is not infer a new mode of struggle from abstract principles but instead try to draw out the implicitly radical significance of the struggles within capitalism (for higher wages, for free time, for public institutions) in support of the conclusion that socialism is part and parcel of the struggle for democracy, and the struggle for democracy (as all political struggles) should be understood along a continuum. Reconceiving the goals of struggle as progressively realizable frees the idea of revolution from the nineteenth century image of it as a one-off cataclysm, opening space for new ideas of organization and political strategy that are neither social democratic nor vanguardist (see Hudis, this volume).

Here again, Lebowitz is an instructive starting point. He notes that even when struggles do not 'transcend the capital/wage labour relation', they can be significant for the life-value of working people's lives because they express the fact that 'a qualitative development ... takes place in the course of such struggle' (2003: 99). The qualitative development is that workers improve the conditions of their own lives, create life-time and life-space for self-realizing activity and mutualistic interaction, and thus both teach themselves that society is not impervious to collective struggle, *and* make their lives better by realizing some elements of the socialist ideal in their day to day reality.

Since every human life is finite, lived by mortal individuals, rev-olutionary politics must take into account both the short and the long term. Immanuel Wallerstein puts the point well: 'People live in the present', he argued. 'Everybody has to eat today, not tomorrow. Everybody has to sleep today, not tomorrow. Everybody has to do all these just ordinary things today, and you can't just tell people that they have to wait another five or ten or twenty years, and it is going to get better ... So you've got to worry about today, but you can't worry only about today' (quoted in Boggs 2012: 197). No one can be expected to sacrifice the whole of their present life for the sake of a distant future that they will never experience. A politics capable of motivating people must demonstrate its capacity to improve workers' lives in their own here and now and not just function as a way-station on the way to a promised transcendence. Hence the struggle for free time by shortening the working day without loss of real wages has historically been (and could become again, if it were taken up once more by a revivified trades union movement) a victory over the power of capital over the whole of human life. So too the struggle for higher wages. If it is understood as a struggle against the power of capital over human life and not an end in itself or instrumental to higher levels of life-destructive consumption of capitalist commodities, it becomes a basis and a building block for more radical demands. Such struggles can become bases and building blocks if they are used as occasions to raise critical questions: why is it that capitalism permits both mass unemployment and resists shortening the working week without loss of real wages? Why is it that real wages have stagnated while corporate profits have soared? Why is it that capitalism continues to ravage the planet (see Holleman, this volume) even though there is an unshakeable scientific consensus that without drastic socio-economic changes a massive life-crisis awaits us in the not too distant future? When workplace struggles are connected to these sorts of questions workers can realize – without being preached at or otherwise dogmatically exhorted to overthrow capitalism – that the real *implications of their struggles* contest the power of capital over human (and planetary) life.

Let us take another example to further illustrate the point – the struggle for universally accessible public institutions. Here too trade unions have historically played a decisive role. What does the creation of universally accessible public institutions mean? The re-channelling of wealth away from private accumulation towards life-requirement satisfaction on the basis of *need*, not the ability to pay. In other words, the funding of universally accessible public institutions through taxation is another inroad against the power of capital over life. When education, health care, access to cultural institutions, and pensions are taken out of the cycle of commodified exchange and made available to all people *on the basis and to the extent of their needs for them*, real life improves: 'The public provision of goods and services, well-managed in a way that fosters sustainable development and social justice initiatives, and which is accountable to the community, significantly improves standards of living' (Fanelli 2016: 86). Such improvements take society some way towards instantiating the principle of socialist society: 'from each according to their abilities, to each according to their needs' (Marx 1875). Of course, public institutions do not *fully realize* that principle, but nor do they *fully ignore it*, as commodified exchange does. Nor are actually existing public institutions free of invidious, often racialized and sexualized, oppressive hierarchies of power (see Sears 2014: 56, 88). Nevertheless, they do represent a victory over what Lebowitz calls the 'mediating power' of capital, i.e., the way it makes people dependent on the possession of money, as opposed to nature and each other, for their life-support.

The road to socialism thus lies along a continuum of struggle against the power capital exerts over people's ability to satisfy their real life-needs and express and enjoy their life-capacities. This struggle brings to light the deepest contradiction of capitalism, that it masks the real relations of dependence of human life on nature and collective labour with its own structurally imposed dependence on access to labour and commodity markets. Once workers peer behind this curtain of capitalist reification, they see that the real purpose of labour is not the production of private money-value for the capitalist, but life-capital – 'the *life wealth that produces more life wealth without loss and with cumulative gain*' (McMurty 2015) – for the need-based appropriation and use of all. Whatever struggles expose this contradiction, recapture wealth and resources for the production of life-capital, and create universally accessible pathways for all to appropriate life-capital are elements of the struggle for a socialist society.

In sum, we have argued that the struggle for socialism must be reconceived as a struggle along a continuum. The 'political economy of the working class', implied but largely absent from *Capital*, focuses on the ways in which organized collective struggle can divert wealth from the circuits of capital to the circuits of collective life-capital through which real human beings preserve and develop themselves. Life can be better or worse in capitalism, and struggle that makes life better without overthrowing it should not be dismissed as 'reformist' but understood as part of a continuum of struggle *towards* socialism. People do not fight, normally, for abstractions or slogans, but for achievable goals that will improve their lives. To radicalize the struggle does not mean radicalizing slogans, but treating each victory as a plateau on which to rest for a moment before extending the counter-logic of public provision, need-satisfaction, and democratic control over wealth and resources further into the life-space and life-time dominated by capital.

While union density has declined in the twenty-first century, there are still millions of workers organized by trade unions, a reserve army of *labour activists* that needs to be activated by a more dynamic and creative leadership – mobilized and in turn led by a more active and interventionist rank-and-file – than we find in most unions. Activating this political potential, like rebuilding a socialist movement, must also be conceived along a continuum of more or less, better or worse, as an antidote to all-or-nothing conceptions of revolution. Marx conceived of the struggle of socialism as an extension of the struggle for democracy and understood that effective struggle must be oriented by concretely realizable goals. As Nimtz concludes, 'Draper's point about Marx's democratic credentials are instructive: "Marx was the first socialist figure to come to an acceptance of the socialist idea *through* the battle for the extension of democratic control from below"' (2000: 299). Neither trade unions nor social democracy has ever consistently posed the problem of democratic control of the economy from below, but instead limited themselves to demands which appear to be nothing but 'capitalism with a human face' (Lebowitz 2003: 168). Nevertheless, as we have tried to show, and as *Capital* implies but does not spell out, struggles within capitalism make a difference to workers' lives. If socialists are driven by the goal of establishing the conditions for the all-round satisfaction of human needs and the comprehensive development and enjoyment of life-capacities, these struggles cannot be ignored and the struggle for socialism rethought as *struggles* along a continuum rather than a once and for all cataclysm.

References

Anderson, K. B. (2010). *Marx at the Margins: On Nationalism, Ethnicity and Non-Western Societies*. Chicago: University of Chicago Press.

Boggs, L. (2012). *The Next American Revolution*. Berkeley: University of California Press.

Brown, H. (2013). *Marx on Gender and the Family: A Critical Study*. Chicago: Haymarket Books.

Draper, H. (1978). *Karl Marx's Theory of Revolution, Vol II: The Politics of Social Classes*. New York: Monthly Review Press.

Engels, F. (1977 [1845]). *The Condition of the Working Class in England*. Moscow: Progress Publishers.

Fanelli, C. (2015). The Radical Keynes: An Appraisal. *Workplace: A Journal for Academic Labour*, 25: 69–81.

Fanelli, C. (2016). *Megacity Malaise: Neoliberalism, Labour and Public Services in Toronto*. Halifax and Winnipeg: Fernwood Publishing.

Gramsci, A. (1917). The Revolution Against *Capital*. https://www.marxists. org/archive/gramsci/1917/12/revolution-against-capital.htm

Lapides, K. (ed.) (1987). *Marx and Engels on Trade Unions*. New York: Praeger Publishers.

Lebowitz, M. (1992). *Beyond Capital: Marx's Political Economy of the Working Class*. New York: St. Martin's Press.

Lebowitz, M. (2003). *Beyond Capital: Marx's Political Economy of the Working Class*, 2nd edition. New York: Palgrave Macmillan.

McMurty, J. (2011). *What is Good, What is Bad – The Value of All Values Across Times, Places, and Theories*. Oxford: EOLSS Publishers.

McMurty, J. (2015). Breaking Out of the Invisible Prison: The Ten-Point Global Paradigm Revolution. http://www.socialistproject.ca/bullet/1085. php

Marx, K. (1864). 1864 General Rules. http://www.marxists.org/archive/marx/works/1864/10/27b.htm

Marx, K. (1866a). *Value, Price and Profit*. https://www.marxists.org/archive/marx/works/download/pdf/value-price-profit.pdf

Marx, K. (1866b). The Different Questions. http://www.marxists.org/archive/marx/iwma/documents/1866/instructions.htm#o6

Marx, K. (1875). *Critique of the Gotha Programme*. https://www.marxists. org/archive/marx/works/download/Marx_Critque_of_the_Gotha_Programme.pdf

Marx, K. (1964). *The Economic and Philosophic Manuscripts of 1844*. New York: International Publishers.

Marx, K. (1986). *Capital, Volume 1*. Moscow: Progress Publishers.

Marx, K. and Engels, F. (1879). Strategy and Tactics of the Class Struggle. https://www.marxists.org/archive/marx/works/1879/09/17.htm

Nimtz, A. H. (2000). *Marx and Engels: Their Contribution to the Democratic Breakthrough*. Albany: State University of New York Press.

Noonan, J. (2009). Free Time as a Condition for a Free Human Life. *Contemporary Political Theory*, 8(4): 377–93.

Noonan, J. (2011). Use-Value, Life Value, and the Future of Socialism. *Rethinking Marxism*, 23(1): 117–34.

Noonan, J. (2012). *Materialist Ethics and Life-Value.* Montreal and Kingston: McGill-Queens University Press.

Sears, A. (2014). *The Next New Left: A History of the Future.* Halifax and Winnipeg: Fernwood Publishing.

Wood, E. M. (2002). *The Origin of Capitalism: A Longer View.* London: Verso.

9

Capital and Ecology

Hannah Holleman

In *Capital*, Marx set out to examine scientifically and critically 'the capitalist mode of production, and the relations of production and forms of intercourse [*Verkehrsverhältnisse*] that correspond to it' (Marx 1990: 90). In so doing he explained systematically why bourgeois civilization and barbarity go hand in hand – a fact taken for granted as much by nineteenth-century elites as by those seeking to transform society (Beckert 2014: 244). Today the ecological and social violence of the system of capital is difficult to comprehend fully, much less bring to an end, without access to analyses benefitting directly or indirectly from Marx's theoretical, methodological and empirical advances. These contributions have profoundly shaped many scholarly and scientific disciplines and been a resource for activists in nearly every progressive and anti-colonial movement of the past century and a half.

Scientists, scholars and activists building on early Marxian traditions continue to make important breakthroughs in our understanding of the relationship between social, economic and ecological crises. Their insights, often with origins in Marx's own work, now seem common sense to many, even those unaware of their intellectual provenance or political implications. Moreover, thanks to the work of ecosocialist thinkers and activists, especially in the last 20 years, there is now a growing knowledge of, and interest in, the role of Marxist and socialist traditions in the development of ecological thought and activism.

As we mark the 150th anniversary of the publication of Marx's *Capital*, this chapter highlights its critical importance for the environmental movement as it seeks a way forward amidst issues such as the ritualized ineffectiveness of international climate negotiations, the segregation of the global environmental movement, and the disorienting onslaught of claims that capitalism will solve, or is solving, the socio-ecological crises it engenders. Connecting these issues, I draw on Marx's work and contemporary analyses to explain what every environmentalist needs to know about ecological imperialism, and the necessity of a deep commitment to transcending the racialized division of humanity and nature at the heart of the ecological rift of capitalism. Such a commitment is the first step towards overcoming imperialist environmental 'politics as usual' in order to transform 'business as usual'.

While many environmentalists are concerned about over-crowded cities, urban slums, poverty and poor sanitation, fewer inquire about the origins of these conditions. Without an historical analysis such as that presented in *Capital*, mass displacement, poverty and inequality seem a natural and inevitable feature of modern society. The general problem is often seen as one of poor communities and countries 'catching up', but the relationship between the wealth of some areas and the impoverishment of others, or the growth of urban slums and the transformation of the countryside (especially the privatization of the commons) is rarely discussed.

As a result, the fact that social domination is prerequisite for ecological degradation is obscured for many environmentalists, and conceptions of environmental justice tend to be shallow and ahistorical. Marx's *Capital* provides the basis for a much deeper understanding of contemporary socio-ecological change and for developing a movement that is honest regarding our history – a movement focused on the reparation of injustice and oppression, working against the logic of capital and building solidarity in the struggle for an ecological society.

Old Dog, New Tricks:
Imperialism and the UN Climate Agreement

The 2015 Climate Change Conference in Paris (COP 21) was widely reported as representing a crossroads for civilization with respect to taking action on climate change. Representatives of 195 nations signed up to an agreement that prominent climate scientist James Hansen called 'a fraud really, a fake ... just worthless words' (quoted in Milman 2015b). In contrast to Hansen and other climate scientists, leaders of the wealthiest countries and of some environmental NGOs have referred to the Paris agreement as a 'turning point'. Kumi Naidoo, then executive director of Greenpeace International, said 'the wheel of climate action turns slowly, but in Paris it has turned' (Greenpeace International 2015). UN Secretary General Ban Ki-Moon declared that the Paris agreement 'set the world on a new path, to a low-emissions, climate-resilient future' (quoted in Worland 2015).

However, rather than imposing immediate cuts in emissions at their source, or supporting the global movement to 'keep it in the ground' (known fossil fuel deposits), the Paris scheme relies on technological and market approaches that the text of the agreement itself admits are inadequate to prevent a rise in emissions and global temperature that climate scientists have referred to as 'dangerous to deadly', especially for the world's poorest people (New York Times 2015; Randerson 2015). But there are other serious problems with the mechanisms outlined, and more broadly with the so-called greening of capitalism.

In May 2016, the 15th session of the United Nations Permanent Forum on Indigenous Issues convened in New York City. Concern for issues related to ecological imperialism were prominent in this series of meetings. Representatives from indigenous communities around the world protested ongoing violations of their rights to land, water, clean air, self-determination and to existence itself. In particular, indigenous leaders described the continuation of old struggles against incursions now routinely taking place under green cover. Calfin Lafkenche, a Mapuche leader from Chile, summarized the points reiterated by other participants:

> We are here today in the UN to stop the offensive of the Green Economy and its market systems of carbon trading, carbon offsets, the Clean Development Mechanism, and REDD+, which constitute a new form of colonialism and have caused conflicts, forced relocation, threats to the cultural survival and violations of the rights of Indigenous peoples, especially the rights to life, to lands and territories, and to free, prior and informed consent. (Indigenous Environmental Network 2016)

The 2015 Paris climate agreement was protested as an embodiment of this new colonialism.

At the UN forum, Alberto Saldamando, human and indigenous rights expert and attorney with the Indigenous Environmental Network, said:

> The Paris Agreement is a trade agreement, nothing more. It promises to privatize, commodify and sell forest and agriculture lands as carbon offsets in fraudulent schemes ... These offset scams provide financial laundering mechanisms for developed countries to launder their carbon pollution in the Global South. Case-in-point, the United States' climate change plan includes 250 million megatons to be absorbed by oceans and forest offset markets. Essentially, those responsible for the climate crisis not only get to buy their way out of compliance but they also get to profit from it as well. (Indigenous Environmental Network 2016)

Moreover, the agreement ignores the production of fossil fuels, which are extracted via methods that often violate indigenous and national sovereignty, and that appropriate and destroy the commons for private profit.

Discussions of solutions to the climate crisis that ignore the broader socio-ecological crises caused by capitalist energy extraction help obscure the deeper injustices of the global energy economy. How do you 'offset' imperialist wars for oil or recent legal changes pushed by energy companies around the world (aided by the US State Department, especially when led by Hillary Clinton from 2009 to 2013) to allow more fracking (Blake 2014)? And what about the displacement of communities and vast ecological destruction that continue as biofuel production expands to fulfil countries' mandates for renewable fuel under the banner of environmental stewardship and meeting emissions targets (Holleman 2012)?

As a result of all such developments, today indigenous communities are faced with a two-sided conflict, described succinctly by Tom B.K. Goldtooth, executive director of the Indigenous Environmental Network:

> For centuries, Indigenous Peoples have suffered from colonialism and genocide. Now the United Nations itself is promoting false solutions to climate change that imperil the very survival of our

peoples and Mother Earth. We are on the frontlines of protracted conflicts with governments and extractive industries that want to steal our land, territories and resources. We are also on the frontlines of climate change and the false solutions to climate change like REDD. (Indigenous Environmental Network 2016)

All of this points to imperialism as central to the ecological crisis, or what Marxists and others refer to as the ecological rift of capitalism. It shows that attempting to address ecological crises without challenging the social order serves to reinforce the undemocratic social relations of capital, simply displacing or shifting crises socially, geographically or temporarily.

Understanding why this is the case under capitalism should be an urgent goal for all environmentalists. If we don't understand the historically specific political and economic dynamics of the society in which we live, we cannot effectively organize, even for reform. Committed organizers for social change, past and present, have understood this. Another urgent and related goal should be understanding why the mainstream environmental movement, in spite of claims to support 'environmental justice', has so far failed to fight consistently in solidarity with the most oppressed communities for a more radically democratic society – for an alternative to a system with such toxic priorities. This lack of solidarity has had grave consequences for the efficacy of the movement and hence for the planet. Along the same lines, why have prominent environmentalists helped political elites declare the Paris agreement a victory and obscure 1) the lack of substantive ecological content in the agreement, and 2) its oppressive and imperialistic implications?

It is these sorts of crucial questions that *Capital* helps us answer, by explaining the historical development of capitalist political economy – the separation of the mass of people from the land, the division of humanity, and how 'the advance of capitalist production develops a working class which by education, tradition and habit looks upon the requirements of that mode of production as self-evident natural laws' (Marx 1990: 899). The following highlights sections of *Capital* that serve as starting points for understanding the continued relevance of Marx's comprehensive research and socio-ecological analysis to today's environmental movement. We begin with Marx's description of the essential, distinctive features of capitalist society and explanation of why, as capitalism displaces alternative modes of provisioning, ecological degradation follows and reformist politics prove unable to keep pace with the destruction.

The Origins of *Capital*

The first chapter of Volume 1 of *Capital* is titled simply 'The Commodity'. Marx begins his analysis with the commodity in the first few chapters because it is the 'economic cell-form' of bourgeois (capitalist) society (1990: 90). Distinguishing the capitalist mode of production from earlier economic forms, for the first time in human history commodity production – production of goods for sale on the market to realize a profit – is generalized, dominating the economic and social landscape.

Money becomes capital in the process of production as it is invested to realize profit, some of which is reinvested for more profit, etc. The cycle endlessly repeats, periodically interrupted by crises. The accumulation of capital, rather than meeting human needs, becomes the predominant end towards which production and all economic activity is geared in capitalist society. Though it is the result of the labour of the direct producers, profit is appropriated and accumulated by those who own and control society's primary means of production (the capitalists), rather than the producers themselves (workers). Because the goal is to increase profit, capitalists are compelled to extract as much labour as possible from workers and to minimize costs by means including lowering wages, externalizing costs of production (including ecological costs), and avoiding taxes.

Moreover, since commodity production implies production for sale on the market, rather than to meet direct needs, selling as much as possible, at the highest price, becomes the priority of every capitalist and another means of extracting wealth from workers. Massive efforts are made and are necessary to coerce or convince people to consume more and more commodities – from destroying or making illegal alternative means of subsistence, to employing a vast network of scientifically sophisticated and manipulative advertising. It doesn't matter, as Marx writes, whether the commodities fulfil a need that 'arises from the stomach or the imagination' (1990: 125). The value of the commodity realized in exchange, as distinct from its actual value in use, becomes the measure of all things.

At the level of society as a whole, the main concern of economic accounting is exchange value expressed in monetary terms. Thus, the opening line of Marx's opus observes that 'the wealth of societies in which the capitalist mode of production prevails appears as an "immense collection of commodities"' (1990: 125). It is the same in our time, with the collection of commodities produced (goods and services) presented as the Gross Domestic Product (GDP) and Gross National Product (GNP) of nations, representing the national wealth, but telling us nothing of the social or ecological consequences associated with each increase in GDP. As political economist and activist Marilyn Waring (1995) analysed so well in her critique of the UN's system of national accounts, even 'misfortune causes growth' in GDP and is recorded as a positive in the ledger. She uses the Exxon-Valdez oil spill as an example. The high costs of legal proceedings, clean up and compensation, as well as the earnings of media companies covering the disaster, all contributed to the growth of GDP.

More recently, in response to the BP oil spill in the Gulf of Mexico, JP Morgan's US chief economist assured readers of the *Wall Street Journal* and others concerned with the health of the economy that, while 'the spill clearly implies a lot of economic hardship in some locations … given what we know today, the magnitude of these setbacks looks dwarfed by the scale of the US macroeconomy', and, 'if anything U.S. GDP could gain slightly from it' (Feroli quoted in Di Leo 2010).

Sociologists John Bellamy Foster and Brett Clark have discussed the distinction made by early political economists between public wealth (consisting of use values such as clean air, water, food) and private riches (monetary gain based in the exchange value of commodities). For example, in 1804 political economist John Maitland, the Earl of Lauderdale, 'argued that there was an inverse correlation between public wealth and private riches such that an increase in the latter often served to diminish the former' (Foster and Clark 2009). In the history of economics this is referred to as the Lauderdale Paradox. Nevertheless, increasing GDP (economic growth) is one of the primary ends towards which politics and economics in capitalist societies are set.

The opening chapters of Marx's *Capital* reveal the mystification of society implied by the reduction of social processes (i.e. labour) to the market value of their product, which is then treated independently of those social processes in economic and policy analyses. Marx decries the ahistorical treatment of capital by bourgeois economists – of the privatization of public wealth (commons) and the fruits of our collective labour – as natural and inevitable. As against the prevailing ideology, he shows the historical specificity of this state of affairs and the true origins of capital.

Marx explains the precondition of our historically unique society, wherein most of us must work for those who own the means of production with almost no control over the conditions or products of our labour, in Part Eight of *Capital*:

> In themselves money and commodities are no more capital than the means of production and subsistence are. They need to be transformed into capital. But this transformation can take place only under particular circumstances, which meet together at this point: the confrontation of, and the contact between, two very different kinds of commodity owners; on the one hand, the owners of money, means of production, means of subsistence, who are eager to valorize the sum of values they have appropriated by buying the labour-power of others; on the other hand, free workers, the sellers of their own labour-power, and therefore the sellers of labour. (1990: 874)

By 'free workers', Marx means those no longer constrained by lords or guilds, no longer connected to the land; they are not free in the broader sense. He makes clear, 'the starting point of the development that gave rise both to the wage labourer and to the capitalist was the enslavement of the worker. The advance made consisted in a change in the form of this servitude, in the transformation of feudal exploitation into capitalist exploitation' (1990: 875). In tracing the historical unfolding of these circumstances Marx provides foundational insight into the origins of the massive expansion of ecological degradation and social violence that are part and parcel of capitalist development, and why transcending such a system is difficult, yet necessary and possible.

The origins of capital, and its control by an elite minority of the population, are explained in the ideological and justificatory myth of 'primitive accumulation'. The myth tells us that those at the top, with accumulated capital, got there through their own industry and abstinence – they worked hard and saved – while others wasted their time or the fruits of their labour. Marx explains that 'in actual history, it is a notorious fact that conquest, enslavement, robbery, murder, in short, force, play the greatest part' (1990: 874). Using England as the primary illustration before extending his analysis to the global level, Marx provides a crucial social and legal history of the forcible removal from the land of the English agricultural population through the process of enclosure and eviction, and their concentration in towns and urban centres. This is a critical contribution and historical corrective as it undermines attempts to naturalize capitalism and class society, and to justify the exploitation of the labour of others, the control of society by political and economic elites, inequality, poverty and environmental destruction.

In the towns and cities, Marx explains by making rather commonplace observations for his time, the newly expropriated of all ages were coerced to labour under the most vile conditions both through legal means that restricted their movements and activities, often involving violent enforcement, and by the privatization of land so that there was no alternative means of subsistence. In sum, 'so-called primitive accumulation ... is nothing else than the historical process of divorcing the producer from the means of production'. Unlike earlier social and economic formations, 'the capital-relation presupposes a complete separation between the workers and ownership of the conditions for the realization of their own labour. As soon as capitalist production stands on its own feet, it not only maintains this separation, but reproduces it on a constantly extending scale' (Marx 1990: 874).

The Ecological Rift

Set in motion in the late fourteenth and early fifteenth centuries, this process of separating the mass of people from the land has enormous social and ecological consequences and continues around the globe. In place of the soil nutrient cycling associated with traditional farming, the displacement of the rural population and the commodification of agriculture meant that increasingly 'essential nutrients were shipped hundreds, even thousands, of miles and ended up as waste polluting cities' (Foster et al. 2011: 350).

Agricultural production for the capitalist market bears no relationship in its social and ecological consequences to subsistence agriculture, or farming to supply local markets. The purpose is different. It is volatile, subject to global market fluctuations. And there is an insatiable quality to it as long as there is money to make, or, because of the role of finance and taxes in agriculture, there are debts to pay. As a consequence, fields are planted when they should rest and herds are expanded when they should be culled, leading to the rapid degradation of the land. By the mid-nineteenth century European scientists were sounding the alarm with respect to 'the loss of soil nutrients – such as nitrogen, phosphorus, and potassium – through the transfer of food and fiber to the cities' (Foster et al. 2011: 350).

Nineteenth-century scientists viewed this disruption of the soil nutrient cycle as a system of robbery. Marx saw this transformation of agriculture under the aegis of capital as an original source of the rift in the metabolism between man and nature, or what we now call the 'ecological rift' of capitalism. He writes that due to the expropriation of the agricultural population from the land,

> Capitalist production collects the population together in great centres, and causes the urban population to achieve an ever-growing preponderance. This has two results. On the one hand it concentrates the historic motive force of society; on the other hand, it disturbs the metabolic interaction between man and the earth, i.e., prevents the return to the soil of its constituent elements consumed by man in the form of food and clothing; hence it hinders the operation of the eternal natural condition for the lasting fertility of the soil. (1990: 637)

In the third volume of *Capital* he reiterates,

> Large landed property reduces the agricultural population to an ever decreasing minimum and confronts it with an ever growing industrial population crammed together in large towns; in this way it produces conditions that provoke an irreparable rift in the interde-

pendent process of the social metabolism, a metabolism prescribed by the natural laws of life itself. The result of this is a squandering of the vitality of the soil, which is carried by trade far beyond the bounds of a single country. (1991: 949)

Analysed most extensively by John Bellamy Foster, along with Brett Clark, Paul Burkett and other scholars and activists, at the heart of Marx's ecological critique of capitalism, 'the central theoretical construct is that of a "rift" in the "metabolic interaction between man and the earth," or in the "social metabolism prescribed by the natural laws of life," through the removal from the soil of its constituent elements, requiring its "systematic restoration"' (Foster 1999: 378).

Marx's concept of metabolism and the metabolic rift developed out of his studies of the most advanced scientific developments of his time (especially agricultural chemistry). He uses the concept of metabolism to describe the material exchange of matter and energy between human society and the rest of nature, mediated by labour, that accompanies production and exchange. As Foster explains:

Since the *Grundrisse* in 1857–1858, Marx had given the concept of metabolism (*Stoffwechsel*) – first developed in the 1830s by scientists engaged in the new discoveries of cellular biology and physiology and then applied to chemistry (by Liebig especially) and physics – a central place in his account of the interaction between nature and society through production. He defined the labor process as the metabolic relation between humanity and nature. For human beings this metabolism necessarily took a socially mediated form, encompassing the organic conditions common to all life, but also taking a distinctly human-historical character through production … Building on this framework, Marx emphasized in *Capital* that the disruption of the soil cycle in industrialized capitalist agriculture constituted nothing less than 'a rift' in the metabolic relation between human beings and nature. (Foster 2013)

Marx's scientific investigations were linked in a holistic and dialectical way to his detailed research on social history and change. The development of capitalist agriculture in tandem with industry, and their impact on workers and the land, were for him central concerns.

Along with his advanced understanding of ecological crises as social in origin, Marx saw how capitalist solutions to crises tended to exacerbate them, making him an early critic of the idea that capitalism could or would go green, and of the deformation of science in capitalist society.

From the perspective of capitalist production, so long as it is profitable, the point is always to continue 'business as usual'. Efforts to address the root cause of crises – which are social in origin, and require social changes to address them – are usually avoided or stifled. Technological and market mechanisms are favoured that might resolve issues in the short run, but ultimately serve to deepen crises in the longer term (the Paris agreement is a recent illustration of this tendency). These mechanisms often depend on increased social disruption and domination. For example, capitalists addressed the early European soil crisis, caused by the expansion of agricultural production for profit, by seeking means to replace the lost nutrients of the soil with fertilizers, rather than rebuilding the basis for long-term soil health and fertility. Consequently, the soil has been increasingly exhausted with science applied more to masking the effects of this exhaustion rather than restoring natural soil fertility.

Today, abuses associated with the modern era's technologically advanced but socially and ecologically regressive farming for profit have led to the subjection of 90 per cent of global agricultural land to erosion, with 80 per cent affected by erosion classified as moderate to severe (Pimentel 2006: 123). From approximately 1975 to 2015 alone, the earth lost a third of arable land due to erosion and pollution (Milman 2015a). In other words, '30 percent of the world's arable land has become unproductive and much of that has been abandoned for agricultural use' (Pimentel 2006: 123). Moreover, the increased application of fertilizers, herbicides and pesticides has led to further crises as they chemically pollute the land and waterways, poison farmworkers, and lead to an evolutionary-chemical arms race as species adapt to pesticide and herbicide application by selecting for resistance to these chemicals.

Marx was an early articulator of the paradox, now routinely observed, that as our technological capability and scientific understanding of ecological crises expands, so do the crises themselves. In relation to the emerging agricultural science of the nineteenth century and the development of agricultural technology, Marx wrote,

> all progress in capitalist agriculture is, a progress in the art, not only of robbing the worker, but of robbing the soil; all progress in increasing the fertility of the soil for a given time is a progress towards ruining the more long-lasting sources of that fertility … Capitalist production, therefore, only develops the techniques and the degree of combination of social process of production by simultaneously undermining the original sources of all wealth – the soil and the worker. (1990: 639)

These issues spread via the rapacious expansion of capitalist agriculture via imperialism, with science often used to facilitate and justify colonial incursions, the extraction of local resources, and the murder, enslavement and starvation of local peoples.

Imperialism, the Ecological Rift and Agriculture

By the nineteenth century the degradation of land in Europe and the eastern United States resulting from the transformation of agriculture along capitalist lines motivated a search for new sources of agricultural inputs and products around the world. The ecological rift was generalized at the global level as the colonial powers sought to compensate for their environmental overdraft at home, feed the growing urban market, and develop new sources of raw materials for industry (e.g. cotton) by combing the earth for new inputs to replace lost soil nutrients in degraded fields, bringing under production new agricultural lands, and seeking new sources of slave or 'free' labour. The violent and ecologically destructive guano trade was one exemplary result of this push, the expansion of tropical plantation agriculture and the development of export-oriented agriculture in white settler colonies was another (Foster et al. 2011; Melillo 2012).

Consequently, '[t]he transfer of nutrients was tied to the accumulation process and increasingly took place on national and international levels' (Foster et al. 2011: 351). Marx observed that globalized capitalist agriculture benefits the 'main industrial countries, as it converts one part of the globe into a chiefly agricultural field of production for supplying the other part, which remains a pre-eminently industrial field' (1990: 579–80). This involved both the violent subjugation of peoples and the destruction of local industry and production. As in their home countries, in the colonies of Europe, Britain, the US and Japan, it took 'a staggering degree of violence' before whole populations were forced to abandon their traditional occupations and cultivate crops for export to global markets (Beckert 2014: 255, 308–9).[1]

Thus far I have emphasized Marx's work on the capitalist transformation of agriculture and how this helped shape his theoretical development. However, his eco-critical analysis of capitalism extends much further, to the broader unsustainable disruption of natural cycles and exploitation of resources and people. In this he was far ahead of his time, and more sophisticated than many contemporary analysts in seeing the interconnections between ecological issues and social oppression.

---

[1] There are many historical analyses further chronicling the details of Anglo-European, Japanese and American imperial incursion into various areas of the globe to expand cash crop agriculture, extract resources, access new sources of labour and pry open markets. Within the Marxist and broader anti-colonial traditions, a vast literature documents how the over-development of the global North is facilitated by the rape and pillage of the global South, with the collaboration of political and economic elites across borders. In line with the arguments of these traditions, and providing a new resource, historian Sven Beckert's prize-winning *Empire of Cotton: A Global History* (2014) makes a great contemporary companion reading to Marx's Capital. Beckert examines in detail the transformation of the global economy and countryside through the lens of cotton production, trade and textile manufacturing. Social scientists often divide the development of capitalism into early mercantile capitalism and later industrial capitalism, but Beckert argues, along lines that reaffirm Marx's historical observations, that the methods of so-called merchant capitalism are better designated 'war capitalism'. He explains that while there are many ideological explanations for why some countries are rich, while others are poor – or in the problematic language of the UN and the World Bank, 'more developed' or 'least developed' – the fact is that countries rich today became so because their 'capitalists and statesmen … built a comparative advantage with a willingness and ability to use force to extend their interests' (2014: 30). This point is crucial to understanding the modern world.

The Racialized Division of Nature and Humanity

In his analysis of primitive accumulation, or the origins of capital, Marx wrote:

> The discovery of gold and silver in America, the extirpation, enslavement and entombment in mines of the indigenous population of that continent, the beginnings of the conquest and plunder of India, and the conversion of Africa into a preserve for the hunting of blackskins, are all things which characterize the dawn of the era of capitalist production … Hard on their heels follows the commercial war of the European nations, which has the globe as its battlefield … These methods depend in part on brute force, for instance the colonial system. But they all employ the power of the state, the concentrated and organized force of society, to hasten, as in a hothouse, the process of transformation. (1990: 915)

By the early 1900s, 'the colonial powers, their colonies, and their former colonies extended over approximately 85 percent of the earth's surface' (Magdoff 1978: 34). All of this, the 'vast quest of the dark world's wealth and toil', was justified, as W. E. B. DuBois wrote, by the gospel of capitalist imperialism, white supremacy, proclaiming: 'whiteness is the ownership of the earth forever and ever, Amen!' (2003: 54, 45).

There is a vast body of research on the way elites in capitalist countries employ racism and gender chauvinism (promoting toxic forms of masculinity) to divide working people and subordinate groups within the wealthy countries, as well as to generate support (and participation via the military) for imperial warfare and domination globally. This has been so effective that modern ideas about race and gender, though socially constructed, have taken on a life of their own, with far-reaching and hateful consequences. The division of humanity associated with capitalist development, along lines of race, ethnicity, nationality, gender and sexuality, has had tremendous consequences for movements. Gender division predates capitalism, though taking on new form in the modern era, with restrictive Anglo-European notions of gender and the family imposed globally via imperialism and colonialism (Lugones 2007). Biological notions of race, however, emerge with the modern era as a justification for colonialism and enslavement (Dunbar-Ortiz 2003).

Marx understood well the consequences of such divisions. In the global economy workers are pitted against one another in a race to the bottom. US workers, for example, are encouraged to blame the even worse exploited Mexican or Chinese workers for their own low wages and lack of good employment. Wage differentials across different groups of workers thus serve to maintain working-class separation and undermine solidarity. This was no different in the nineteenth century.

Among other preyed upon lands and peoples, England colonized Ireland in order to make of the country 'a mere pasture land which provides the English market with meat and wool at the cheapest possible prices' (Marx 1870). Marx studied the ecological and social consequences of colonization. Colonial agriculture depleted Irish soils while masses of newly displaced Irish people were forced by the British to emigrate to the Americas and to England, creating a surge of extra workers that suppressed wages in their new home countries, even while the bosses maintained a wage hierarchy. This wage hierarchy allowed English workers to feel better than the Irish while at the same time living in fear of being downgraded to Irish wage levels. Such fears fuelled the anti-Irish prejudice drummed up by elites who demeaned and demonized the Irish to justify colonization and mistreatment, and to prevent a collaborative revolt.

This divided workers within countries and between them. Marx wrote: 'this antagonism is artificially kept alive and intensified by the press, the pulpit, the comic papers, in short, by all the means at the disposal of the ruling classes. *This antagonism* is the secret of the *impotence of the English working class*, despite its organization. It is the secret by which the capitalist class maintains its power. And the latter is quite aware of this' (1870, emphasis in original). Moreover, the divisions extended across the Atlantic with the 'antagonism between Englishmen and Irishmen' acting as 'the hidden basis of the conflict between the United States and England. It makes any honest and serious co-operation between the working classes of the two countries impossible' (1870). Marx saw the artificial divide between the Irish and English as similar to that between poor whites and blacks in the United States. For these reasons, among so many others, Marx saw the defeat of colonialism as a necessary and urgent step towards any serious social change. In this are crucial lessons for today's environmental movement.

Ecological Imperialism and the Movement Today

The current pace and scale of ecological degradation is unfathomable without recognizing the history and persistent reality of ecological imperialism. The rest of the world has not willingly volunteered its resources to the richest countries, nor to the richest in every country, so that 'over-consumption' by some becomes a problem at the same time too many cannot afford basic access to food and water. Nor have the rest of the world agreed to host the rich world's garbage or offer their land as carbon sequestration sites for the effluence of the affluent, even if the political and economic elites of certain countries have undemocratically made decisions to facilitate such schemes for a cut of the profit.

Rather, the military, political and economic might of the original colonial powers, in concert with class divisions in the global South, continues to mean that the terms of environmental policy and trade favour the interests of elites in the global North in particular (and most), but also elites in the global South (Smith 2016). Colonialism and postcolonial economic conditions have led to the vast and under-compensated draining of natural wealth from, and export of toxic waste to, the global South (Pellow 2007). The imperial destruction of local industries and economies to eliminate competition and orient production in colonies towards the demands of the industrial and retail centres of the global North set up a pattern of unequal exchange between nations that is still with us today (Foster and Holleman 2014). This unequal ecological and economic exchange has accumulated in the form of a debt owed the global South by the North. If valued properly even in market terms, the economic and ecological wealth drained from the South should repay all the Southern countries' debts many times over – much of which is odious in any case, contracted by Southern elites in collaboration with Northern financiers and contractors.

Resolving this situation requires tackling head on the imperial system of capital. The mainstream environmental movement has been hamstrung by disorienting claims that capitalism can solve the ecological crisis, and by misplaced faith in technology, 'green' or fair-trade products, and international climate agreements.

In looking towards political and economic elites for salvation, and often relying on them for funding, significant segments of the movement are cut off from those with the greatest interest in transforming the system, the global working class and dispossessed. This means they are not engaged in the arduous but necessary task of overcoming the historical divisions imposed by the racialized division of nature and humanity at the heart of the ecological rift of capitalism. Mainstream conceptions of environmental justice remain narrow, focusing on inequality in terms of outcomes of environmental harms or the need to diversify movement leadership, rather than addressing the roots of social divisions and inequalities.

Addressing these issues requires moving beyond superficial approaches to historical changes associated with imperialism and capitalist development. These have too often allowed environmentalists and other activists, as historian and Professor of Native American, Women's, and Ethnic Studies Roxanne Dunbar-Ortiz wrote, to 'safely put aside present responsibility for continued harm done by that past and questions of reparations, restitution, and reordering society' (2015: 5). Superficial approaches to addressing racism, indigenous oppression and other forms of social domination preclude the possibility of a deeper solidarity across historical social divisions. However, this kind of solidarity is exactly what we need to build a people's movement capable of overthrowing the status quo and making change that is socially and ecologically restorative and just.

In *Capital* and other works Marx lays the foundation for making sense of past and present ecological imperialism. Understanding the centrality of ecological imperialism to capitalism, and the necessity of transcending both, is key to dispelling the misguided assumptions of many mainstream environmentalists – in particular – that the liberal state will safeguard our environmental future through regulations at home or international agreements, that environmental justice is compatible with the workings of capitalism, and that capitalism can resolve the ecological crises confronting the planet today.

Moving beyond these assumptions, perhaps better labelled ideological and ahistorical myths, leaves us confronted with the necessity of transcending the logic and system of capital. This does not mean we abandon struggles for crucial reforms, such as meaningful environmental policy and social changes that reduce the elite monopolization of politics, support the self-determination of all peoples and an end to imperial incursion, help end racist police brutality, and stop the widespread violence against women, immigrants, refugees, activists, LGBT people and other targeted communities. These reforms and others are necessary to alleviate suffering, fight oppression, extend democracy and address urgent ecological crises. However, in capitalist societies all progressive changes only partially address their targets and are subject to constant attack and roll back. Therefore, they must be viewed in terms of a broader strategy towards revolutionizing society. In other words, our efforts can only be meaningful in the end if, in social and ecological content, they 1) promote substantive material and political equality, in other words, aim for the self-empowerment of the associated producers (this means democracy extended into the economic sphere); 2) entail the end of oppression and exploitation in all its forms; and 3) have the ultimate goal of the realization of a society in which 'the free development of each is the condition of the free development of all', and in which the social metabolism connecting human beings to 'the universal metabolism of nature' is governed in a rational way (Marx and Engels 1998; Marx 1990).

These are the goals of ecosocialism today, guided by the recognition that 'only a socialist future holds out the hope for a sustainable one'. However, as the activist and writer Chris Williams concluded:

because something is necessary does not make it inevitable. Organization lags behind the urgency of the need. The urban and rural working classes that make today's economy operate need to become organized into a political force that can take charge of the productive machinery and democratically redirect it towards the sustainable satisfaction of human need. Only by organizing and fighting for change on this class basis will the possible future become a real one. (2010: 239)

References

Beckert, S. (2014). *Empire of Cotton: A Global History*, New York: Knopf.
Blake, M. (2014). How Hillary Clinton's State Department Sold Fracking to the World. *Mother Jones*, http://www.motherjones.com/environment/2014/09/hillary-clinton-fracking-shale-state-department-chevron

Di Leo, L. (2010). Oil Spill May End Up Lifting GDP Slightly. *Wall Street Journal*, http://blogs.wsj.com/economics/2010/06/15/oil-spill-may-end-up-lifting-gdp-slightly/

DuBois, W. E .B. (2003 [1920]). The Souls of White Folk. *Monthly Review*, 55(6): 44–58.

Dunbar-Ortiz, R. (2003). The Grid of History: Cowboys and Indians. *Monthly Review*, 55(3), http://monthlyreview.org/2003/07/01/the-grid-of-history-cowboys-and-indians

Dunbar-Ortiz, R. (2015). *An Indigenous People's History of the United States*. Boston: Beacon Press.

Foster, J. B. (1999). Marx's Theory of Metabolic Rift: Classical Foundations for Environmental Sociology. *American Journal of Sociology*, 105(2): 366–405.

Foster, J. B. (2013). Marx and the Rift in the Universal Metabolism of Nature. *Monthly Review*, 65(7), http://monthlyreview.org/2013/12/01/marx-rift-universal-metabolism-nature

Foster, J. and Clark, B. (2003). Ecological Imperialism: The Curse of Capitalism. *Socialist Register*, 40: 186–201.

Foster, J. and Clark, B. (2009). The Paradox of Wealth: Capitalism and Ecological Destruction. *Monthly Review*, 61(6), http://monthlyreview.org/2009/11/01/the-paradox-of-wealth-capitalism-and-ecological-destruction

Foster, J. B., Clark, B. and York, R. (2011). *The Ecological Rift: Capitalism's War on the Earth*. New York: Monthly Review Press.

Foster, J. B. and Holleman, H. (2014). The Theory of Unequal Ecological Exchange: A Marx-Odum Dialectic. *The Journal of Peasant Studies*, 41(2): 199–233.

Greenpeace International (2015). Kumi Naidoo of Greenpeace Responds to Paris Draft Deal. http://www.greenpeace.org/international/en/press/releases/2015/kumi-naidoo-cop21-final-text-paris-climate

Holleman, H. (2012). Energy Policy and Environmental Possibilities: Biofuels and Key Protagonists of Ecological Change. *Rural Sociology*, 77: 280–307.

Holleman, H. (2015). Method in Ecological Marxism. *Monthly Review*, 67(5), http://monthlyreview.org/2015/10/01/method-in-ecological-marxism

Indigenous Environmental Network (2016). Carbon Offsets Cause Conflict and Colonialism, *IC Magazine*, https://intercontinentalcry.org/carbon-offsets-cause-conflict-colonialism

Lugones, M. (2007). Heterosexualism and the Modern/Colonial Gender Order. *Hypatia*, 22(1): 186–209.

Magdoff, H. (1978). *Imperialism: From the Colonial Age to the Present*. New York: Monthly Review Press.

Marx, K. (1870). Letter to Sigfrid Meyer and August Vogt in New York. https://www.marxists.org/archive/marx/works/1870/letters/70_04_09. htm

Marx, K. (1990 [1867]). *Capital, Volume 1*. New York: Penguin.

Marx, K. (1991 [1863–65]). *Capital, Volume 3*. New York: Penguin.

Marx, K. and Engels, F. (1998 [1848]). *The Communist Manifesto*. New York: Monthly Review Press.

Melillo, E. D. (2012). The First Green Revolution: Debt Peonage and the Making of the Nitrogen Fertilizer Trade, 1840–1930. *American History Review*, 117(4): 1028–60.

Milman, O. (2015a). Earth Has Lost a Third of Arable Land in Past 40 Years, Scientists Say. *Guardian*, http://www.theguardian.com/environment/2015/dec/02/arable-land-soil-food-security-shortage

Milman, O. (2015b). James Hansen, Father of Climate Change Awareness, Calls Paris Talks 'a Fraud'. *Guardian*, http://www.theguardian.com/environment/2015/dec/12/james-hansen-climate-change-paris-talks-fraud

New York Times editorial board (2015). The Road to a Paris Climate Deal. 14 December, http://www.nytimes.com/interactive/projects/cp/climate/2015-paris-climatetalks/scientists-see-catastrophe-in-latest-draft-of-climate-deal

Pellow, D. N. (2007). *Resisting Global Toxics: Transnational Movements for Environmental Justice*, Cambridge, MA: MIT Press.

Pimentel, D. (2006). Soil Erosion: A Food and Environmental Threat. *Environment, Development and Sustainability*, 8(1): 119–37.

Randerson, J. (2015). A Story of Hope: The Guardian Launches Phase II of its Climate Change Campaign. *Guardian*, https://www.theguardian.com/environment/2015/oct/05/a-story-of-hope-the-guardian-launches-phase-two-of-its-climate-change-campaign

Smith, J. (2016). *Imperialism in the Twenty-first Century: Globalization, Super-exploitation, and Capitalism's Final Crisis*. New York: Monthly Review Press.

Waring, M. (1995). *Who's Counting? Marilyn Waring on Sex, Lies and Global Economics*. Montreal: National Film Board of Canada.

Williams, C. (2010). *Ecology and Socialism*. Chicago: Haymarket.

Worland, J. (2015). World Approves Historic Paris Agreement to Address Climate Change. *Time Magazine*, http://time.com/4146830/cop-21-paris-agreement-climate

10

Imagining Society Beyond *Capital*

Peter Hudis

Few problems weigh more heavily upon humanity today than developing a viable alternative to capitalism. The increasing levels of income inequality worldwide, coupled with massive destruction of the environment and increasing social alienation, are threatening to undermine the very basis of human and natural existence. As capitalism reverts to ever more regressive forms of intolerance and social control – as seen in the reaction of numerous European powers to the influx of millions of refugees from Africa and the Middle East and the rising threat posed by nativist and racist currents in the US body politic – the need for an alternative vision that can give direction to the aspirations of those dissatisfied with the existing state of affairs is especially palpable.

Nevertheless, meeting this challenge is far from easy, not least because radical theorists and activists tend to draw their poetry from the past – even when it no longer serves much of a purpose. For many decades innumerable figures on the Left have argued that it is utopian and even futile to delineate the specific form and features of a post-capitalist society, since historical materialism commands us to engage in a critique of the existing conditions from which it can immanently emerge. But the argument is inherently self-refuting, for two reasons. First, if the analysis of present-day conditions is of such overriding importance, why act as if we are still living in the mid nineteenth century, when Marxism took shape as a reaction against 'utopianism'? Why repeat the truths of a different era instead of grappling with those of our own? Is it really so self-evident that traditional objections to envisioning a new society retain their validity in the twenty-first century, after almost 100 years of aborted revolutions, Stalinism and failed efforts at socialist transformation? And do not today's 'material conditions' suggest that one of the greatest barriers standing in the way of effective anti-capitalist action is a crisis in imagining an alternative to a society dominated by the all-pervasive power of capital? Second, if the central task of Marxist theory is defined as critically analysing existing realities, why presume that a comprehensive discussion of a possible postcapitalist future is out of order? Is it not possible to articulate future forms of life that are embedded, however implicitly, in the terrain of the present? If one wishes to argue that the future is immanent within existing material conditions, one must be logically consistent enough to acknowledge the need to articulate what that future is. To the extent that dialectical thought delineates normative values from objective realities, the critical analysis of the latter cannot help but compel the conceptualization of the former in some way.

The fundamental problem we face today is that the alternative to the state of affairs that goes by the name of capitalism is very far from clear – perhaps less clear than ever. At one time it may have been possible to claim that the abolition of private property and the 'free' market would free humanity from the incubus of capitalism, racism, sexism and class domination. Yet today this is no longer possible, given how the logic of capital proliferated in societies that abolished private ownership of the means of production and an unregulated market. Capitalism has proved to be far more resilient than many of its radical critics anticipated, in large measure because the alternative that was supposed to replace it proved so threadbare when it came to delivering on the promise of liberation. Given the realities of *our* life and times, we clearly need to think out a more adequate conception of an alternative to capitalism than has hitherto been available.

To meet this challenge, we will need to marshal many theoretical and conceptual resources. I wish to argue that we need *begin* with Marx – precisely because his work constitutes the foremost and irreplaceable critique of the capitalist mode of production. Since his body of work is *dialectical*, in so far as it views every social formation and development from the perspective of its tendencies towards transformation and dissolution, it has much to tell us about what constitutes a post-capitalist society. That Marx refrained from writing 'blueprints' about the future and disparaged utopian speculation that was not grounded in a careful analysis of actually existing social realities does not mean that he lacked a distinctive conception of socialism and communism. Nor is it the case that it was only in the twentieth century that the true nature of 'socialist' or 'communist' society became clarified, by followers of Marx such as Kautsky, Lenin, Preobrazhensky, Mao et al. As I show in *Marx's Concept of the Alternative to Capitalism* (Hudis 2012), Marx's body of thought contains vitally important discussions of the nature of a postcapitalist society that have been overlooked by his critics as well as followers. Now that we have his complete works, the *Gesamtausgabe* (MEGA-2), before us, it becomes possible to reconstruct, from both his published and unpublished work, an overall outline of his concept of a postcapitalist society with an eye to how it addresses today's search for pathways to surmount capitalist value production.

Two points concerning *dialectical* methodology need to guide our investigation from the outset: 1) It only becomes possible to develop a genuine alternative to capitalism if we first grasp what does *not* constitute an alternative. As Spinoza long ago remarked, 'all determination is negation'. Thinkers from an array of traditions – both friendly to and hostile to Marx – have presumed that the abolition of private property and unregulated commodity, labour and financial markets represents *the* point of divide between capitalism and socialism. This chapter will show that such a position has no basis either in Marx's texts or in actual social realities. In fact, much of what called itself 'socialism' and 'communism' over the past 100 years owes little or nothing to Marx's understanding of the transcendence of capitalism. 2) Although Marx developed a distinctive conception of a socialist/communist alternative, it is not grounded in *a priori* assumptions regarding the nature of the good life or in an ideal type to which history *ought* to conform. Like Hegel, Marx holds that the object generates its own categories of knowledge. He studiously adhered to the Hegelian notion that 'Logic has nothing to do with thought *about* something which stands outside by itself as the base of thought ... the determinations are not just of the knowing subject but are rather determinations of the object [*Gegenstand*]' (Hegel 2010: 29–30). In carrying through this perspective into a critical analysis of his object of investigation, *capital*, Marx discloses a form of domination that shackles human creativity while at the same time containing immanent possibilities for its transcendence. That Marx spent most of his life delineating the logic of capital should not be seen as a substitute for elucidating a concept of communism but rather as the necessary path for doing so.

A further *historical* point grounds our analysis: Marx used many phrases to refer to a postcapitalist society – 'communism', 'socialism', 'positive humanism', 'communal production', 'realm of free individuality', 'free association', etc. These terms are completely interchangeable in his work. The notion that 'socialism' and 'communism' are distinct forms of society or phases of historical development is alien to Marx's work and only entered the lexicon of 'Marxism' after his death.

I will here demonstrate these claims by looking briefly at four moments in Marx's work – his *Economic and Philosophical Manuscripts* of 1844, the *Grundrisse*, *Capital*, and his 1875 *Critique of the Gotha Program*.

Marx's effort to envision an alternative to capitalism was grounded in a specific conception of humanity's social being. In his early writings he argues that freedom is not something that merely *ought* to exist but is rather an *ontological* characteristic of the human being. He writes, 'No man combats freedom; at most he combats the freedom of others' (Marx 1975a: 295). Marx's conception that we find freedom *in* our social being rather than *from* it – elaborated shortly afterward in his concept of humanity's 'species-being' – became his standard for critically evaluating political and economic realities. By measuring social reality against the potential disclosed by our species-being, Marx establishes the normative criteria for critically judging the most mystifying aspects of capitalism while discerning the *necessity* for a form of life that can transcend it.

At the same time, Marx developed a *distinctive* understanding of what constitutes a *viable* alternative to capitalism through his indebtedness to Hegel's dialectic of negativity. The basic idea of communism – an equitable distribution of the product through the abolition of private property – long predates Marx. For Marx, however, abolishing private property is a necessary but *insufficient* condition for liberation. This is because it leaves untouched the alienation in the very activity of labouring. Marx develops this in his *Economic and Philosophic Manuscripts of 1844* by making use of Hegel's insight that since all negation is dependent on the object of critique, the transcendence of alienation proceeds through 'the negation of the negation'. Marx writes that the 'vulgar communist' infatuation with abolishing private property is only a first, 'abstract' negation that shares with capitalism an infatuation with *having* instead of *being*; it 'is only a retrogression, a sham universality' (Marx 1975b: 295). *It does not by itself lead to what he calls 'positive humanism, beginning from itself* (1975b: 342).

Significantly, Marx does not demonstrate this by simply noting that class relations can remain unaltered even when property forms are significantly transformed (a point that is surely implied by his analysis). He goes further, by calling attention to the impact of the 'vulgar communist' infatuation with collective property on *gender* relations. The effort to define emancipation by the replacement of private ownership with collective ownership, he writes, 'finds expression in the brutish form of opposing to *marriage* (certainly a *form of exclusive private property*) the *community of women*, in which a woman becomes a piece of *communal* and *common* property'. Indeed, 'It may be said that this idea of the *community of women gives away the secret* of this as yet completely crude and thoughtless communism' (Marx 1975b: 294). The treatment of women as an object of communal possession is hardly an advance upon traditional marriage, since '*greed* re-establishes itself and satisfies itself, only in *another* way'. This proves, for Marx, the fundamental defect of the vulgar communist infatuation with property forms, since 'The direct, natural, and necessary relation of person to person is the *relation of man to woman* ... In this relationship, therefore, is *sensuously manifested*, reduced to an observable *fact*, the extent to which the human essence has become nature to man, or which nature to him has become the human essence of man' (1975b: 295–6). Relations between the sexes serve as the measure, he argues, for the validity (or lack thereof) of any critical stance assumed by those taking issue with existing society. Therefore, 'in the approach to *woman* as the *spoil* and handmaid of communal lust is expressed the infinite degradation in which man exists for itself' (1975b: 295).

It may seem that issues of gender have little to do with the central object of investigation in the *1844 Manuscripts* – the nature of labour in *class* society. However, Marx opposes class society because a product of human activity – society itself, with its accompanying social division of labour – takes on a life of its own and confronts the individual subject as a person apart that imposes its will irrespective of his and her actual needs and desires. This *inversion* of subject and object, which Marx sees as also expressed in Hegel's idealistic mystification of the state as the subject rather than the predicate of human activity, is a critical normative principle employed in his analysis of capitalism.

He opposes any formation in which individuals become dominated and constrained by social relations and products of their own making. In *The German Ideology*, Marx and Engels write that with the division of labour, in which human 'activity is not freely but naturally divided', 'man's own act becomes opposed to him as an alien power over and above him, which subjugates him instead of being controlled by him' (Marx and Engels 2014: 89). And the first historical expression of this social division of labour, Marx and Engels contend, 'is the family, where the wife and children are slaves of the husband' (2014: 87). Marx therefore objects to 'vulgar communism' because its infatuation with replacing private with collective property leaves unchanged the alienated and inverted character of man/woman relations that characterize all forms of class society. Any form of social change – even one that goes by the name of 'communist' – that does not transform the most fundamental of human relationships remains untenable.

The object of Marx's critique therefore goes much deeper than property forms. As he writes in 1844: 'For when one speaks of private property, one thinks of dealing with something external to man. When one speaks of labor, one is directly dealing with man himself. This new formulation of the question already contains its solution' (Marx 1975b: 281). Here we see Marx's thoroughgoing *humanism*. Focusing on altering forms of property – that is, on a *product* of labour – does not get to the critical issue, since it still deals with 'something external to man' while leaving untouched that which is *interior* to it – the human relations at the point of production and between the sexes. By shifting the object of critique from property forms to the deeper level of production relations, Marx is able to touch the nerve of human relations – and those that not only concern *class* but *gender* as well. This 'new formulation of the question already contains its solution' in so far as the alternative to the existing state of affairs is now posited as new human relations that are no longer characterized by subject-object inversion.

Marx therefore concludes that to reach a truly *free* society the focus on negating private property must itself be negated, by achieving a thoroughgoing transformation of the social relations of production. On these grounds he contends (in 1844) that *genuine* 'communism is the position as the negation of the negation' (Marx 1975b: 306).

In his writings of 1844 to 1846, Marx's analysis calls into question *all* relations 'in which the human being objectifies itself inhumanly, in opposition to himself' (Marx 1975b: 331). The focus in his subsequent work on the need to uproot the *class* relations of existing society is part and parcel of envisioning a transformation of *human relations*. This is a far cry from the conventional fixation on property forms and market relations that characterizes many radical tendencies – both in his time and long afterwards.

Moreover, 'private property' does not simply refer to *private* or *individual* ownership of the means of production. For Marx, 'private property' denotes the ownership of the means of production by a minority at the expense of 'the vast majority' (Marx 1976: 495). The *Communist Manifesto* refers to this as the '*class* property' of the bourgeoisie.[1] In contrast, far too many have assumed that it is sufficient to abolish individual ownership and transfer control of the means of production to the state. But what happens if this state is not democratic, and if the workers and peasants are not in *actual* control of the means of production? Property forms are *juridical* relations, whereas the fundamental issue for any Marxist is *production* relations. If a bureaucratic clique controls the latter, it is hard to see how collective ownership of the means of production *in the Marxian sense* can be said to exist. On these grounds Marx often takes issue in his work with statist socialists who assume that the transfer of ownership titles from private individuals to some sort of undifferentiated 'collective' entity constitutes socialism.

Marx's concept of a postcapitalist society is therefore derived not only from a detailed criticism of capitalist social relations but also from a critique of left-wing tendencies that adopted variants of 'socialism' and 'communism' at odds with his own. This is also evident from his criticism of Pierre-Joseph Proudhon's effort to 'transform' capitalism by promoting an equitable distribution of the social product by 'organizing

---

1   'The abolition of existing property relations is not at all a distinctive feature of Communism … The distinguishing feature of Communism is not the abolition of property generally, but the abolition of bourgeois property. But modern bourgeois private property is the final and most complete expression of the system of producing and appropriating products, that is based on class antagonisms, on the exploitation of the many by the few' (Marx and Engels 1976: 498).

exchange' and introducing an equality of wages. Marx contends that this not only fails to address the problem of alienated labour; it also seeks to define the 'new' society by universalizing the principle of wage labour that adheres to the old one. Proudhon fails to see, Marx contends, that calling for labour to be accorded equal monetary value fails to break with capitalism's drive to reduce labouring activity to an undifferentiated equivalent, 'abstract labour'. Hence, 'Proudhon only transforms the relationship of the present-day worker to his labor into the relationship of all men to labor. Society is then conceived as an abstract capitalist' (Marx 1975b: 280).

Marx develops this further in his mature critique of political economy. He shows that the aim of capitalism is not to generate material wealth or satisfy use values. It is to augment exchange value. Use values are *finite* magnitudes – one can only use so many shoes, clothes or foodstuffs. Exchange value, however, is a potentially *infinite* magnitude. This is because exchange value is the phenomenal manifestation of *value*. The value of a commodity is based, not on the actual amount of time that it takes to produce it, but on the *average* amount of time that is *socially necessary* to produce it. A worker may spend ten hours making a product, but that does not mean she has engaged in ten hours of value-creating labour. If the average amount of time that is necessary, on the world market, to create that product is only six hours, the extra four hours of labour performed by the worker creates no value. As a result, the worker is constantly pressured to produce in accordance with an ever-shifting social average – *socially necessary labour time*. The worker is not in control of time; time instead confronts the worker as a 'person apart' and subjects her to *its* will. As the Marxist-Humanist philosopher Raya Dunayevskaya put it,

> Socially necessary labor time is the handmaiden of the machine that accomplishes the fantastic transformation of all concrete labors into one abstract mass. Constant technological revolutions change how much labor time is socially necessary ... All must subordinate themselves to the newly-set socially necessary time to be expended on commodities. (2000: 105).

This means that actual, concrete labour is *not* the source of value in capitalism. The source of value is instead *abstract* labour – a specific *form* of labour that is governed by a social average that is indifferent to the sensuous needs and character of the labourer. The split between concrete and abstract, undifferentiated or homogeneous labour defines capitalism and has an egregious impact on all facets of human and natural existence.

Remarkably, many commentators on Marx continue to overlook his cardinal distinction between value and exchange value as well as his understanding of the dual character of labour – even though Marx considered the latter his 'unique contribution' to the critique of political economy. Elizabeth Grosz, for instance, writes:

> The specificity of labor becomes homogenized into a system in which the commodity produced by that labor gains its value outside of itself, by being made equal to something else (its exchange-value). Through the mirroring of labor in the form of body of the commodity, through its embodiment as use-value, which is then homogenized through exchange-value, differences in labor are ordered into system of hierarchical structure. (2004: 37)

On the contrary, Marx holds that labour becomes homogenized *prior* to the exchange of the commodity, in so far as it is subjected to the 'discipline' of socially necessary labour time *in the very process of production*. That homogenization is what makes generalized commodity exchange possible. Concrete and abstract labour are not two discrete moments of labour – one when the product is produced and the other when it is exchanged – but occur *simultaneously* when confronted with the 'hierarchy' of socially necessary labour time. To claim otherwise leads one to presume that 'organizing exchange' in lieu of transforming production relations can uproot capitalism.

Does the pressure to conform to an ever-changing abstract average ever end? Is there any *finite* limit to the drive to obey the dictates of value production? Surely not, since what dominates humanity is an *abstract* average that, by definition, escapes finite limits. From capital's standpoint there is 'never enough' value extracted from workers. No sooner is a given amount of value created in making a product than the socially necessary labour time further declines – which *de-values* part of what was earlier counted as the value of the product. Workers must produce more in less time to keep up with the level of value production in the previous cycle. *This process is never-ending.* Value production, by its very nature, is an endless quest for an infinite magnitude.

It goes without saying that natural resources are a finite magnitude. But ignore all of that, says capital: since we cannot produce more in a shorter amount of time without exploiting more natural resources, that is just the price that has to be paid for economic progress. The result is that the natural environment is considered a mere 'externality' that is not factored into the cost of production. *This process of exploiting and raping nature is as relentless as the drive to augment value itself.*

Capitalism therefore is based on a specific modality of time – abstract universal labour time – that confronts the body of associated producers as a person apart. It is the first (and for Marx the last) abstract form of social domination, in which time ceases to be grounded in contingent conditions and circumstances but rather assumes a fixed, objectified form that is indifferent to the sensuous needs of individuals.

This issue of time brings us to the heart of Marx's critique of capital – and of how he understands its transcendence. Being alienated from the product of labour – and being dominated by it in turn – is bad enough. But time possesses an interiority that grounds, and thereby makes possible, any fashioning of an external, spatial object. Time, as Kant shows in his First Critique, is 'the immediate condition of the inner intuition (of our souls), and thereby also the mediate condition of outer appearances'. Moreover, 'no object can ever be given to us in experience that would not belong under the condition of time' (Kant 1998: 181). Time – *lived* time, with all of its flux and variation, is that which is most *interior* to our subjective experience. It is constitutive of our very being-in-the-world. As Karel Kosik put it, 'Man knows his mortality only because he organizes time, on the basis of labor as objective doing and as the process of forming socio-human reality. Without this objective doing in which man organizes time into a future, a present, and a past, man could not *know* his totality' (1976: 123). In capitalism, however, we become alienated from our subjective experience of time in so far as it takes on a fixed, frozen, objectified form. Time now confronts the individual as an abstract, impermeable, objective power that bends the activity of labouring to its determinateness. Humanity no longer organizes time, as in pre-capitalist societies; time now organizes humanity. As a result, we no longer *know* the world as being a result of our own subjective activity. The social totality becomes mystified; human relations take on the form of relations between things, and things seem to take on a life of their own, as if the awoken from the dead. We become alienated from that which grounds our very experience of the world.

Herein lies the inner core of Marx's critique of capitalism. It is a critique of capitalist value production that goes much deeper than a mere opposition to private property and 'market anarchy' – though he surely opposes both! In capitalism, he writes, 'we should not say that one man's hour is worth another man's hour, but rather that one man during an hour is worth just as much as another man during the same hour. Time is everything, man is nothing; he is at the most, time's carcass' (Marx 1976: 127).

By identifying the central contradiction of capitalism in his critique of political economy, Marx is led to spell out a distinctive conception of a postcapitalist society – one that is markedly different from the 'socialist' and 'communist' alternatives developed both in his time and by those who claimed to govern in his name afterward.

Since Marx locates the central problem of capitalism as consisting in the fact that 'individuals are subsumed under social production, which exists outside them as their fate', a new society represents *the inversion of this inversion* by 'subsuming social production under the individuals who manage it as their common wealth' (Marx 1986: 96). He spells this out in a remarkable passage in the *Grundrisse* where he states that in socialism or communism 'the general character of labor would not be given to it only by exchange', since

the communal character of production would from the outset make the product into a communal, general one. The exchange initially occurring in production, which would not be an exchange of exchange values but of activities determined by communal needs and communal purposes, would include from the beginning the individual's participation in the communal world of products. (Marx 1986: 96)

Value production – which for Marx is specific to *capitalism* and capitalism *alone* – renders human relations *indirectly* social, since people are connected to each other through abstract forms of domination, such as money. In contrast, in socialism or communism labour takes on a 'general character' *prior* to the exchange of products, on the basis of 'the communal character of production' itself. This occurs through the free, democratic deliberation of the producers who control the means of production – not nominally, but actually. Once this occurs, generalized commodity production comes to an end. In other words, exchange value – which is the phenomenal expression of value production based on abstract labour – is eliminated *as soon as* new, *freely* associated, non-alienated conditions of labour come into existence. Freely associated individuals distribute the elements of production – including the amount of time that they do or do not invest in their social reproduction – through a plan based on their needs instead of being governed by forms that operate independently of them, such as the state or the market.

In a postcapitalist society labour becomes *directly* social since the decisions and actions of the human being, not an autonomous force that exists outside of them (such as exchange value), mediates their interaction. Marx refers to this in the *Grundrisse* as 'the realm of free individuality'. This leap into the realm of freedom is made possible by capital itself, which generates a multiplicity of new needs by developing the productive forces on an unprecedented scale. It goes without saying that these new needs arise in an alienated form and context. Some of these needs may even be dangerous or superfluous. But once the value integument is stripped away it becomes possible to release the forms of the new society that are immanently contained in the old one. And among the most important of these is the multiplicity of needs themselves. Marx does not envision a new society as a regression to the 'natural simplicity' of pre-capitalist life, let alone one of material impoverishment. *He envisions a new society as making possible 'a totality of human manifestations of life'* (Marx 1975b: 299). Value production creates the material conditions for this spiritual possibility, even as it constrains its actualization. The object generates its own categories of knowledge – in this case, the very knowledge of a postcapitalist society that surmounts the horizon of value production.

Marx further delineates this in Volume 1 of *Capital*, in 'The Fetishism of Commodities and its Secret'. The fetishism of commodities is dispelled neither by the discovery of labour as the source of value nor the proletariat as the revolutionary class. This is because 'the social relations between [the producers'] private labors appear as what they are, i.e. they do not appear as direct social relations between persons in their work, but as material relations between persons and social relations between things' (Marx 1977: 165–6). He writes that since commodity fetishism is 'adequate' to the concept of capital, its mysteriousness can be dissolved only by examining the present from the vantage point of 'other forms of production'. He then writes, 'Let us finally imagine, for a change, an association of free men, working with the means of production held in common…' (1977: 171). In this future postcapitalist society, products are 'directly objects of utility' and do not assume a value form. Labourers decide how to produce, distribute and consume the total social product. One part of the social product is used to renew the means of production; the other part 'is consumed by members of the association as means of subsistence' (1977: 172). He invokes neither the market nor the state as the instrument through which this distribution of the elements of production is achieved. Instead, there is a freely planned distribution of labour time by those who are no longer subjected to socially necessary labour time.

Although Marx speaks of a 'parallel' with commodity production in that 'the share of each individual producer in the means of subsistence is determined by his labor time' (Marx 1977: 172), he is *not* suggesting that socialism or communism is governed by *socially necessary* labour time. There is a vast difference between the latter and *actual* labour time. Socially necessary labour time imposes itself as a person apart, irrespective of the sensuous needs of individuals, whereas actual labour time is the sensuous activity of individuals mediating their relations with nature. There is a parallel with commodity production *only in the sense* of an exchange of equivalents, in that one contributes a given hour of labour to the community and receives from it goods and services produced in that same amount of time (a given hour of labour). But since there is no social average that governs the exchange, commodity production as such comes to an end.[2]

---

2   The distinction between actual labour time and socially necessary labour time is of cardinal importance, since conflating the two leads to the erroneous conclusion that Marx posits value production as continuing to operate in a postcapitalist society. Georg Lukács made this erroneous conflation in his *Ontology of Social Being and The Process of Democratization*. He writes, 'For Marx, labor exploitation can exist under socialism if labor time is expropriated from the laborer, since "the share of every producer to the means of production

Marx further specifies this conception of a postcapitalist society in his 1875 *Critique of the Gotha Program*. The *Critique* introduces, for the first time in his work, a distinction between a lower and higher phase of communism. Of the lower phase, he writes, 'we are dealing with here a *communist* society, not as it has developed on its own foundations, but on the contrary, just as it emerges from capitalist society'. At this initial phase 'the producers do not exchange their products; just as little does the labor employed on the product appear here *as the value* of these products, as a material quality possessed by them, since now, in contrast to capitalist society, individual labor no longer exists in an *indirect* fashion but *directly* as a component part of the total labor' (Marx 1989: 85). Generalized commodity exchange is possible only if there is a commensurate social substance – abstract labour – that enables the diverse array of products of labour to be universally exchanged. But with 'common ownership' of the means of production, abstract or alienated labour comes to an end. Since abstract labour is the substance of value, value production also comes to an end even *at this initial phase of socialism*.

Marx is pointing to a radical breach between capitalism and even the most 'defective' or initial phase of the new society. 'Socialism' or 'communism' does not represent, for Marx, a more equitable *distribution* of value. *It represents the abolition of value production itself*, from its initial moment of emergence. This is still only an initial phase, however, since an exchange of equivalents continues to prevail – albeit in a radically changed form: 'The individual producer receives back from society – after the deductions have been made – exactly what he gives to it. What he has given to it is his individual *quantum* of labor.' Individuals receive from society a voucher or token that they have 'furnished such and such an amount of labor (after deducting his labor for the common funds)' and through it obtain from 'the social stock of means of consumption as much as the amount of labor costs' (Marx 1989: 86). This recapitulates what he had earlier said about the new society in *Capital*. Marx is again *not* suggesting that the worker's labour is computed on the basis of a social *average* of labour time.

---

is determined by his labor time" ... For Marx, the law of value is not dependent upon commodity production ... according to Marx these classical categories are applicable to any mode of production' (Lukács 1991: 120–1).

Here, labour time simply refers to the amount of actual hours of work performed by the individual in a given community.

Nevertheless, the form of remuneration in the lower phase is *defective*, since it is based on a *quid pro quo*. The individual receives from the community what he puts into it, in the form of actual hours of labour time. Exchange *value* is abolished, but exchange based on an 'equal standard' – *actual amounts* of labour time – persists. This equal standard or right, Marx acknowledges, 'is still in principle *bourgeois right*'. That is because 'the right of the producers is proportional to the labor they supply'. Since some may work longer hours than others there will be inequities in the amount of remuneration that they receive. The application of an equal standard – remuneration according to actual labour time – produces *unequal* results. Classes cease to exist, but not social differentiation based on levels of remuneration. This is unfortunate, but inevitable, since 'Right can never be higher than the economic structure of society and its cultural development which this determines' (Marx 1989: 86). In contrast, when we reach a higher phase of communism, a completely different principle prevails – 'From each according to their ability, to each according to their need' (1989: 87). No longer is remuneration based on the amount of labour time contributed by the individual. Actual labour time ceases to be a measure of social relations. No 'equal standard' of any sort applies to a higher phase. *The realm of bourgeois right and natural necessity is therefore left behind.* The producers simply withdraw from the common storehouse what they need, and they give to society what they can, based on their natural and acquired abilities. This involves no *quid pro quo*. But this can only emerge once we have fully rid ourselves of the birthmarks of the old society.

Marx's conception of the phases of communism should not be confused with 'the dictatorship of the proletariat', which he defines as a *political* transitional stage *between* capitalism and communism. As he clearly states in the *Critique*: 'Between capitalist and communist society lies the period ... in which the state can be nothing but *the revolutionary dictatorship of the proletariat*' (Marx 1989: 95). The latter represents the democratic control of society by the 'immense majority', the producers, who use political power as a lever to eliminate class domination by revolutionizing the social relations of production. Engels spells out the thoroughly democratic character of this political transition stage in his critique of the 1891 Erfurt Program: 'If one thing is certain it is that our party and the working class can only come to power under the form of a democratic republic. This is the specific form of the dictatorship of the proletariat' (Engels 1990: 227). Marx and Engels use the term 'dictatorship' as it was understood in Roman law – as a magistrate elected by the Roman Senate for a limited period of time to deal with an emergency and whose rule is disbanded upon its termination. As Norman Levine has argued (2015: 74–80), it has nothing to do with later Leninist conceptions of a prolonged 'transitional phase' led by a political party that monopolizes power. The political transition period discussed by Marx is *not* a distinct form of society, since it comes *between* capitalist and socialist or communist society. It is instead a political *stage* in which the old mode of production is undermined and negated through an ongoing revolutionary process. Once this process is completed the dictatorship of the proletariat becomes superfluous, since with the abolition of class society and value production the proletariat is abolished alongside all other classes. What then emerges is the first or initial phase of communism, in which a completely new form of production relations prevails.

To be sure, Lenin made a vitally important contribution in his 1917 *State and Revolution* by returning to Marx's 1875 *Critique* (as well as *The Eighteenth Brumaire of Louis Bonaparte*) in order to spell out the need to *smash* and not simply take over the existing capitalist state (his admonition has hardly been followed by many 'socialist' revolutions since then). However, Lenin muddied the waters considerably in writing: 'What is usually called socialism was termed by Marx the "first," or lower, phase of communism' (1972: 90). Marx, in fact, makes no such distinction; socialism and communism for him are interchangeable terms. Moreover, Lenin argued, 'bourgeois law in regard to the distribution of consumer goods inevitably presupposes the existence of the bourgeois state, for law is nothing but an apparatus capable of enforcing the observance of the rules of law' (1972: 90). Whereas Marx conceives of the distribution of the social product being achieved through the collective deliberation of the producers, Lenin apparently cannot conceive of how this is possible without the existence of a centralized state. He therefore insists that in 'the first phase of communist society, all citizens are transformed into hired employees of the state'. But Marx nowhere mentions the existence of a state in discussing distribution according to labour time in the lower phase of communism. *Nor could he mention it, since the state is based upon the division of society into classes – which no longer exists in socialism or communis*m. Furthermore, Marx does not state (as does Lenin) that 'All citizens become employees and workers of a single country-wide state "syndicate." All that is required is that they should work equally, do their proper share of work, and get equal pay' (Lenin 1972: 92). This concession to the existence of wage labour in 'socialism' is nowhere found in Marx's *Critique*.

Lenin's interpretation has important consequences, as seen in how it continues to place blinders upon accurately rendering Marx's text to the present day. One recent study contends: 'We build communist society *upon its own foundations* by developing new communal relations of production that subordinate the private ownership of labor-power by creating a new state' (Lebowitz 2015: 71).[3] Here not only is the state imported into the lower phase of communism – it exists in a higher phase as well! The state is now fetishized to the point of making it an eternal fact of human existence.

By confusing the 'dictatorship of the proletariat' with the initial phase of the new society, post-Marx Marxists have assumed that the state – which in some form prevails in the political transition period – also continues to dominate in socialism/communism. That this was never Marx's position, however, is clear from his actual writings, which nowhere equate socialism or communism with state domination. For Marx, the state is an 'excrescence' of class society that is superseded in socialism.[4]

The closer we explore Marx's body of work with fresh eyes, the more insights we find regarding what constitutes the alternative to capitalism. Here I have only been able to point to a few of the many

---

3   My emphasis. The italicized phrase is highly significant, since it makes it clear that Lebowitz is referring to Marx's discussion of a *higher* phase of communism (in Marx's words) 'as it has developed on its own foundations' (Marx 1989: 85).

4   'Maine ignores the much deeper point: that the seeming supreme independent existence of the State is itself only seeming and that it is in all its forms an excrescence of society; just as its appearance itself arises only at a certain stage of social development, it disappears again as soon as society has reached a stage not yet attained' (Marx 1972: 329).

places where Marx delves directly into this. At the same time, what is no less striking is the enormous distance that separates Marx's view of a postcapitalist society from what has been attributed to him by his critics and many of his followers. An immense layer of conceptual debris heaped upon Marx over the past century has helped to conceal the true nature of his liberatory project. Now that so many alternatives that ruled in its name have exhausted themselves, it is time to *return to the source* and work out the meaning of his insights for our life and times. To be sure, the fact that Marx said something does not make it true. But isn't it time for us to become clear on what he actually said? In doing so, we may discover that it isn't true because he said it; rather, it is important that he said it because the realities we have experienced for the past 100 years show that it is true.

References

Dunayevskaya, R. (2000). *Marxism and Freedom, from 1776 Until Today*. Amherst, NY: Humanity Books.

Engels, F. (1990). A Critique of the Draft Program of 1891. In *Marx-Engels Collected Works*, Volume 27. New York: International Publishers.

Grosz, E. (2004). *The Nick of Time: Politics, Evolution, and the Untimely*. Durham, NC: Duke University Press.

Hegel, G. W. F. (2010). *Science of Logic*. Cambridge: Cambridge University Press.

Hudis, P. (2012). *Marx's Concept of the Alternative to Capitalism*. Leiden: Brill.

Kant, I. (1998). *Critique of Pure Reason*. Cambridge: Cambridge University Press.

Kosik, K. (1976). *Dialectics of the Concrete: A Study on Problems of Man and World*. Dordrecht-Holland: D. Reidel.

Lebowitz, M. A. (2015). *The Socialist Alternative: From Gotha to Now*. New York: Monthly Review.

Lenin, V. I. (1972). *The State and Revolution*. Moscow: Progress Publishers.

Levine, N. (2015). *Marx's Rebellion Against Lenin*. New York: Palgrave Macmillan.

Lukács, G. (1991). *The Process of Democratization*. Albany, NY: SUNY Press, 1991.

Marx, K. (1972). *Ethnological Notebooks*. Assen: Van Gorcum.

Marx, K. (1975a). Debates on Freedom of the Press. In *Marx-Engels Collected Works*, Volume 1. New York: International Publishers.

Marx, K. (1975b). *Economic and Philosophic Manuscripts of 1844*. In *Marx-Engels Collected Works*, Volume 2. New York: International Publishers.

Marx, K. (1976). *The Poverty of Philosophy*. In *Marx-Engels Collected Works*, Volume 6. New York: International Publishers.

Marx, K. (1977). *Capital, Volume 1*. New York: Penguin.

Marx, K. (1986). *Grundrisse*. In *Marx-Engels Collected Works*, Volume 28. New York: International Publishers.

Marx, K. (1989). *Critique of the Gotha Program*. In *Marx-Engels Collected Works*, Volume 24. New York: International Publishers.

Marx, K. and Engels, F. (2014). *Marx and Engel's German Ideology. Manuscripts: Presentation and Analysis of the Feuerbach Chapter*. New York: Palgrave Macmillan.

Marx, K. and Engels, F. (1976). Manifesto of the Communist Party. In *Marx-Engels Collected Works*, Volume 6. New York: International Publishers.

Marx, K. and Engels, F. (2014). *Marx and Engels' German Ideology. Manuscripts: Presentation and Analysis of the Feuerbach Chapter*. New York: Palgrave Macmillan.

Notes on Contributors

Carlo Fanelli teaches in the Department of Politics and Public Administration, Ryerson University, Canada. He is the author of *Megacity Malaise: Neoliberalism, Public Services and Labour in Toronto* (2016), and editor of *Alternate Routes: A Journal of Critical Social Research*.

Silvia Federici is a feminist activist, teacher and writer. She was a co-founder of the International Feminist Collective and the Committee for Academic Freedom in Africa. She is the author of many essays on political philosophy, feminist theory, cultural studies and education. Her published works include: *Revolution at Point Zero: Housework, Reproduction, and Feminist Struggle* (2012); *Caliban and the Witch: Women, the Body and Primitive Accumulation* (2004); *A Thousand Flowers: Social Struggles Against Structural Adjustment in African Universities* (2000); *Enduring Western Civilization: The Construction of Western Civilization and its 'Others'* (1994). She is also Emerita Professor at Hofstra University.

Peter Gose is a Canadian anthropologist whose graduate studies were at the London School of Economics. He has taught at the University of Lethbridge and the University of Regina and currently works at Carleton University. His early research as an ethnographer of the Peruvian Andes explored how peasant mortuary and sacrificial rituals articulate relations of production, property and political power. In the late 1980s, he turned to historical research on ritual and political power under the Incas. From 1993 to 2008, he did archival research on ancestor worship as a key mediating practice in relations of indirect colonial rule in the Andes. More recently, he has conducted archival research for a project on 'purity of blood' racism in Spain and its Andean colonies. His most abiding theoretical interests are in practice theory, hegemony theory, Marx and hermeneutics.

Hannah Holleman is Assistant Professor of Sociology at Amherst College. Her current book project, *Dustbowls of Empire*, reinterprets the 1930s Dust Bowl as one dramatic regional manifestation of a global socio-ecological crisis generated by the realities of settler colonialism and imperialism. She is the author of numerous articles focused on social theory, political economy and environmental sociology. Her work has appeared in the *Journal of Peasant Studies*, *Rural Sociology* and *Monthly Review*, including the award-winning 'Weber and the Environment: Classical Foundations for a Post-Exemptionalist Sociology' in the *American Journal of Sociology* (co-authored with John Bellamy Foster).

Peter Hudis is Professor of Humanities and Philosophy at Oakton Community College. He has written extensively on Marxism, Hegelian philosophy and critical race theory, and is the author of *Marx's Concept of the Alternative to Capitalism* (2012) and *Frantz Fanon: Philosopher of the Barricades* (2015). He is general editor of *The Complete Works of Rosa Luxemburg* (Verso), three volumes of which have appeared so far.

Anej Korsika is a freelance author writing for various Slovenian and international journals. He is currently completing a PhD in philosophy. He has edited the student newspaper *Tribuna*, was a member of the Marxist think-tank Workers and Punks University, and one of the co-founders of the Initiative for Democratic Socialism Party that is now a member of the United Left parliamentary coalition. He is currently active with the League of the Balkan Left and The Eighth of March Institute.

Jeff Noonan is Professor of Philosophy at the University of Windsor. He is the author of three books, *Critical Humanism and the Politics of Difference* (2003), *Democratic Society and Human Needs* (2006), and *Materialist Ethics and Life-Value* (2012), and more than 50 peer reviewed articles and book chapters. He also writes regularly for his local alternative press and progressive websites in Canada and abroad, and maintains an active blog at www.jeffnoonan.org. He is a long time socialist activist and is currently President of the Windsor University Faculty Association.

Prabhat Patnaik has taught at the University of Cambridge, where he was a Fellow of Clare College, and at the Jawaharlal Nehru University, India. He is currently Professor Emeritus at the JNU, having retired in 2010 from the Sukhamoy Chakaravarty Chair that he held there. Between 2006 and 2011 he was the Executive Head of the Planning Board of the southern state of Kerala in India. His main research interests are in the areas of macroeconomics and development economics. His books include *Whatever Happened to Imperialism and Other Essays* (1995), *Accumulation and Stability Under Capitalism* (1997), *The Retreat to Unfreedom* (2002), *The Value of Money* (2009), *Re-Envisioning Socialism* (2011), and *A Theory of Imperialism* (co-authored with Utsa Patnaik, 2016).

Justin Paulson is a political sociologist and critical theorist at Carleton University, where he teaches in the Department of Sociology and Anthropology and the Institute of Political Economy. He was trained at the University of California, Santa Cruz, and his areas of research include Marxist theory, theories of political economy, and social movements. He is an active member of the editorial boards of *Studies in Political Economy* and *Mediations*.

William A. Pelz is an academic historian who specializes in European and comparative labour history. His previous books include *A Peoples History of Modern Europe* (2016), *The Eugene V. Debs Reader: Socialism and Democracy* (2014), *Karl Marx: A World to Win* (2012), *Against Capitalism: The European Left on the March* (2007), and *The Spartkusbund and the German Working-Class Movement* (1988).

Ingo Schmidt is a Marxist economist and a socialist activist. Originally from Germany, he is currently the academic coordinator of the Labour Studies Program at Athabasca University, Canada. His books include *Varieties of Neoliberalism* (in German, 2008), *Social Democracy After the Cold War* (co-edited with Bryan Evans, 2012), *Rosa Luxemburg's 'Accumulation of Capital'* (in German, 2013), *The Three Worlds of Social Democracy: A Global View* (2016), and *Capital@150, Russian Revolution@100* (in German, forthcoming).

Chris Smith is Professor of Organisation Studies and Comparative Management, School of Management, Royal Holloway, University of London and has research interests in labour process theory, knowledge transfer through the transnational firm, comparative analysis of work and employment and professional labour. He is currently researching the organization of the labour process in Chinese factories and the 'Chinese Business Model' abroad. He has been active in the International Labour Process Conference for many years. Recent book publications include *China at Work* (co-authored with Mingwei Liu, 2016); *Working Life: Renewing Labour Process Analysis* (co-authored with Paul Thompson, 2010); *Creative Labour: Working in the Creative Industries* (co-authored with Alan McKinlay, 2009).

Paul Thompson is Professor of Employment Studies in the School of Management at the University of Stirling. He has a long association with labour process theory and research, and is currently Convenor of the International Labour Process Conference. His book *The Nature of Work* (1983, 1989) played a key role in defining and diffusing the labour process debate in the UK and internationally. His more recent contribution to labour process scholarship has focused on the changing nature of worker resistance and the impact of financialization on capitalist political economy and work relations.

Index